ATHLETICS
THE GOLDEN DECADE

ATHLETICS
THE GOLDEN DECADE

TONY WARD

Macdonald
Queen Anne Press

A QUEEN ANNE PRESS BOOK

First published in Great Britain in 1991 by
Queen Anne Press, a division of
Macdonald & Co (Publishers) Ltd
Orbit House
1 New Fetter Lane
London EC4A 1AR

A member of the Maxwell Macmillan Pergamon
Publishing Corporation

Design – Peter Champion and Deborah Holmes

British Library Cataloguing in Publication Data
Ward, Tony
    Athletics: the golden decade.
    I. Title
    796.0941

    ISBN 0–356–19679–8

Typeset by Leaper & Gard Ltd, Bristol

Printed and bound in Great Britain by
BPCC Hazell Books
Aylesbury, Bucks, England
Member of BPCC Ltd.

CONTENTS

ACKNOWLEDGEMENTS

Millions of words were written about the golden decade of British athletics and I am grateful to all those writers and journalists whose work prompted and sometimes corrected doubtful memory or gave an extra insight into momentous events.

More particularly I acknowledge the valuable background provided by some of the biographies of the period: *Ovett, An Autobiography* (with John Rodda); *Running Free* (Sebastian Coe with David Miller); *Fatima, The Autobiography of Fatima Whitbread* (with Adrianne Blue); *Zola, The Autobiography of Zola Budd* (with Hugh Eley); *Made in America* (Peter Ueberroch); *Linford Christie* (with myself).

A number of people were kind enough to be interviewed for the book and I am indebted to Allan Wells, Peter Coe, Neil Wilson of the *Independent,* John Bryant, formerly of *The Times* and *Sunday Correspondent,* John Rodda of the *Guardian,* Don Anthony, Andy Norman, Les Jones, Alan Pascoe, Brendan Foster, Kriss Akabusi, Dick Palmer and Arthur McAllister. I had brief conversations with Roger Black and other international athletes that gave valuable background. I thank, too, Stuart Barnes of the PA for the idea.

I would like to mention specifically the work of a number of excellent writers on athletics who provided me with material, namely Cliff Temple, Eric Olsen and Hal Higdon of that late and much lamented American publication *The Runner.* Cliff's writings in *Running* and *The Sunday Times* were also of enormous benefit. I would also thank the editors and publishers of *Running* magazine, *Athletics Weekly* and *Athletics Today* for permission to use some of the material I have written for them during the past decade. Thanks too to Jeremy Brooks of the *South African Sunday Times* for his help in obtaining cuttings concerning the murder of Frank Budd.

My appreciation also goes to that magnificent statistician Ian Hodge for perusing the text for statistical errors (while I do take full responsibility for any that remain!) and to Geoff Irvine and Angie Bainbridge of the Bagenal Harvey Organisation for their support. I thank, too, Caroline North of Queen Anne Press for her faith in the project.

Finally, I thank my wife Gwenda, not only for her memory of the conversation which forms the chapter *Sporting Salem*, but also for the suggestion that this might be the way to tackle a difficult subject. I thank her for her support during the writing of this book and also my son, Tim, for his patient understanding of his father's absences during its evolution.

Tony Ward
May 1991

PICTURE CREDITS

Allsport: 52, 67, 69B, 87B, 90, 95T, 116, 123, 129, 177, 179, 181, 215, 218, 231. *Colorsport*: 13T, 21T, 44T&B, 101, 105, 131, 134, 150T&B, 154T, 183T&B, 198, 217, 233. *Empics*: 237. *Professional Sport*: 21B, 169. *Mark Shearman*: 17, 78T&B, 82, 97, 111, 113, 125, 154B, 190, 209, 226. *Bob Thomas*: x, 9, 13B, 62, 69T, 87T, 95B, 206.

Jacket photographs   Front: *Colorsport* (top) *Allsport* (bottom)
                     Back: *Mark Shearman*

The Publishers have attempted to observe the legal requirements with respect to the rights of suppliers of photographic materials. Nevertheless, persons who have claims are invited to apply to the Publishers.

PROLOGUE

We sat under a large, colourful parasol, out of the hot afternoon sunshine, in the outdoor section of the restaurant of a small marina. Beside us expensive yachts and motor cruisers rested upon a somnolent sea. Above us, a quarter of a mile away, the edifice of the modern Gradski Stadium awaited the influx of spectators and competitors, still two hours away.

My companion, Hans-Joachim Waldbrol and I were in Split, on the Adriatic coast of Yugoslavia, for the 1990 European Championships; he for his newspaper, the *Frankfurter Allgemeine*, I with the Great Britain team. We were there, on this Thursday in late August, to talk about the extraordinary British triumphs of the previous days. Hans had his notebook open on the table and when we had finished our indulgence of pancakes and coffee I knew that I would have to begin answering the question that he had first posed the previous evening: what was the secret of our success?

I had flown into Split a week earlier with a team in an ambivalent mood. All the signs were that we could be equally as triumphant as we had been in Stuttgart, four years earlier, but this time there was one overriding difference: media, and therefore public, expectancy was running very high. The previous Sunday one journalist had written "let's start counting the medals now". Such presumptuous confidence had its downside; it could sow seeds of complacency and ensure that if our athletes did, for all sorts of reasons, fail to win the clutch of gold medals expected of them, the flop would be a very public one. By this fourth day all such worries were past. We had won five gold medals in style, three on the previous evening, and we knew there were more to come, that our anthem would vie with that of the German Democratic Republic at the daily victory ceremonies. As Hans and I sipped our *cappuccinos* we mulled over the situation in Germany and he told me of the fear amongst West German athletes, especially the women, that in a reunified team the following year they would be totally excluded by the previously state-trained, pampered athletes from the east.

Finally, as the sun dipped towards the horizon, we began to talk about the previous decade and the golden years of British athletics, unprecedented in the century-long history of the sport ...

Britain's women's 100 metres hurdles winners in the 1990 Commonwealth Games in Auckland. (L-R: Lesley-Ann Skeete (England, bronze), Kay Morley (Wales, gold) and Sally Gunnell (England, silver).

1
MOSCOW SHOWDOWN

We flew eastwards, high above cirrus clouds, towards what was for so many a city as forbidden as Lhasa – Moscow, setting for the Games of the XXII Olympiad. This Aeroflot flight, it turned out, was my entry to the greatest era in British athletics, a decade or more of drama, of triumph and disaster, both as impostor-like as Kipling ever imagined. Had I known it my mode of arrival lacked a certain panache for such an occasion. We flew in on an Ilyushin, the Skoda of the airways.

The passenger list was athletically intriguing and would have graced any Agatha Christie novel. There was Gay Ovett, the young mother of Steve, the world record holder for the mile and the European 1500 metres champion. Eighteen days earlier in the tiny, compact Bislett Stadium in Oslo, he had run the fastest mile the world had ever seen. Gay sat with her husband. They were a tense, quiet couple, made nervous perhaps by the presence of the confident, garrulous Peter Coe, father–coach of Sebastian, who the year before had set three world records in forty-one days; two at Bislett, the third in Zurich. Ovett had snatched the mile away and equalled the 1500 metres but now they were to meet in the massive Lenin Stadium in Moscow, a drama in two acts. In athletics terms it was the ultimate showdown, and flying to witness it was a man who had run in the Olympics decades before anyone else on the flight had been born. Frail now at ninety-one but mightily compos, Philip Noel-Baker, ex-Cabinet Minister, Nobel Peace Prize winner, was travelling to lend his support to the most boycotted Games in Olympic history. With him was his "minder", short, dumpy, jolly Don Anthony, former hammer-thrower for Britain, like a well-fed cockerel guarding a favoured hen.

It was a cheerless flight. Sustenance was of a low order, entertainment non-existent. Stewardesses marched up and down the centre aisle with fixed smiles, but as Elton John later had it, with eyes as cold as Christmas in the middle of the year. I chatted with Peter Coe about coaching and coaches, about Cerutty and about Stampfl, rivals of two decades or so earlier, and thought of his own rivalry with Harry Wilson, Ovett's long-established coach. All of this contention between families and coaches had been fuelled and fanned, some said invented, by the media, until even the protagonists themselves had begun to believe in it. A dour stewardess interrupted our conversation with a severe-looking packet of sandwiches and an empty plastic cup – lunch. I thought sexist thoughts – if fate willed that she and I should be the last persons on earth then it would be the end of civilisation as we knew it. Don Anthony, in a moment of telepathy, interrupted his minding to turn round and grimace. Even his non-agearian charge, who was to display an amazing libido on this trip, was unimpressed.

Peter Coe was a thin, bony, bespectacled man. It was no surprise to learn that he had been a Wandsworth Wheeler in his younger days, just after the war, partial to fifty-mile time trials before breakfast (even now on the landing of their London house is a bicycle machine in case the seventy-year-old has some flight of fancy). Of Sebastian he said: "By fourteen I knew I had a good 'un, by sixteen I knew I had a world-beater." It was an oft-repeated, well-worn phrase. "Seb was a slow developer," he went on, "small and slight. It comes from my side of the family. So, of course, it was vital that he be brought on slowly."

As he stood around bleak Yorkshire running tracks and at the end of wind-swept, muddy cross-country courses he was presented with much conflicting advice.

"It was difficult to separate fact from fiction," Peter said as he munched, but did not look too closely at, his sandwich, now accompanied by a cup of very un-English tea. "By the time he was fourteen I'd decided to coach him myself. I'd always been very close to him and I thought, 'If anyone knows this lad's mind, I do.' "

By this time there was confusion on the plane. Some of the travellers insisted that their itinerary – we were all on a package tour, the only way to get to the Games unless you were a competitor – indicated that they were visiting Leningrad. The rest of us were bound for Moscow. We consulted the stewardesses, but their very limited English became non-existent, the smiles a little more fixed. Garbled messages suddenly came over the intercom, fasten-seat-belt and no-smoking signs flashed on, and we descended through cloud, totally uncertain as to which airport awaited us below. We peered through the windows but learned nothing. Suddenly, over the intercom, a voice announced in loud, clear English: "Welcome to the Soviet Union. Welcome to Leningrad."

In truth, we were lucky to be there at all, whether competitors or spectators. Since Detroit had withdrawn its application to stage the Games back in 1974, leaving the field clear for Moscow, there had been a mounting campaign to have them moved elsewhere or boycotted. This had been supported especially by Jewish organisations in Britain and America, deeply concerned for the plight of their people in the USSR. The fate of dissidents was also in people's minds. The invasion of Afghanistan in the closing days of 1979 became a focal point for the campaign and in the ensuing six months the British Olympic Association and particularly its Chairman, Sir Denis Follows, and Secretary General, Dick Palmer, came under extraordinary and unprecedented political pressure from Margaret Thatcher's nine-month-old Conservative government and its media acolytes. Luckily, the BOA was prepared. On his return from his annual fortnight's holiday in Italy the previous year, Denis Follows had called Dick Palmer into his office.

"My boy," he said, "I've been thinking about this problem and all these letters we're receiving. I think what we should do is to have a resolution of the BOA which will set out our policy quite clearly."

They called a meeting of the Association and after diffidence in some quarters (the BOA still had a quota of admirals and generals on its committee) it was agreed to attend the Games in Moscow because, in essence, not to attend would deny individuals the right to make the choice. It was a policy that was to stand the Association in good stead over the following months.

On 17 January President Jimmy Carter announced his wish that the USA boycott the Games and one week later Mrs Thatcher followed suit. Immediately the political pressure began, with the BOA meeting with various government ministers, including a bullish Michael Heseltine. Some MPs formed a "Hands off Afghanistan" committee; inevitably Norris McWhirter and the Freedom Association joined in. The right-wing Press sounded off a continuous cacophony of anti-Moscow Games propaganda. At the Winter Olympics in Lake Placid the CIA were very active in trying to persuade national Olympic Committees to join the boycott. Cyrus Vance, the US Vice-President, was so intent on attacking the choice of Moscow at the IOC session that he totally forgot to perform the opening ceremony, for which he had been specifically invited.

Public opinion was running 70/30 against British participation and the BOA, on its return from Lake Placid, was mostly fire-fighting. In desperation it called together a number of media notables to help try and turn the tide. The advice given was tough, but as it turned out, absolutely correct. Get Denis Follows out of the firing line – the Press was starting to lampoon him – and ask competitors to do the talking. Almost immediately the Foreign Office withdrew the Olympic attaché which it normally appoints. On hearing this, the Irish Olympic Committee telephoned to offer the use of its man. Then Sue Reeve, a long-jumper and civil servant, announced that she was being refused leave of absence. Geoff Capes told the BOA that his Chief Constable was putting him under pressure. The government stated that British Airways would not carry spectators to the Games. Sebastian Coe confirmed his intention to compete and immediately, like many other athletes, began to receive unpleasant mail. While training one evening he was harangued by an army officer until his father intervened. Colin Moynihan persuaded fellow-rowers to urge a wavering rowing association to take part. In a six-hour House of Commons debate, in which sport gained more time and attention than it was to receive in the rest of Mrs Thatcher's term, thirty Tory MPs ignored a three-line Whip and abstained. Suddenly the pendulum had swung; the public, in an opinion poll, showed a complete turnaround, 70/30 in favour of Britain's attendance. The BOA, with its courageous and firm stand, had won through.

Relationships within the Ovett household were not harmonious that summer of 1980. Steve had met and fallen in love with Rachel Waller two years before, but jealousies had been aroused by her arrival. "My parents were so intensely involved in making their son successful," he was to write in his autobiography, "that women became an intrusion." Clearly though, the Olympic Games and Steve's chances must not be affected and the disagreement, and what seemed an inevitable confrontation, were tacitly postponed.

Steve had had an immensely successful season leading up to the Olympics, culminating in two superb runs in Oslo, taking Coe's world mile record with the first and equalling his 1500-metre record with the second. In many eyes this made him favourite for the 1500 metres – he had an unbeaten string of forty-three victories – with Seb (who had set a 1000-metre world record at the first Oslo meeting) favourite for the 800 metres. Their clash was a showdown that had not been witnessed since the fifties when Roger Bannister and John Landy battled it out at the Vancouver Empire and Commonwealth Games.

Peter Coe and I share a room at the immense Isolovo Hotel on the outskirts of Moscow, a massive structure of ten thousand bedrooms, ready, most weeks, to welcome to the capital city the most successful workers from around the Soviet Union as a reward for beating quotas. On the first evening, after a dinner of plain fare, we decide on a stroll. We hand in our room key at the reception and are handed in return three key-cards, together with an insight into the extraordinary bureaucratic thinking that dominates Soviet life.

"No," Peter says, "only two people. Not three." He looks at one of the cards. "No Mr Barnes." We both smile encouragingly.

"No Mr Barnes?" says the receptionist.

"No Mr Barnes," we chorus.

Looking worried she quickly withdraws the cards and goes away to consult. Soon three or four people stare at us from another reception area. They are joined by two more. Then an interpreter comes over.

"You have three beds in your room," she announces.

"No, only two," I say. "No Mr Barnes."

She doesn't believe us. An old man, one of the hotel's commissionaires, joins the throng. His wartime medals clink as he limps over. There are now eight people in deep consultation.

"May I see your room?" asks the interpreter.

Of course they can. We cram into a lift and ascend to the eighth floor. There the party is joined by the formidable figure of the floor concierge. We fling open the door and wave triumphantly towards the two beds inside. There is a further lengthy debate. Finally, the interpreter turns to us and says: "Will you mind if we move you to another room?" The only way the system can cope is to go back to square one. We move.

The British athletics team arrived at Moscow airport amidst a great furore. Photographers milled around, flashbulbs popping every few seconds. Reporters, many of whom had never seen the inside of an athletics stadium in their lives, shouted inane questions. Steve Ovett, still back in Britain, had fuelled speculation with an exclusive interview in a Sunday paper: he had said that he felt he had a fifty-per-cent chance in the 800 metres and a ninety-per-cent chance in the 1500 metres. The temperature was rising nicely. Of course there were other medal hopes – Daley Thompson was the new world record holder at decathlon and Allan Wells, the dour, muscular Scot, was expected to do well in the sprints – but the middle distances had always been the blue-riband events of track and field, the ones on which public interest focused.

Peter Coe is on a high. It is his and Seb's first Olympics, a factor that is to prove crucial later in the week. He has tremendous expectations that his son will achieve the coveted double, a feat last accomplished sixteen years earlier in Tokyo by the New Zealander, Peter Snell. I harangue him fiercely, to try to keep his feet on the ground.

"Hello," he answers a telephone call, "this is Peter Coe here, Sebastian Coe's coach."

"What do you mean?" I cry when he replaces the receiver, "'Sebastian Coe's coach.' You're his father!"

"I put a hell of a sight more into creating the athlete," he says, "than into creating the son."

He dresses in a collar and tie under his track suit and I call him a "poofter", but all to no avail. Peter Coe is determined to enjoy his first Olympics. He leaves for a more central hotel after two days.

The opening heats of an Olympic event rarely cause surprises, unless somebody is tripped or falls. The 800 metres saw the usual removal of the chaff from the wheat. Because of the boycott it was difficult not to qualify for the semi-final. Coe and Ovett both strolled in and so did Beyer, the man who had roared past them both to take the gold medal in the European Championships in Prague two years earlier. The third British runner, Dave Warren, also went through. The next day saw the three semi-finals. Beyer went out, Warren qualified and both Seb and Steve cruised through safely. Nothing had happened to mar the first confrontation.

Peter and Sebastian Coe sat at dinner in the large but excellent international restaurant in the Olympic Village, after the semi-final. As always, the hubbub, the noise of so many languages, was immense. Peter considered his job completed; now he was just the valet, as he termed it, waiting upon his athlete's needs. Suddenly, with a quick flash of anxiety, he realised that something was wrong. Seb stared at his meal, uninterested, then glanced up and caught his father's eye. The immense pressure, the world-wide expectation that only an Olympic Games can produce, had arrived.

"Cool it," Peter said quickly, "don't run the race now."

Seb thought that people who had told him of such anxieties had exaggerated. He had been to a European Championships and a European Cup final and thought that he could cope. Now he realised that nothing that had gone before could have prepared him for this. He had his worst night's sleep ever, listening to his heart thumping away, staring out into the darkness, watching the dawn of his fateful day rise.

As the morning wore on he constantly sought company. Part of the shock was the suddenness of the pressure. He had felt a twinge when visiting the huge empty stadium shortly after his arrival but mostly he had been relaxed, happy, enjoying the Moscow sunshine. At lunch he felt disoriented, ungainly. He knocked over his cup of orange juice, dropped his cream carton into his coffee. He didn't want to be alone. As he and Peter left for the stadium, Brendan Foster, who had run his last international race in the 10,000 metres, noticed them both in almost frenetic conversation. He thought it strange, for on such occasions an understanding silence between coach and athlete is normal; the waiting is almost over, the job done.

Steve Ovett, meanwhile, had had a good night's sleep. He had arrived in Moscow later than the rest of the team, two days before the first round of the 800 metres. He had settled into the Village, rooming with two coaches, Ron Holman and his own mentor, Harry Wilson. The atmosphere was relaxed, jokey even. They shared the making of the tea.

Steve was recognised as the supreme competitor. He had experienced a very tough schedule in the Montreal Olympics four years earlier, where he had run fifth in the 800 metres final and reached the semi-final of the 1500 metres, five races in all. He had won the inaugural World Cup 1500 metres in Düsseldorf in 1977 and had recovered from the shock of Beyer's win in Prague to take the gold medal in the metric mile. There was no doubting the man's pedigree and the fact that his invaluable Montreal experience would stand him in good stead here.

He went for an early morning run with Wilson – once around the Village, about three miles. It was important, he knew, to keep to his routine of two runs a day. His body, maybe even his mind, expected it. Then he left, with his friend and training partner, Matt Patterson, to meet his parents at the Ukraine Hotel, a vast, monumental building in the centre of Moscow with a foyer like Grand Central Station. It was an occasion for small talk; the moment of truth was almost upon them, in more ways than one. They wished him good luck and he returned to the Village.

He had a good lunch and then talked with Harry, almost mechanically, about possible tactics. Steve, only half listening, nodded occasionally. It was routine, had happened twenty, thirty times before but it was important, for if the ritual had not been performed Steve might have started to worry. He slept a while in the afternoon, then carefully packed his kit and boarded the bus to the stadium.

The three British athletes warmed up for the final. Dave Warren had run magnificently to reach it but had had his supreme moment. Steve Ovett warmed up on his own, bothered slightly by television crews. Coe was still disoriented, detached even. Finally, preparations over, they walked with their coaches and British team management to the check-in point, exchanged final niceties and then went over the long bridge that separated the warm-up track from the stadium, quickly dubbed by the competitors 'The Bridge of Sighs'.

They were packed into a tiny, stuffy room and had to sit and wait, shaking muscles, trying to stay loose. There were nods, brief handshakes, murmurs of good luck. Finally they were told to rise and leave for the arena, Indian file. As they emerged into the huge stadium, athletes, sweating, exhausted, forlorn, passed them, returning to the inner bowels, failure written across their faces, for the medallists had been shepherded away for the victory ceremony. The runners broke file and strode up and down the home straight or into the first bend. Then they were summoned to their marks.

We sat high up in the stadium, amidst a hundred thousand people. The fever that had gripped the world's media about this event had even caught the Soviets. Coe was the favourite of most of the British Press; his was the clean-cut, sporting image. Most importantly he talked to them. Ovett was cast in the role of the bad guy, who treated the press impishly and who, for five years now, after a bad experience, had been disinclined to meet them.

The gun went. Ovett was in lane two, Coe on the outside. The break from lanes came at the start of the back straight. It is a tense, dangerous moment in a two-lap race, the runners desperately jockeying for the best positions. There was some barging and pushing, Ovett doing more than his share. The crowd made a collective comment. As the first lap unfolded Ovett was still trying to extricate himself from a boxed position; Coe, running wide, was keeping out of trouble. The bell rang; Brazil's Alberto Guimaraes was leading, but the pace was extremely slow, 54.3 seconds. Ovett was sixth, Coe last. Dave Warren had a moment of glory, dashing into the lead, taking Kirov the Soviet runner with him. Ovett chased hard but Coe stayed where he was at the rear of the field. As far as he was concerned it was the critical moment of the race. Kirov took the lead going into the final bend and the crowd rose and roared.

Coe now began to make his move, but he was ten metres away from the leader. Kirov led into the final straight but Ovett was poised at his shoulder, wondering where Coe was, then chastising himself for not going flat out, for almost willing a repeat of Prague. He drove hard, took the lead and went away. It was almost an anti-climax and Steve thought that too. Behind him Coe was desperately making up ground, overtaking Guimaraes and an inspired Kirov to take the silver. But Steve had won, and thought: "You're Olympic champion. What's all the fuss been about?"

The British Press stood and looked at each other shell-shocked. The unbelievable had happened; the world record holder, the man who was, on paper at least, fifteen metres faster than anyone else in the field, had been beaten. It was an extraordinary reaction, far from the euphoria that a British gold and silver should have invoked. Peter Coe was stunned, wondering where he had gone wrong. He had seen the anxiety signs the day before but was inexperienced, facing an entirely new situation. He hadn't known what to say and in the end had said nothing.

Seb said that he felt relief after the race rather than disappointment and this was symptomatic of his condition, of the anxiety syndrome that he had just suffered. He just wanted to get away, anywhere, but there were the formalities to go through; the dope-testing, the medal ceremony, the incessant demands of the photographers. He received his medal – Clive James, then television critic of the *Observer*, said that Seb looked as if he had just been given a turd. The kindest comment you could have made was that he looked grim. The Olympic anthem was played (the British decided not to allow *God Save the Queen*) and it was all over.

Steve suddenly began to overheat and almost became unconscious in the dope-testing room. The moment passed and he ignored it, but many were to remember it four years later in Los Angeles. That evening he had a small

Steve Ovett beats Nikolai Kirov and Sebastian Coe to win his only Olympic gold medal.

celebration with his parents at the Ukraine, though since it was after hours they could not obtain any food.

Every morning of the Games a fleet of buses stands outside the Isolovo ready to whisk us all to the Lenin Stadium or any of the other venues in Moscow. By them stand smiling, efficient Intourist guides with clip-boards. Every morning we smile back and say: "No thank you, we prefer the Metro." They leave nonplussed and we proceed to the station, walk down the clean stone steps, past the bent, old peasant women whose sole job it is to keep them clean and on to the immaculate platforms. A digital clock shows the seconds ticking away until the arrival of the next train, never more than three minutes away. Specially for the Games a voice in English announces over an intercom the station you are at and the next one. It is brilliantly efficient and one makes instant comparisons with the London Underground and its antiquated carriages, its graffiti, its dirt and grime – until one remembers that people had done exactly the same with Mussolini's railway system.

One day Don Anthony and I stand on the train travelling to the city centre and an old man stands alongside us, carrying a battered briefcase. It is Army Day and he wears his medals. Judging by the reek of vodka he has had a celebration. Don and I chatter away in English and then he suddenly catches our eye.

"English?" he says haltingly. "Shakespeare, good; Galsworthy, good; football, Wolverhampton Wanderers, Tommy Lawton!"

We smile and shake his hand and he beams. We look around for a KGB man but no one stirs. At the hotel there is an amazing system whereby you can be telephoned direct to your room and vice-versa. Amazing – until you realise the significance of it and wonder where in the hotel Boris sits and listens.

Living on the outskirts of Moscow we seem completely free of the stultifying security of the inner-city hotels and the Village. The shadow of Munich and the killing of the Israeli athletes seems destined to hang like a pall over the whole Games.

For the Scottish sprinter Allan Wells the hype surrounding the Coe–Ovett confrontations was absolutely ideal. He and his wife Margot slipped into Moscow with the team, unnoticed and unheralded. He was lucky to be there. Two and a half weeks before the Games he had badly ricked his back whilst training and only treatment four times a day got him to Moscow in a fit state. It had been a scary time. On the day after he had sustained the injury he tried jogging and was forced to stop after a hundred metres, the intense pain making his body run with sweat.

Allan's background was like that of no other British sprinter, for he was born in Edinburgh, the home of Scottish professional running, venue of the famous Powderhall Handicap. The early coaching that he received was from the "pro" trainers. Their regimented, disciplined approach suited his personality, which was complex. The Allan Wells who arrived in the Soviet capital was an automated sprinter, programmed by his wife–coach Margot and himself, no detail left to chance, no avenue unexplored, a man determined to stick rigidly to the schedule that had been laid down. He shared the same Village accommodation with Sebastian Coe and there was, in some ways, a striking similarity between the two athletes. Peter Coe and Allan were both engineers and Margot and Peter were related to their charges. The father would finally lose his job because of the time he devoted to the son's running; the wife had given up her international career to help her husband.

In the days before the opening heats of the 100 metres he trained carefully and as he did so he reflected back on his life and the trail that had finally led to Moscow. He remembered his early days as an engineer when he had become flustered over a job and a foreman had said to him: "Look at the drawing, laddie, decide what you want to do, get it into your head, look at the drawing again. Do it three times." What had it been – two minutes' worth of advice? Yet it had stayed with him all his life. Precision planning, the week-by-week build-up and above all the trials, that unique feature of Powderhall training, the flat-out, full-distance runs against the clock, a routine he was to maintain right up until the end of his career.

In Moscow he slept only four and a half hours every night and being the man he was this made him fret, for good nights' sleeping was an essential part of the plan. As he lay in his bed, willing slumber, he remembered another focal point that had turned his career around. It was towards the end of a training session at Meadowbank Stadium, in Edinburgh. The group had worked hard but now came the time for the trial. He had become friendly, even close, to another Scottish sprinter, Drew McMaster, and as the time came for the race, he went over to chat with him. McMaster cut him dead, completely ignored him, and a light dawned on Allan as surely as if the sun had suddenly risen above Arthur's Seat. This was the reality then, the hard, competitive edge that the coach desired. There was no room for sentiment in this world. He decided just to go through the motions of the race, because he had no chance. His attitude was wrong, he knew that now and would change it. He became a Jekyll and Hyde figure, a self-confessed sod in training. In the gym, on the track, at his famous speed-ball work-out, he determined to be a perfectionist. He became obsessed with performing always at his best. To achieve this he relied more and more on Margot, his mentor, his prop, his coaching eye. Steadily he improved, this Scottish loner, won the 200 metres at the 1978 Commonwealth Games in Edmonton and now he was here, chasing the title "the fastest man on earth".

The aim had not always been Olympic gold, but simply to get himself in physical and mental shape to do his best. The political pressures of the previous six months – he too had received some nasty mail – had made him even more determined to do well. His firm of marine engineers had given him six months off to prepare and this had made him realise that these races would be the most important that he would ever run.

When he learnt the draw for his opening heat Allan told Margot that he was going to go out and set his mark on the event by beating Don Quarrie. The great Jamaican had defeated him over 100 metres in Edmonton and still had a world-wide reputation. All Allan's concentration was on this first race, he was looking no further forward. He blasted out, held his form and duly finished half a metre up on Quarrie.

He collected his gear, left the stadium, took the bus back to the Village, rested and then returned the same way, back to the warm-up track, all on a meticulously planned timetable. He knew when to leave the room, which bus to catch, knew that a special bus lane from the Village to the stadium ensured that there would be no delays. When he arrived he warmed up and then, accompanied by team manager Nick Whitehead, himself an ex-Olympic sprinter, who seemed to know what and what not to say before a race, he crossed the long bridge into the stadium for the second round.

It was a tough draw. There was Crawford, the defending champion; Lara, the Cuban; Mennea, from Italy, who had set a new world 200-metre record the previous year; and the Bulgarian, Petrov. Three of them would reach the final – but they were led home by Allan Wells in a new British record of 10.11 seconds.

"Well," he said to Margot, "we've all showed our hand. But I've done it once and I can do it again."

That night he ran the final over and over in his mind as he suffered his insomnia, and he did not lose it once.

He won his semi-final and Margot, watching from the stand, thought it his greatest-ever run. Allan needed convincing because it had felt so easy. He was a muscular type of sprinter, heavily reliant on power and drive and he liked to feel it. This run had felt too relaxed, he hadn't been pushed, the second man, Lara, being a metre behind.

Again he left for the Village and his absence caused a slight panic amongst the British team management. Suddenly attention was focused away from the 800 metres, for it seemed that only Silvio Leonard, the Cuban champion, stood between Allan Wells and the gold medal. "Where is he?" they kept asking Margot. "Is he all right?" When she found him he was lying on his bed, reading *Forty Years of Murder.* It would take his mind off the race, he said, but also keep him aggressive!

Margot and Allan felt that everything was on schedule when they returned to the stadium for the evening final. On the warm-up track the two Cubans, Lara and Leonard, were preposterously practising starts, with the latter three

Allan Wells' lunge for the line (left) just beats Cuba's Sylvio Leonard and makes him the oldest ever Olympic 100 metres winner at twenty-eight years and three months.

The serious Scotsman permits himself a lap of honour.

metres ahead at thirty. It was all part of the psychological ploys that had been in evidence all week. Mennea spying on Wells's training; Crawford pretending to lose his spikes and shouting abuse at Quarrie. Before he reported in for the final, Allan went to the lavatory in a small pavilion by the warm-up area. As he stood there he thought, not for the first time in his life, what the hell are you doing here? You're putting yourself through murder. And then he prayed to God to give him the strength to win the gold.

He said good-bye to Margot. "I feel really good," he said.

"Go out and show them what you can do," she replied. "See you after the race."

"I'm going to do everything I can do," he said.

He was marched away and felt as if he were being taken in front of a firing squad. He went into the little room where the finalists assembled before they emerged into the heady atmosphere of the stadium. As they waited the Russian Aleksandr Aksinin went out for a moment and when he returned he was without his shorts and on his slip there was a red mark, presumably meant to look like blood. Allan thought, this guy is trying to have us on. He looked away and made sure that Aksinin noticed his contempt for this tactic.

His draw for the race was not good. His chief rival, Leonard, was in lane one, Allan in lane eight. He tried not to worry, he was programmed for this moment. It was the culmination of years of sacrifice in his life.

There was a false start and Allan was glad of it for he was poorly away. Lara next to him was credited with the flyer. They were away the second time, and again Allan had a slow reaction. Leonard started well and was leading. By fifty metres the Scotsman felt on his own, at eighty he glanced over and saw Leonard. He told himself to drive hard, keep form and dip at the finish as he had planned. It was the dip, the lunge finish, that gained him the gold by inches, for even the clock showing hundredths of a second could not separate them. At twenty-eight years three months he became the oldest ever 100 metre Olympic winner. History, in a way, had repeated itself, for Britain's only other Olympic sprint champion, Harold Abrahams in 1924, had employed such a finish to win the gold.

Confusion reigned for a time as to who had won. Initially the photographers thought it was Leonard but when Allan watched the replay on the giant scoreboard he was convinced that he had got the verdict and embarked on a lap of honour. Half-way round it he suddenly worried that maybe he hadn't won and that he would look very foolish. It was typical of the man.

Despite the fact that he won the silver medal in the 200 metres with another British record, the race was something of an anti-climax. Each round was a psychological struggle. He felt more and more drained. Mennea, the champion, had made an early exit from the shorter sprint. He was so worried by the man the Press inevitably dubbed the "Flying Scotsman" that he had spent a long time consulting with the double champion of Munich, the Russian Valeriy Borzov. In the final Allan, as he went to his blocks, again wondered what he was doing there, why he was putting himself through the mangle for a second time. It was a frequent thought for this very serious man, for whom the slightest deviation from a meticulously planned programme meant an angst of worry and doubt, who needed the continual reassurance that Margot, his tough, streetwise wife, was able to give him. In the end, to gain his gold, Allan Wells had had to conquer more than seven other sprinters.

The very large wife of a Very Important Person angrily waves her accreditation and demands entrance to the huge, six-thousand-bedroomed Hotel Rossiya. Imperturbably, the military security team manning the X-ray and other checking equipment at the doorway ask her once again to step through the security beam. For the tenth (or is it fifteenth?) time she does so. The machine bleeps. She cannot pass.

Her anger boils over and her ample bosom heaves as she raves. Mr Brezhnev should hear of this. It is unthinkable. She is not only a VIP but a VVIP. She has to go to an important meeting. Her husband will be worried. Their machine must be faulty. They must allow her through.

All this falls on stony ground with the Armenian-speaking soldiers. They smile encouragingly and offer her another chance under the beam. Perhaps this time it will give an all-clear. She barges through, eyeing her large, black handbag that has cleared X-ray and awaits her. The machine bleeps.

After three-quarters of an hour an interpreter arrives and the large lady, now subdued and close to tears, is persuaded to subject herself to a strip search.

Five minutes later she emerges, passes clear through the beam and awaits her magnificent, steel-ribbed corsets as they pass through X-ray.

The Rossiya housed all the media, and all the main officials visiting the Games. Security was ultra-tight. Guests would rush out of the exit to wave farewell to one of their visitors, turn to re-enter the hotel and then realise their mistake. They had to walk around the block, as large as London's Green Park, to regain entrance on the other side. For those of us on the fringes of the city there were no such problems; we were free to come and go as we pleased. We ran in the nearby park, past the local markets with their inevitable queues. We talked to students who wanted to practise their English. We rode the Metro, went to the Bolshoi, visited the Gum shop and the Kremlin.

The only problem was the bureaucracy. For each meal we had to produce a chit. No chit, no meal. The food deteriorated as the two weeks went by but we thought, what the hell, the citizens would give their right arm for the meals we were being served with.

Philip Noel-Baker is having a whale of a time. He is the symbol of recognition that the Soviets badly need and so he is fêted and interviewed ad infinitum. *Don Anthony introduces him to some young Australian nurses and I gaze astounded across to their table as they chat away whilst Philip has his hand firmly gripping the upper thigh of a vivacious blonde, who seems totally unperturbed – indeed, probably feels very safe.*

As Steve Ovett headed in a taxi towards the Ukraine Hotel to celebrate his gold medal with his parents, the athletes in the final event of the decathlon were willing themselves around the red rubberised track, faces drawn, bodies aching, for three and three-quarter laps, to end their two days of competition. The winner had already been decided, unless he fell over or dropped out. It was Daley Thompson, at twenty-one the youngest winner since Bob Mathias in 1948. He had led since the opening event, the 100 metres, the previous morning. His main challengers were two Soviets, Kutsenko and Zhelanov but they had struggled to match him in vain. Another Soviet, Katschanov, had challenged for seven of the ten events before crashing out, in tears and pain, with a pulled calf muscle during the pole vault.

Thompson at this stage of his career was a chirpy, cheeky young man. He had already won a Commonwealth title and early in 1980 had set a new world record of 8622 points at Götzis in Austria, surpassing the previous best by the American Bruce Jenner by just five points. This Olympic title in Moscow was the beginning of six golden years for him, years in which he was to prove himself one of the greatest athletes the world has ever seen.

Yet he was also to prove an enigma. To me his quirky personality, his normal persona, never matched in any way his physical attributes nor his great competitive nature. His friends and acolytes fiercely defended him, especially his attitude to the media which was uncompromisingly anti. No one seemed to have the courage or will to point out or correct his anti-social behaviour, which was frequent. He lived for decathlon. He loved the bonhomie of the event, the camaraderie. It has been his *raison d'être* and ten years on from Moscow, in the twilight of his career, he seems reluctant to leave the stage. In the Lenin Stadium he set the fastest time in the 100 metres, and in all his subsequent decathlons it was the yardstick by which we were to forecast his performance.

The day after his Moscow triumph, Sue Gough, an athletics aficionado *and I take Daley's Auntie Doreen to lunch at Stalin's favourite restaurant on Gorky Street. Allan Wells had said after his win that he wished he could cut his medal in two to give half to Margot. In some ways Auntie Doreen, a small, almost frail woman, deserves the whole for without her efforts in bringing him up it is doubtful whether Daley, an abandoned, angry young man, would have been there at all.*

The vanquished await the arrival of gold medal-winner Daley Thompson in the decathlon 1500 metres.

High up on a balcony in one corner a string ensemble plays. The meal is excellent and pleasant and it is difficult to believe we are where we are. Auntie Doreen has been bewildered by the past two days when Daley has gone centre-stage on the world arena and become the Olympic champion. In her hotel strangers kept coming up and congratulating her.

"People keep staring," she says over her bortsch, "it's so embarrassing."

I look at her, this kindly, down-to-earth woman, to whom, as my grandmother would have said, there is no "side". At this time she has no measure of the man she has reared, that will come later; she only knows that he has done something of which she can be intensely proud. The last thing she will have thought of will have been to claim any credit for herself.

"If there's any justice in the world," I say to her, "after the next New Year's Honours, you should be Lady Doreen."

The final day of the Games saw the second act and finale of a drama of which any Greek dramatist would have been proud. As the heats and semi-finals of the 1500 metres had evolved, the anticipation and excitement had mounted amongst the British contingent and the media.

After the 800 metres Seb had escaped from the stadium as quickly as he could, comforted by his father and by David Miller, then a sports writer with the *Daily Express* and later to be his biographer. He had spent a sleepless night with Peter trying to analyse what had gone wrong, trying to pick up the pieces. The next morning he set out for a long run, to shake everything out of his system. He was trailed by a whole car-load of British photographers, all hanging out of the windows, cameras poised, rather as in a Keystone Cops movie. A tabloid carried a picture next day titled "Trail of Shame".

An additional problem had been created by Peter. Holding court in the international area of the Village, where the media and team members can meet, he gave the Press his opinion. Seb had "run like an idiot", a sentiment that he had expressed to his son shortly after the race. It was a true assessment and one that any coach would have been duty-bound to relay. Whether it was wise to confirm it to the assembled hacks was another matter. But he also said: "I'm ashamed. I feel humiliated." The words were splashed over the next day's papers and this annoyed Seb. But his anger was tempered by the fact that he felt he had let his father down. Speaking ten years later Peter Coe explained that the words referred to himself. He was ashamed that he had not prepared Seb properly, he was the one that was humiliated – but of course, it was misconstrued.

The general media opinion was that Ovett had proved himself the "complete middle-distance runner" and Britain's greatest. Coe was dismissed as being all right for one-night stands in Oslo and Zurich but not able to stand the hurly-burly of major championships. Ovett was a firm favourite to complete the double.

Steve Ovett, after he had crossed the line in the 800 metres and regained his composure, had found himself staring into a television camera. Elated by his easy success he drew the letters I-L-Y in the air and mouthed the word Rachel. It was, as he said, a simple, loving gesture over the satellite. The media in Britain galvanised itself into action and besieged Rachel's home in Maidstone. The publicity that followed was intense and led to a family row in Moscow when Steve went to visit the Ukraine Hotel the day before the 1500 metres final. Ever since Gay Ovett's arrival in Moscow there had been a phony atmosphere that concealed, for the sake of Steve's running, the tensions based on jealousy that had been building up over the preceding months. Pictures of the attractive Rachel on the front page of tabloids broke the dam. Home truths were uttered; Steve stalled. He would not discuss it until after the final. A break came a month or so later, bitter and long-lasting. Gay and Steve Ovett would only be reunited nine years on after she had seen him break down on television following controversy at the AAA Championships.

The sun beat down on the Lenin Stadium for the heats of the 1500 metres. Again it should have been a matter of discarding the also-rans but the Press area was full. In the first heat Steve Cram, a curly-haired Geordie from Hebburn, qualified with a desperate sprint finish. In the third Coe led nearly all the way and finished an easy second to Fontanella of Italy. The fourth heat saw Steve Ovett matched against the East German, Jurgen Straub. The pace was fast; Steve had forty-three consecutive wins behind him and Straub wanted to take him on. There was a desperate battle over the last lap which Steve won but in a time which everyone knew must have sapped his energy. We looked at each other; what on earth was he playing at? It was a question that he was to ask himself in more rational moments later.

Ovett won his semi-final waving at the crowd in a time almost seven seconds slower than his heat. The nineteen-year-old Cram made the final by inches in fourth place. In the other semi Coe met Straub and in a rumbustious race seemed once more to display tactical ineptitude. On the final bend he found himself boxed in and had to show aggression and produce an acceleration that gave his forlorn supporters some hope. He finished ahead of Jurgen Straub by inches, with the Frenchman Marajo third.

For the latter half of the Games Moscow had produced a mini-heatwave. The final day saw a clear blue sky and a hot sun. The stadium was packed. "I've got to come back and climb the mountain again," Coe had said. He had known that this race was going to be tough, but he had made it that much tougher by his display in the 800 metres.

The preliminaries over, carried out amidst the cries of British supporters who seemed evenly divided between the two main protagonists, the runners crouched over the curved starting line at the end of the first bend. The gun went and the race was under way. Straub and Coe were the early leaders, but the pace was woefully slow and anxiety crept into our minds. With such a slow pace it would be easy to get boxed in at a vital moment. The field was bunched together after one lap, the time over the minute. The second lap was even slower, and the digital clock at this point displayed a time that was slower than in Bannister's famous mile, slower even than in Walter George's great run almost a hundred years before. But the stakes here were very high indeed.

Straub was now leading, Coe and Ovett were almost literally breathing down his neck, and the tension in the hot stadium was rising. The pace was so slow it was almost like watching the runners in slow motion. Then for the second time in two years an athlete from the German Democratic Republic intervened in the destinies of these two great British middle-distance runners. In the European it had been Beyer; now Jurgen Straub, the tough ex-steeplechaser, put in a sustained burst with over half the race to go in a courageous bid for glory. The cadence of the runners quickly speeded up, physical and mental adjustments were made. They were no longer bunched but in a line, Straub leading, Coe second, Ovett third. In the stand Peter's heart leapt, for he knew the race was now tailor-made for Seb. But Ovett was still there, in contention.

The bell rang: Straub led them round the penultimate bend, then sprinted again down the back straight, gaining momentarily a three-metre lead over Coe. Seb gradually closed the gap and was poised to overtake on the final turn, Ovett still close behind. The crowd rose, roaring encouragement. This was the true race, the one they had longed for, the two greatest runners in the world locked together in a death-or-glory finish in an Olympic final. Seb burst past Straub, put in a "second-kick" and went clear. Now we waited for the Ovett drive to the tape – but it did not come. Coe ran on and crossed the line, his arms open wide as if in supplication, his face a mixture of pain, excitement and finally triumph. Behind him Straub grimly fought Ovett for the silver medal and won. Coe sank to his knees in immense relief. He had won, he had redeemed himself. The stadium, the Press box were in pandemonium. It had been one of the greatest finals ever. Coe and Ovett never met in competition on equal terms again.

Seb Coe's face tells the story of the two-act drama in Moscow, from receiving a silver medal that could have been "a turd"...

...to the joy of his triumph in the 1500 metres.

2

IF IT'S WEDNESDAY, IT MUST BE ZURICH

After the final of the 1981 American championships in Sacramento, California, two sweating figures spoke to the media. They were the winner, South-African-born Sydney Maree and the runner-up, Steve Scott. They praised each other in time-honoured, sporting fashion; Maree added that he was proud to have won his first American title and said how grateful he was to be allowed the opportunity to compete on the world stage. It was all conventional, polite post-race utterance until the subject arose of their respective forthcoming European tours. Then their faces lit up and their voices became animated as they spoke of the prospect of races with Coe and Ovett, both of whom they believed were eminently beatable. They could hardly wait for the moment, a few days hence, when they would board the jumbo jet to fly to the European circuit, which traditionally began in Oslo with the Bislett Games.

One of the rituals of the Bislett was the barbecue held the afternoon before in co-promoter Arne Haukvik's garden on the outskirts of Oslo, which always included generous helpings of the first strawberries of the season, often flown in from more southern and warmer climes of Europe. Here gathered the élite of the world's athletes and the attendant media, in a jocular and relaxed mood, the tensions and tiredness of the demanding European circuit having not yet set in. The meeting traditionally set the European season in motion. American athletes poured in on flights from Boston, New York and Los Angeles, relieved to be rid of their collegiate programmes where they often ground themselves into the track for Ivy League pride. The national championships marked the end of all that and after it began the rush to Europe, with its illegal but lucrative "spectaculars".

In 1981 all was as usual. Smoke from the barbecue drifted skywards, its pungent smell enticing. Arne moved affably around the different groups in a straw trilby hat that one might hope he wore only once a year. I sat and chatted with Harry Wilson, who was there with Steve Ovett, who called him Tiger, mainly because he looked least like one. We reminisced about Geoff Dyson, a colossus in the world of coaching, who had died five months previously. Scattered around the garden were Steve, relaxed and happy with Rachel; Scott, the American miler, and John Walker, the 1976 Olympic champion, the first man below 3:50 for a mile. Clearly something was brewing in the middle-distance world. Standing apart from the rest, in earnest conversation, were Sven-Arne Hansen, the hard negotiator for the meeting, and Pete Petersons of Nike, the shoe company, who also ran an athletics club in the States. Petersons was anxious to get one of his runners, Tom Byers, into the 1500 metres, but the Norwegians were reluctant. They already had a world-class field of ten runners. The target was the world record, jointly held by Coe and Ovett. Walker and Scott, who had missed Moscow because of the boycott, thought they had something to prove. Ovett wanted the record for his own. Sven-Arne knew it was a buyer's market.

"However," he said, through chewed strawberry, "we need someone who can run 2:52 for the first twelve hundred metres." He stared hard at Petersons; he had been careful not to use the words "hare" or "pacemaker".

"My man can do that," Petersons said quickly. "He ran 3:36.35 a couple of weeks ago."

Sven-Arne made an offer for Byers that Petersons couldn't refuse and the conversation moved on to more general topics.

The following evening all roads led to the Bislett Stadium for one of the annual summer treats for the citizens of Oslo. It is a small, compact track of only six lanes. The crowd is close to the action and the athletes love it. More world records have been set there than in any other stadium on earth. The last had been Ovett's world mile record the year before.

Carl Lewis had won the long jump in a rather subdued fashion: Allan Wells had not recovered from a virus and had lost the 200 metres to the American, Dwayne Evans; Harald Schmid, the extraordinary German 400-metre hurdler, had beaten the Kenyan, Mike Boit, in the 800 metres; but all these events were merely *hors-d'œuvres* to the main course, the metric mile. Arne Haukvik, still in his straw trilby, introduced the runners trackside. Each athlete waved in appreciation of the approving applause of the crowd. Having suitably built up the tension, Arne stood back and the runners prepared to get down to the business.

From the gun Byers took the lead with only an Ethiopian, Wodajo Bulti, for company. After completing one lap Bulti and Byers, his long, blond hair flowing behind him, were some fifteen metres ahead of the pack in a moderate time. After two laps, the two front runners were some fifty metres ahead of the rest, who clearly had taken a collective decision to race each other rather than go for the record. It is interesting how such moments occur, for obviously no one utters his thoughts as they circumnavigate the track. In this instance, reputations were at stake. Walker and Scott wanted to beat Ovett; Steve wasn't going to make any sacrifices to let them do it.

Byers duly arrived at 1200 metres in 2:53.09, some sixty metres up on the great stars behind him. Bulti had faded back into obscurity. At this stage the pacemaker usually bows out gracefully, but Tom Byers, with a glance backward, must have considered the distance behind, the distance ahead, his condition and the growing enthusiasm of the crowd for what they considered was his audacity; he decided to keep going. He entered the straight still thirty metres up but looking desperate, lactate pouring through his body, painfully slowing him down. Ovett led the charge behind him. We were now on our feet, yelling him on. The field closed and closed but Byers staggered over the line the winner and collapsed amidst great cheers and laughter. He had run the last lap nine seconds slower than Ovett but his courage had paid off. It had been the little hare's day. Did Sven-Arne mind? Of course not. It was good entertainment; the crowd loved it, and they would come back next year.

The Gateshead International Stadium is crowded as the teams march in for the opening ceremony of a four-sided international match. The crowd stand, the anthems are played, including that of Ethiopia, whose runners are making their first visit to this part of Britain. The teams march off and we all settle down to enjoy the meeting. I am doing a public-address commentary and introduce the runners for the opening event, the 800 metres. The two Ethiopian competitors seem to be absent. The time set for the race passes and the crowd fidgets a little. Then from the walkie-talkie of the controller, who sits next to me, comes a tinny voice.

"Andy Norman says the Ethiopians are refusing to run. We played the wrong anthem. We played that of the Haile Selassie era. Andy is still talking to them. Hold the start."

I apologise for the slight delay but give no reason for it. Then a further communication arrives.

"Andy says that the Ethiopians will run if the crowd can hear their anthem. He says they want to come up and sing it to them." There is a pause. "Andy says to tell Tony, the crowd mustn't laugh."

It is one of those moments in life when, as the saying goes, it's down to you.

"Ladies and gentlemen," I say over the PA system, "I am sorry to tell you that we have done a great injustice to our guests here in Gateshead, the runners from Ethiopia. We have inadvertently played the anthem of the despot Haile Selassie. The Ethiopian runners would like you to hear their new revolutionary anthem and they are going to sing it to us now. Please be upstanding."

The citizens of Gateshead stand and listen, without so much as a giggle, to the most dreadful caterwauling heard in their town for many a year. At the end they cheer and stamp their feet and the Ethiopians wave back. If the singing hasn't been totally appreciated, the sentiment behind the protest has. I summon Andy to a walkie-talkie: "Don't you ever," I tell him, "bloody well do that to me again!"

The year 1981 was one of those off-championship years when the athletes can relax, choose their meetings, earn some still under-the-counter money and have a good time. The tensions of Moscow behind them, Ovett and Coe set out on a record-breaking spree that was unprecedented and has yet to be surpassed. In between they served Britain and Europe well in the European and World Cup competitions. Although they chased the records they studiously avoided each other all that season. Under glittering floodlights, beneath balmy summer skies, the green digital figures on trackside clocks displayed times that had never been seen before. The crowds loved it and television called for more. The promoters were now the kings of athletics, and extraordinary sums changed hands surreptitiously. It was Coe who set the record bandwagon rolling with an 800-metre run in Florence in June that many believe is the greatest world record. Nine years on it still stands, surviving the assaults of a generation of two-lap runners.

It was the first time in the event that any athlete had been under 1:42, a milestone in itself. When Coe set it, it placed him 1.71 seconds faster than anyone had ever run before; only the Brazilian, Joachim Cruz, has come close since, back in 1984. Seb said of his own feat:

"It's getting under 1:42 that is the great thing for me. It was as hard a race as I have run for a long time. In the last thirty metres I was beginning to tie up but apart from that there was no problem. You give so much in Olympic year. Mentally, you get to the end of it and you are a bit dry."

He was back to what, in the end, he liked doing most. But he was a tougher athlete mentally after the Olympic experience, and it showed. He moved on to Oslo and whilst Steve Ovett failed to break his own record in the Dream Mile, Seb ran what remains the definitive 1000 metres, and that moreover with a badly blistered foot. After the run and the lap of honour he sat down to inspect it with the Norwegian doctor, surrounded by a bevy of photographers, including Britain's Monte Fresco, a jovial Jewish lad and an excellent cameraman. The bloody foot was displayed to view with a piece of blistered skin hanging down. A few winced.

"Hang on," said the doctor, "we'll soon whip that off."

Monty viewed the scene. "Never mind Seb," he said. "I had a bit off the end once – you'll get over it!"

In Lausanne, with the screams of English teenage girls on holiday ringing in his ears, Steve Ovett was badly paced and missed his own record. He made other attempts in Budapest and Fana in Norway, producing fantastic runs but receiving no accolades. Then, in August, came nine days that shook the world of miling.

The *Weltklasse* in Zurich's Letzigrund stadium is widely acknowledged as the world's finest athletic meeting. With powerful finance behind him through the assurance of world-wide television coverage, the promoter, Andreas Bruger, can almost command the attendance of the very best athletes. The stadium is always packed to its 28,000 capacity, most standing as at a football match. Seb Coe had visited Zurich several months before to plan the mile race, wanting them to have timekeepers at 1500 metres, looking for a double record attack. A week before, Tom Byers, the unexpected hero of the earlier Oslo meeting, joined Coe for practice as his pacemaker. Byers' instructions were to run a 3:44 pace for as long as he could.

As in Oslo, Byers went immediately into the lead, followed by Coe, and after a first lap on schedule, they were disengaged from the rest of the field. After two laps Coe sensed that Byers was fading and took up the running. Now he had only the crowd to aid him, but it was enough and he finished in 3:48.53. Ovett, recovering at home from a slight injury, could only sit and telewatch.

Exactly a week later, on one of his favourite tracks in Koblenz and wearing his treasured red Soviet team vest, Steve Ovett struck back. There was some controversy when he asked for the race to be switched from 1500 metres to a mile; in the end the promoter, Freddy Schaefer, had to do what so many promoters were having to succumb to: stage both races. Steve Scott won the shorter race within half a second of Ovett's record and then, paced by one of the most dependable men ever, Bob Benn, Ovett set a new mark of 3:48.40. But the climax was to come in Brussels two days later.

The *Ivo Van Damme Memorial* is named after one of Belgium's greatest-ever athletes, the silver medallist in the Montreal Olympics 800 and 1500 metres, who died tragically in a car crash in December 1976. It is held at the Heysel Stadium in Brussels, a venue which was to have other, tragic, connotations later in the eighties. The field that assembled for the 1981 Golden Mile was a formidable one – Scott, Maree, Byers from the USA; the Irishmen Coghlan and Flynn; John Walker; Wessinghage of Germany and Mike Boit. The man they had to beat was Seb Coe. Coe had not run since Zurich; the rest had been padding around Europe. He was, he said, too tense in the *Weltklasse* and had rested. He half suspected that Ovett might turn up for the race. Byers had promised to do a better job of pacemaking than he had done in Zurich, where he had been suffering from a cold.

The pace was perfect this time, Byers keeping to the schedule, Coe shadowing him, and of the rest only Boit in attendance. Coe slipped into the lead with five hundred metres left, but this was not to be a solo effort such as he had had to produce in Zurich, for still running in his wake was Boit. Coe pulled away down the home straight and flashed past the finishing line so quickly that he failed to see the clock. As he turned he saw the huge stadium scoreboard flashing "Record du Monde" and he knew that he had done it. The time was 3:47.33. Miling standards had been revolutionised. Craig Masbach had run 3:54.31 at the meeting in Lausanne. In 1979 it would have ranked him amongst the world's top twenty milers of all time. In the Swiss race he finished tenth. By the end of 1981 twenty of the twenty-five fastest miles ever run on a track had been achieved in that year.

It was Sebastian Coe's superlative season. He had set four world records, two of which were to last the decade. He was now a celebrity, and was a guest on *Desert Island Discs*, which some thought the ultimate accolade. The world seemed his oyster, but though he was to achieve further greatness, he was never to run as fast again.

Steve Ovett had run superbly, without in the end matching Coe. His wedding to Rachel, with Andy Norman as best man and Matt Patterson, Harry Wilson, Freddy Schaefer and Arne Haukvik in attendance, seemed like the end of a Fred Astaire movie where the hero gets his girl.

We take a holiday in Italy and then drive on to the World Cup in Rome. This is a mistake. Seven years before I had spent two weeks in the city for the European Championships, when Brendan Foster had run his finest-ever race to win the 5000 metres. It had been an exotic two weeks at the Excelsior Hotel (on company expenses) when I had met my second wife, Gwenda. We should have remembered that when travelling by taxi, the person sitting in the front seat would always turn round to face the back-seat passengers, who would always have their eyes closed.

Each drive is a repeat of the chariot race in Ben Hur. *In the middle of the day you have your foot hard on the accelerator, tyres screaming in a desperate attempt to shake off the three Fiats that are inches off your back bumper, headlights on beam, horns blaring a perpetual cacophony. Shouts are exchanged, victory signs seem rampant. And as you roar through red lights at 100 kilometres an hour and approach black-habited nuns and little old ladies on quite useless pedestrian crossings, the* carabinieri *lean back on their motor cycles nonchalantly manicuring their nails. Well, that's how it seems. It is always a relief to flop down in the* Stadio Olimpico, *beside the Tiber River.*

Twenty-one years earlier the sporting world had descended upon Rome for the Olympic Games. Abebe Bikila, a bodyguard to Haile Selassie, had run in bare feet and won the marathon for Ethiopia, finishing amongst the ancient ruins in the city centre. At the stadium, Wilma Rudolph had sprinted to gold three times and Herb Elliott, that extraordinary Australian miler, had won the 1500 metres in devastating fashion. Older enthusiasts still pointed to the place where his old, craggy, eccentric coach Percy Cerutty had stood on the moat wall and waved a towel to signal that Herb was on for a world record. Now everyone was back in Rome for the second World Cup. British athletes were well represented in the 1981 European team. Earlier in the season, in Zagreb, they had had their finest European Cup, the men's team finishing third, their best-ever position, and the women third-equal on points.

Ovett and Coe won their races convincingly but the real pressure was on Allan Wells. Inevitably, after his Olympic win people pointed out that the Americans had not been competing and hinted that, if they had been, he would not even have won a medal. He had convincingly disproved that argument at Cologne after the Olympics and by winning the 1981 IAAF Golden Sprint series in Berlin's Olympic Stadium, defeating the men who would have represented the USA in Moscow. In Rome he was to face the new American sprint sensation, Carl Lewis. Better known as a long-jumper, Lewis had clocked evens for the 100 metres, the fastest time recorded at sea level. The confrontation was not to be. Lewis, nursing a hamstring injury, was never a contender and jogged in last. Wells's shock opponent turned out to be Ernest Obeng, a Ghanaian domiciled in Britain, running for Africa. He made the start of his life and led the Olympic champion by two metres at seventy. Wells just caught him on the line.

The most majestic winner was Edwin Moses, clocking his seventy-fifth consecutive victory in the 400 metres hurdles. He looked like an ancient African prince, his movements slow, graceful and controlled. His domination of the event was total.

On the Friday night, the first evening of the competition (which attracted 180,000 people in total to the stadium) the 10,000 metres had been run, between heavy showers. It featured an Ethiopian, an East German and an American. The American was Alberto Salazar, better known as a marathon runner, and it was the night that he learned, as had David Bedford a decade before him and Ron Clarke before that, that the last laps of a 10,000 are where the running turns into racing. He had finished third, with a personal best, but had been outkicked. Werner Schildhauer of the GDR had won with Mohamed Kedir second. The race had been watched, imperturbably, by Miruts Yifter, the Olympic winner, the man dubbed by David Coleman on his BBC Television commentary "Yifter the Shifter". Much ado had been made in Moscow about the uncertainty of Miruts's age, some even suggesting that he was over forty. Nigusie Roba, an Ethiopian coach with the African team, took the opportunity to put the record straight at the World Cup.

"I have spoken with Miruts's father," he said. "Rumours that he is middle-aged are unfounded. He was born on 15 September 1944." Two years later the birthdate was changed again.

The USA team won seven men's events and two women's and there was anger amongst them about their country's fruitless boycott of the Olympics. Evelyn Ashford won both sprints and was convinced she could have won gold in Moscow. Likewise, Moses, Lewis, Greg Foster. "I'm angry," Evelyn said at her Press conference, "I know I could have done well." And the boycott had been instigated by an ex-cross-country runner who jogged around Camp David.

The big shock of the World Cup was not Ernie Obeng's run, nor Kathy Cook finishing second to Ashford and beating Marlies Gohr in the 100 metres, nor even Seb Coe jogging the History and Peace Mini-Marathon around the landmarks of the Eternal City on the Sunday morning. It was Steve Ovett attending the post-race Press conference. The British journalists were so surprised that they could hardly lift their ballpoints. It was the first time in four years that Steve had consented to meet such a large contingent of sporting hacks.

"Well, I've enjoyed the season," he said, "even though I have not been training as hard ... My rivalry with Seb is a fabrication of the Press. There is no personal grudge, but I don't see him much so we can hardly be called friends ... The Fifth Avenue Mile? I'm told it's all downhill so there will be no problem. And if we get into any trouble we can call a cab."

The proposed Fifth Avenue Mile (won by Sydney Maree a week or so later) had caused some concern in Rome. Fred Lebow, its originator, had been angrily told by the ageing Adrian Paulen, the crotchety IAAF President, in his harsh Dutch accent: "Maybe now we should have a hammer throw at Columbus Circle." But Paulen was very much the outgoing President. Did he jump or was he pushed? Officially, he retired to be replaced by the urbane Turin lawyer, Primo Nebiolo, who had been heavily canvassing for the job for two years, with commercial support. But the rumour was that once he was convinced he had a majority of the votes he or his assistants went to Paulen and told him that he faced defeat. They advised him to retire. The old man took it badly but could not risk humiliation.

In truth, the sport needed Nebiolo as much as he desired the job. In Rome athletics faced a crisis and Paulen was too much a conservative, a man of the old traditions, like his predecessor, Lord Burghley; he could not understand that an official revolution was required if the sport was to be saved from the pro-moters, entrepreneurs and agents who lurked just on the sidelines.

Already the amateur laws were a travesty; athletes were being paid appearance and bonus money in the European meetings with little attempt at secrecy. In Britain, proposals for cash prizes and open athletics had been rejected at an AAA Extraordinary General Meeting, but that decision had been declared null and void by its legal advisers. In the end the British Board's delegates to the Rome Congress were instructed to support the IAAF Working Group on

Eligibility which proposed the abolition of the term "amateur", the setting-up of trust funds for athletes, the awarding of cash prizes at international invitation meetings and allowing athletes to benefit financially from advertising and endorsements. It seemed as far away as the moon from the athletics depicted that year in the film *Chariots of Fire*.

In sombre session the Congress met and made no decision. There was heavy opposition from the East European countries. Everyone needed time to consider the proposals. Banner headlines indicating that the world of athletics had come to its senses and that Coe and Ovett would soon be millionaires proved to be premature. A special Congress would be held in Athens the following year.

The pace of change in the sport, both in Britain and internationally, was accelerating and it seemed fitting, in a way, that those to whom such changes would be anathema were gently passing away. Dyson, Britain's first professional Chief Coach, had died in February; Guy Butler, an Olympic bronze medallist of the twenties, went a month later and finally Lord Burghley, the epitome of the amateur, President of the AAA, Olympic champion of 1928, died in November. These were men of a bygone age, an age of sporting chivalry. Two years before he died Dyson ended a lecture thus:

"The radicals of one age are the reactionaries of the next! Forty years ago, I was one of an iconoclastic vanguard; but now, on some matters, take my station with a small conservative rearguard! It seems that each generation tries to make of the world the kind of place it dreams it should be. However, I suggest, each, when its day is done, comes to regret at least a part of the work of its own hands."

3

ATHENIAN JOYS AND WOES

"Where have I gone wrong? I've let the lad down."

The anguished voice and face belonged to John Anderson, coach to David Moorcroft. We were standing alongside the track by the finish line in the superb new 80,000-seater stadium on the outskirts of Athens. It was the final day of the 1982 European Championships. Moorcroft, the world record holder for the 5000 metres, a favourite for the title, had just finished third and had left the track, crestfallen and dejected. In truth the problem was more psychological than physical. He had known as he had jogged around on the warm-up track that he was not at his best, and was out of sorts with himself.

"Come on, John," I said, "you know better than to shoulder all the blame." But he would not be consoled.

I had flown into Athens the day before from a sports trade fair in Munich to find the British team in low spirits. At that moment we had only two champions, Daley Thompson and Keith Connor. The week had belonged to the Germans, both East and West. In all they were to collect forty-one medals between them.

On the morning of the final day I had sat on the terrace of the Hotel Cecil, the British team headquarters, drinking coffee with coaches Harry Wilson and Ron Holman. We were analysing the race to come and Moorcroft's chances but we were also reflecting on the turnaround in Britain's middle-distance fortunes since the euphoria of the year before. Steve Ovett had run into a church railing the previous November, badly smashing the ligaments and muscles behind the knee. He had had an operation almost immediately but complications had set in and he had not resumed running until March. In May, amidst a good deal of hype, a three-race series involving the two Olympic champions was announced. It stalled before the first event, Seb having to withdraw through injury. Steve ran well early season but then suffered from food poisoning during a trip to Paris and later badly tore a hamstring, which put him out for the year.

Seb Coe had arrived in Athens the clear favourite for the 800 metres. After seemingly cruising through the heats, he had taken the lead in the final; but as everyone was sitting back, ready to applaud the gold medal that he so badly wanted, the West German, Hans-Peter Ferner, stormed past like a man possessed to take the title. As in Moscow the athletics world was stunned. Peter immediately flew Seb back to London for tests which disclosed that he was suffering from low-level glandular fever. So British running hopes rested on this last day with two men, David Moorcroft and the twenty-one-year-old Steve Cram. Harry Wilson was doubtful about Moorcroft's chances and with great prescience saw Thomas Wessinghage, the West German doctor, as the real favourite.

David had had an extraordinary year, weird even. On his own admission he was not, off the track, an aggressive, competitive person. Early in 1982, however, he underwent a mystifying personality change, becoming belligerent, masochistic, not only in his athletics but in his social and home life as well. His wife Linda and coach John Anderson were both, in varying degrees, to bear the brunt of it. He felt frustrated and angry. He brooded at home. His normally warm and gregarious nature changed to silence and introversion. It was a mystery to him and those around him. Perhaps the realisation that he was twenty-nine and had not achieved his full potential had suddenly come to him; that he had come so far for so relatively little. Next year he would be thirty, time was running out. Maybe that sparked his aggressiveness. His training went brilliantly.

He went to Oslo and ran a sub-3:50 mile, only the third Briton to do so. Afterwards he talked over his problems with John Anderson and felt that he had made progress towards solving them. He returned to Oslo, ostensibly to try to break Brendan Foster's eight-year-old 5000 metres British record. From early on in the race, with nobody willing to take the lead, Moorcroft went to the front and started reeling off laps, not at British record pace but on *world* record schedule. He moved further and further away from the rest of the field. The crowd watched with increasing excitement as he seemed likely not just to break Henry Rono's record but to obliterate it. He won in 13:00.41, a tantalising few metres from immortality, yet almost six seconds faster than Henry's best.

As he went to his marks in Athens, though, David knew that he was not the man who had run so brilliantly at the Bislett. He was suffering from an ear infection which made him feel out of sorts. A storm had come down off the mountains and lashed the track, which made him feel worse. The early pace was slow, the runners bunched. For a while he took the lead but to no definite purpose. As he described it afterwards, he was "living a nightmare". It was obvious from the conservative pace that the last lap would be fast, and when Wessinghage took over Dave was fifteen metres behind. He had run a dreadful race. The German was a worthy champion.

Perhaps by the time he got to Athens, David had reverted to his old self, believing that with his world record he had finally fulfilled his potential. Maybe you did need to be totally competitive to succeed at the very highest level. Six years later in the Nihon training camp before the Seoul Olympics, Daley Thompson was being his usual combative, belligerent self and those who knew him were rubbing their hands. It was a good sign, they said. The question is: who would you rather have, Daley Thompson or David Moorcroft?

Steve Cram, on the other hand, ran brilliantly in the 1500 metres. What impressed the experts were his quick thinking and his courage. Again from the gun nobody seemed prepared to make a commitment and after two laps the whole field was still bunched together. A hundred metres further on Graham Williamson was tripped by Abascal of Spain and in the ensuing confusion Steve took off, building up a sizeable lead. He was aided in his run for home by watching the huge TV screens at the end of each straight. His lead dwindled but never faded away.

Although he was still young Steve brought a lot of experience to these championships. Brendan Foster recalled that back in 1978 he and Cram were travelling to Crystal Palace for the Emsley Carr Mile. The youngster, seventeen years of age, had run a 3:42 1500 metres but still Brendan wondered what this schoolboy was doing in the famous race. As it turned out the two of them had a battle for third place down the home straight which Brendan just won by overtaking Steve at the finish.

"I wouldn't have made it," he said, "but for the fact that I just could not have stood the humiliation at home at being beaten by a schoolboy from just around the corner!"

Steve ran a creditable 3:57.43 to become the world's fastest seventeen-year-old. After the race he was untying his spikes, collecting himself together. Brendan approached him.

"Do you fancy going to the Commonwealth Games?" he said. There was one place left; Moorcroft and Hutchings had already been selected.

"Oooh, yes," said Steve.

"Do you think you're ready?" Brendan persisted. "Do you think you'll learn from the experience?"

"Yes, I do," Steve replied.

Brendan went up to Andy Norman and John Martell, two of the top AAA officials. "Look," he said, "I'm the next qualifier in the 1500 metres but I'm doing the five and ten. I'd like the place to go to this kid. He's from Hebburn, he's run well and it would do him a lot of good for the future."

"That sounds like a good idea," Norman said. "Just a minute." He went away and reappeared a few moments later. "That's okay."

Brendan went back to Steve, who was still warming down. "You're in the Commonwealth Games," he said.

"Thanks very much," Steve said and continued jogging round. It was the way of the British athletics world in those days.

Steve travelled south on the train with Mike McLeod, the experienced 10,000 metres runner, to join the team flying to Edmonton, Canada. Once the train pulled away from the station he was disconcerted to see Mike pull a six-pack of lager from his bag. At Darlington Mike's coach climbed on and also produced a six-pack. They turned to Steve and handed him a can. "Here you are, kid," they said. He made it last all the way to London.

In Edmonton he observed and learned. Later he was to say to Brendan that he noticed that the athletes who went to the parties and discos were not the same ones who won the medals. He'd noticed that Dave Moorcroft and Brendan, who were sharing a room, were not into the heavy socialising, they were there to do the business. Two years later he was living the Olympic experience and now he was European champion.

Another who had gone to an Olympic Games and gained invaluable experience was Daley Thompson. He celebrated his eighteenth birthday when he competed in Montreal and finished eighteenth. In Athens, he put in a superlative decathlon, not only winning the title but regaining his world record which he had lost to the West German, Jurgen Hingsen. It had been an extraordinary summer for the event. First, in Götzis, Daley became the first man to better 8700 points. In August Hingsen beat that record by nineteen points. Now, in Athens, Daley scored 8743 points, well over two hundred ahead of his opponent. In the 100 metres he ran his best-ever, non-wind-assisted decathlon time, 10.51 seconds, and the *aficionados* knew that he was on song. After the third event, the shot put, Frank Zarnowski of America's *Track and Field News* wrote: "At 12:44 on the first day, it's all over." It was, and Daley joined that élite band of British athletes who had held Commonwealth, European and Olympic titles at the same time.

Keith Connor, domiciled at university in the USA, travelled back to Europe for the championships and won Britain's first-ever title at the triple jump. He leapt to a magnificent 17.26 metres in the first round to take the lead, watched two athletes creep up on his mark whilst he nursed an injured ankle and then added three more centimetres in the fifth round to assure himself of the gold medal. At his post-race interview he offered an insight in to the world of triple-jumping.

"Pain?" he said. "I jump with pain in every competition and I'm no great hero. Sometimes I give into it as I did a couple of times tonight but on that fifth jump fear of Grischenkov [who came second] catching me drove me to push it out of my mind."

In the days before the track and field events began the world's top athletics administrators gathered in Athens for the special IAAF Congress that would decide the future of the sport. Britain's contribution to the debate was going to be critical. The man chosen to make the important speech was Andy Norman, already a dominant figure in European promotional circles, who was fast dragging British athletics into the latter half of the twentieth century without, it must be said, too much protest.

What Andy realised was that if the Congress rejected the proposals for open athletics that had been put forward a year earlier in Rome, the sport would be at the mercy of those who knew nothing about athletics, cared nothing about athletics and whose main aim would be the making of the proverbial fast dollar. The people who would have to be won over would be the East Europeans. He approached John Rodda of the *Guardian* and asked for help in moulding his thoughts into a cohesive, telling speech. Rodda agreed but forgot about the arrangement as he hurried around Athens gathering information for his preview of the championships. He had a long and highly convivial evening with colleagues before going to bed in the early hours. At eight-thirty the next morning the telephone by his bed in the Hotel Olympic gave a loud, shrill ring that did nothing for his instant headache. It was Andy in the foyer, ready for action.

For the next few hours Rodda sat on his balcony in the sunshine, dark glasses hiding the fearful glare, orange juice moistening his dry mouth, listening to the emphatic, unmistakable voice of Andy Norman hammering home crucial points. He converted them into tough, cogent words and sentences in his mind and transferred them to the typewriter in front of him. Finally, Andy took away the speech that was to convince the world of athletics that it must move to reality, and John Rodda went back to bed.

In the end the Congress accepted the vast majority of the proposals but baulked at prize money, which many felt was going too far down the road to outright professionalism. Hiding payments to athletes behind high-sounding words – "subventions" and "trust funds" – kept, if only slightly, the myth of amateurism alive at international level. The IAAF had gone down the road of appearance money and nine years on many feel it was a grave mistake.

"It has meant that athletics has been geared for quantity and not quality," Brendan Foster said, nine years later. "It has meant that, unlike the past, achievement is not rewarded. In some ways it has changed the nature of the sport."

But that was for the future. The delegates left Athens knowing that for the time being at least, they had kept control of the running of international athletics.

A few weeks later many of the British athletes were on the other side of the world, in Brisbane, Australia, competing for various parts of the British Isles in the very relaxed atmosphere of the Commonwealth Games. England, Scotland, Wales, Northern Ireland – the Isle of Man even. Daley Thompson retained his decathlon title, Steve Cram won the 1500 metres and Allan Wells gained the 100 metres that had eluded him in Edmonton.

Back in England, Don Anthony took an urgent telephone call summoning him to the bedside of Philip Noel-Baker. The marvellous old man was apparently close to the end of his life. Don rushed round to South Eaton Place. Philip lay propped up on pillows, as white as the sheet he lay on, suddenly looking all of his ninety-two years. His eyes were closed. By his side were his granddaughter, his secretary and his nurse.

"Philip, can you hear me?" Don asked.

"Very well, my dear Don," said the great man in a wonderfully clear voice.

"You're a lucky man," said Don, "you're surrounded by young ladies."

"Nothing more stimulating, my dear Don, than the company of beautiful women," said Philip.

Then his voice became faint and the bedside group looked at each other and collectively thought: last words. They leant forward for posterity.

"What was Allan Wells's time for the 100 metres in Brisbane?" asked the man who had paced both the youngest and oldest Olympic 1500 metres champions to their gold medals.

Disconcerted, Don had to think. "Ten point-o-two," he finally said.

There was a silence. "Hm," said Philip. "Allan lacks concentration. He'll have trouble in the two hundred."

A few hours later he died peacefully.

In Brisbane, Allan was going for a sprint double that had always eluded him. In Moscow he had won the silver in the 200 metres and in the World Cup he had finished second. He battled hard down the home straight with Mike McFarlane of England. They both lunged across the line together, and the photo-finish camera could not separate them. For the first time in the history of the Games there were joint champions. Somewhere out there, an old man smiled knowingly as he gazed down on the unique medal ceremony.

4

ENDURING PASSIONS, EVERLASTING TORMENTS

The enduring passion that millions of runners have for their obsession was vividly brought home to me in 1985 when I talked to Erich Segal, the celebrity author of *Love Story*. We met in the lounge of the Connaught Hotel in London's Mayfair. A representative of his publisher sat nervously by, but she need not have worried for we were not there to talk about *Love Story*, neither the book nor the film, nor about his new novel *The Class*, nor about his professorships at Harvard and Yale. We were there to talk about his running and the most traumatic moment of his life, the moment a doctor turned to him and said: "It's not in your head, it's in your leg. I'm sorry, Erich, you are never going to run again."

"It was," Erich said, "a deadly pronouncement." He sat there in blazer and white flannels, a diminutive man with a receding hair-line, neat, tidy, slightly nervous. He had hobbled in on time for our appointment. "Only one pronouncement could have been worse," Erich went on. "In fact, if he had said I'd got three hours to live I would have gone out and run for those three hours."

It was at Harvard, as a student, that he had taken to distance-running and within two years of the coach looking at his frail frame and immediately assigning him to the distance squad, he had run his first Boston Marathon. Boston, with its decades of history, its legends, its heroes won him over completely. It was 1955 and for the next twenty years Erich was there, on Patriots' Day, in the town square at Hopkinton, lusting for the race to begin.

"I decided after that first run that this was for me but that I had better start preparing properly for it. Living in Boston I trained specifically for the marathon. In order for me to conquer my fear of Heartbreak Hill [the Newton Hills on the outskirts of Boston], once a week, fifty-two weeks a year, I did repeat hard runs up it. So when I came to it, during the race, it was my friend

Professor, novelist and former marathon-runner Erich Segal.

and not my foe. I had prepared myself, Pavlovian-style, to run up Heartbreak."

-He had once met the domineering exiled Hungarian coach, Mihaly Igloi, who raved at his charges: "Keel yourselves! Keel yourselves!"

Erich smiled deprecatingly at the memory. "It was not for me. I took more to the methods of the New Zealand coach, Arthur Lydiard." This meant running a lot of miles and by the early sixties, when he was now a teaching fellow at Harvard, he was running upwards of a hundred miles a week.

In his twenty-five years of running Erich had won but one race. It was an ultra-running event of thirty-three miles distance, a trial for the American team to run in the London to Brighton. It was held on the outskirts of Washington DC and right at the end, near Bethseda Naval Hospital, he found himself in the lead. He kept looking round for the legendary distance runner, Ted Corbett, but couldn't see him.

"I didn't know what to do, you see," he said. "I'd never won a race before. I said to myself: 'Erich, you've a mile to go, there is nobody near you, don't screw this up.'" He didn't, but then he increased his training so much that his legs seized up and he never made the British race.

He ran forty marathons. He taught Frank Shorter, who disdainfully watched him grinding out laps on the Yale indoor track, up to eighty of them for a ten-mile run. "You'd have to be an idiot to run a marathon," he said. Erich plodded on and years later Shorter won a memorable Olympic marathon victory in Munich and, legend has it, fired the running boom.

This, then, was the man who was fated to live a chilling, almost Faustian existence, a denial of everlasting bliss. In the mid-1970s he hurt his leg so badly he was paralysed for a year with a compressed peroneal nerve and underwent unsuccessful surgery. He has limped ever since and will do so until he dies. He cannot run properly.

"I'm like a ruptured duck," he said wryly. "If ever I try to run for a bus I feel like handing out stickers to people saying 'I once used to run normally, you know.'"

He was, like Marlowe's hero, tormented with "ten thousand hells" in his deprivation. He lives part of the year in London and part in Boston. He chose to buy a house in Hampstead, near Parliament Hill Fields, massive parkland with a synthetic track in the middle. This was before his operation. It was a fateful mistake.

"I cursed myself," Erich said. "I created my own Dante-like Inferno in moving to an area where there are runners day and night. A runner's paradise can be a hell for an injured man and I see people running *all the time*. When I get up for breakfast, when I come home late from the theatre, I see people running."

I could feel the intensity of his trauma as he stirred in the leather armchair.

There was nothing of a consoling nature one could say, and I did not attempt it. If he is in Boston on Patriots' Day, he leaves town. If he is in New York on the day of the Marathon, he flies back to Boston. London will not see him for its great race. As his wife Karen drives him around, he told me, he points to the joggers. "There's one," he will say. "Look, there's another …" It is an infinitely soulful comment. She turns to him. "I know, Erich," she says, "I know."

That Erich Segal would exchange his fame and fortune for the chance to run again there is no doubt. He was a serious runner, and once ran eighteenth in the New York Marathon when it was almost a private affair in Central Park. But then running began to be popular in the United States. People had seen, on network television, Frank Shorter's run in Munich and a form of emulation arose. By the mid-seventies there were 6,000,000 people running or jogging in the USA; by the eighties this total grew to 30,000,000. Less and less was running around the streets considered, as Erich put it, "an eccentricity bordering on pathology".

Fads and fashions take some time to cross the Atlantic and interest in Britain for the whole of the seventies was confined to a hard core of thin, emaciated, often wholly unattractive individuals who seemed to revel in the most masochistic conditions – infernally steep hills, mud up to the ankles and bracken that ripped at the calves. If you had told a hardened marathon runner in 1970 that 90,000 people would actually want to run twenty-six miles twenty years hence and that 25,000 would do so he would undoubtedly have looked for the men in white coats. But as Coe and Ovett were lighting up the running tracks of Europe, in Britain were seen the first stirrings of a massive urge to run and jog. The genesis of this was, in fact, the New York Marathon of 1979. Then in its fourth year, it was the brainchild of an eccentric, bearded Transylvanian Jew named (in America) Fred Lebow. From small beginnings Lebow had built the race up and this year it had 12,000 starters. Across the Atlantic an equally eccentric figure was having his interest roused. Chris Brasher, craggy and inelegant, sat in the bar of the Dysart Arms, his local in Petersham in Surrey and also the headquarters of Ranelagh Harriers, smoking a pipe and sipping at a pint of real ale. He listened to tales of this race, which covered five boroughs of New York and attracted thousands – the enthusiasm of the crowd was so great, it was said, that you dare not stop running. This was not quite true, as I was to find out three years later. Intrigued, Brasher and his fellow orienteering enthusiast, John Disley, decided to run a tour to New York.

They both ran, and were fascinated by the race that began out on Fort Wadsworth, near the Verrazano Narrows, curled through the city and into the heart of Manhattan, finishing in Central Park. Lebow had negotiated television coverage, the first time that a marathon had appeared on TV outside the Olympic Games.

It is something of an understatement to say that Chris Brasher is not everybody's cup of tea. His autocratic style, his total belief in his own view-point, his abrasive manner, his often dismissive attitude to hard-working, dedicated colleagues have not endeared him to all. But most would allow that they have a love-hate relationship with him, that these characteristics are the down-side of a man who is also single-minded, imaginative, has impossible dreams and fulfils them and who, above all, loves running. Without Brasher there would have been no London Marathon.

Disley is his side-kick, the quiet man of the duo which has for a decade kept the marathon on course and built it up to be not only a race of world-wide stature but a huge fun-party throughout the capital.

They were both steeplechasers back in the fifties, both had an ongoing love affair with the mountains and with nature. Disley won a bronze medal in Helsinki in 1952. Brasher came to prominence by being one of the pacemakers in Bannister's sub-four-minute mile in 1954. Two years later though, in the Melbourne Olympic Games, he first showed the attributes that were so evident twenty-three years later: tenacity, cussedness, self-belief. He won the gold medal in the steeplechase and survived a disqualification.

He returned from New York in 1979 fired with a burning ambition to stage a big marathon in London. He wrote about it for his newspaper, the *Observer*, which took up the cause. Two lunches were staged at the *Observer* offices involving prominent figures from the Greater London Council, the police, the Sports Council and the AAA. At the second lunch, after ample vintage claret had loosened rigid thinking, John Disley produced a draft of a route that used the Thames as a handrail, started in one hemisphere and ended in another, took in many of London's historic landmarks, came down the Royal Mall, curled in front of Buckingham Palace and ended on Constitution Hill. As with his Olympic run no one gave Brasher's dream a chance; but it was so ambitious, so marvellous, so absolutely right that even the police – who were faced with the prospect of shutting down many of London's main thorough-fares for a whole day – became enthusiastic. The London Marathon was born.

Brasher is a character, a man of cultivated inelegance, wild Wastwater rather than stockbroker Surrey. What Brasher's detractors seem to miss is that he is so entertaining, a veritable one-man show. In 1983 I was scheduled to interview him in the Dysart Arms. After the appointed hour cryptic messages were relayed from the bar concerning his progress from County Hall, then the headquarters of the Marathon. Finally he arrived, an hour and a quarter late, in a corduroy suit, a white-spotted red silk handkerchief tied around his neck and wearing a blue cap not unlike Lenin's. His spectacles glinted in the lights of the inn. He collapsed into a chair.

"Christ!" he said in his slightly rasping voice, "it was the bloody wheel-chairs."

For one alarming moment I imagined a disabled demonstration on Rich-mond Hill, snarling the home-flowing commuter traffic, but then I realised that he was referring to the great debates that were going on at that time about wheelchair participation in the Marathon and that this had delayed him. His mild blaspheming was not in any sense aimed at the disabled but was more a reflection on his late arrival. Over our pints of real ale we discussed the Mara-thon and that year's controversy, which was the accusation that Brasher and Disley were using the race to promote their commercial interests, which concerned the distribution of a brand of American running shoe. The topic had been the subject of an article by Duncan Campbell in the *New Statesman*. He denied any impropriety.

"One of your staff at the Marathon told me," I said, "that in the morning you'll be bawling them out for an alleged mistake or for something that you feel is not going right and by lunchtime you'll be buying them a pint in a nearby pub."

"Quite right," Chris said, suddenly grinning, "life is too short to harbour a grudge."

"John has said," I went on, "that problems are created by sequential thought." Chris's eyes twinkled at this. "That you will jump from point A to point C or D whilst the rest of them are still considering point B. Would you therefore consider yourself mercurial?"

As he considered the word, Brasher sipped at his ale and puffed vigorously at his pipe, as if signalling to some Apache chief on the other side of the room.

"No, no, no, no, no," he said in a familiar, vehement style of rebuttal, the words coming like machine-gun fire. I was surprised at his reply, for the Oxford Dictionary lists "mercurial" as implying eloquence, ingenuity and the possession of an aptitude for commerce. Without those qualities the London Marathon would have been but a pipe-dream.

On 29 March 1981 just over 6,000 runners left Greenwich Park to embark on the first London Marathon. They were led home on Constitution Hill, in the slight misty rain, by two men, a Norwegian and an American, who decided on a dead-heat: Inge Simonsen, a twenty-one-year-old physiotherapist and Dick Beardsley, a twenty-four-year-old Minnesotan farmer. Crossing the finishing line together they caught the imagination of millions of television viewers, thousands of whom were to apply for the race the following year.

Both runners showed up for the tenth anniversary celebrations in 1990, though Beardsley was lucky to be there. The previous November he had sustained multiple injuries when the leg of his overalls became trapped in the power take-off shaft of a tractor. He suffered extensive damage to his ligaments, cartilages and tendons. He was lucky to escape with his life and there were fears that he would never walk again. They were unfounded and he, operating without crutches and braces, believes that he will defy the doctors' verdict and run recreationally again. Not for him the traumatised life of Erich Segal, though every day is now a bonus.

Joyce Smith, a forty-three-year-old grandmother, won the first women's race and became the first British woman to run under two and a half hours. She ran even faster to win again in 1982. Eight years later she was planning a comeback assault on the over-fifty world record.

As the decade wore on the winners of the London seemed to assume less and less importance. The times of Ingrid Kristiansen and Grete Waitz, chasing as they were the elusive two hours twenty minutes marathon, were awaited with eagerness by the *aficionados*. It is gratifying to have five British winners – Hugh Jones, Mike Gratton, Charlie Spedding, Steve Jones and Alastair Hutton – but in the end it is the 170,000 and more finishers in its ten years to whom the marathon truly belongs.

At the end of each Marathon there is a party for the helpers, or rather, representatives of them for there are thousands who man feeding-stations and carry out hundreds of other mundane but vital tasks. Here the prizes are presented and up come amazing people, sixty- and seventy-year-old men and women who have not only completed the course from Greenwich to Westminster Bridge (the finish since 1982) but have run times that only two decades or so earlier would have been highly respectable for runners one-third of their ages. Lithe, bright-eyed and bushy-tailed, they seemed to have found the true elixir of life. The London Marathon, like all the great marathons, is a race that challenges not only the physique and physiology of men and women of all ages but also their very souls. As they run through London past a million or more people urging and cheering them on they will discover something new about themselves, that they are different people at the finish from those who stood bleary-eyed in the early morning mist near Blackheath. We watch them, some in fancy dress as pirates or waiters or horses or nurses pushing prams. They pass Big Ben, sight the finish gantry and raise their arms aloft in personal triumph, be it in three hours or six, and we find our blood stirred and our throats choked; for what Brasher and Disley did was write their own Fanfare for the Common Man.

Running saw not only thousands upon the streets of London, New York, Rotterdam, Boston and Chicago, but also smaller groups, sometimes singly:

Dick Beardsley and Inge Simonsen, the joint winners of the first ever London Marathon in 1981, celebrate their victory.

Massed London Marathon runners cross Tower Bridge, urged on by spectators.

across the Himalayas for 2,000 miles; along the Great Wall of China; through the Klondike Trail; on Alpine mountains; or through the Death Valley in California with sauna-like temperatures up to forty degrees centigrade and zero humidity along its 140 miles. They ran, not just for twenty-six miles but for twenty-four and forty-eight hours, round running tracks and shopping malls. They ran for days on end from Los Angeles to New York, from John O'Groats to Land's End as if they were searching for the Holy Grail; perhaps, in a way, they were.

If the seventies saw the beginning of the running boom in America, the eighties saw the emancipation of women in running. When the first Olympic marathon for women was staged in Los Angeles in 1984, members of women's political groups lined the route, realising the importance of the occasion. Since Roberta Gibb and Kathy Switzer battled to invade that bastion of male running, the Boston Marathon, back in the sixties, it had literally and figuratively been a long, hard road. Though other women's championships had been staged, this was the ultimate acceptance. Six women epitomised this emancipation, this drive against male prejudice as to what women could or could not achieve. They were two Norwegians, a glamorous New Zealander, an English grandmother, a Portuguese and an American of extraordinary courage and tenacity.

In 1978 Grete Waitz left her home in Oslo and travelled to New York for the Marathon, a rather reluctant guest at the feast. She had felt that she was coming to the end of a fairly illustrious career – a World Cup winner at 3000 metres and World Cross-Country champion – and her husband and coach Jack had persuaded her to try the marathon before she finally retired. Fred Lebow met her at Tavern-on-the-Green at a Finnair hospitality pre-race function and was disappointed to find that the furthest she had run before was twenty kilometres – just under half the distance. Doubting her ability to finish, he cast her from his mind as he tackled the thousand and one problems that arise in the hours leading up to the race. The next time he saw her was at the awards ceremony in the evening when she was celebrating a win in 2:32:29.8, a new world record by over two minutes. But she had suffered a thousand agonies in achieving it.

In the latter stages she had begun to hurt badly. The course was marked in miles, not in the kilometres that she was more familiar with, and this combined with her inexperience at the distance had led to a certain amount of disorientation. She entered Central Park pained in every muscle, bone and sinew, racked with exhaustion. She had three miles to go and had she been aware of that she would have dropped out. Instead she kept believing that the finish line must be over the next hill, round the next bend. She finally completed the race, glancing up at the digital clock, inexorably ticking the seconds and minutes away above the finish gantry. The time meant nothing. She had two ambitions; one to find Jack to yell at him for putting her through such agony and the other to find a bed, any bed, to lie down on and who knows, perhaps to die.

She recovered, received the plaudits that were her due and began a new running career at the age of twenty-five. She has won thirteen of her nineteen marathons – nine New York, two London. In 1983 she won the World Championship race in Helsinki and in 1984 was the Olympic silver medallist. A year after her début she was back in New York becoming the first woman to run under two and a half hours. But there were now others in the wings, and in 1981 a new star was discovered in the marathon firmament.

One writer has described Alison Roe, from Auckland, New Zealand, as Meryl Streep with a 70 maximal oxygen uptake. The likeness is certainly striking. She was born in Northcote, a suburb of Auckland, amidst volcanic and windswept countryside, where the hills are so steep that the locals have an almost permanent forward lean through walking up them. Not far away are the Waiatarua mountains, legendary in running folklore, where the coach Arthur Lydiard trained his charges and where later Rod Dixon, Dick Quax and John Walker also honed themselves to world-class perfection. Roe had been a sports all-rounder who gravitated to running at seventeen and was spotted by Gordon Pirie, then living in New Zealand, as manic in coaching as he was in running.

"Pirie," Roe said, "would have me believing I would make the Olympics in a week."

She survived the experience, married Richard Roe and entered the world of road-running. Her first marathon in Auckland was completed in just under three hours; in 1981 she won Boston in 2:26:46. The following October she ran New York and set a new world record of 2:25:28.8. Alberto Salazar had set a world best in the men's race. It was New York's greatest Marathon Day. It was also Roe's last triumph; racked by injury she is the only one of the magnificent six not to survive running into the nineties.

Second to Roe that day was Ingrid Kristiansen. Born in Trondheim on the north-west coast of Norway and with an athletics history similar to Waitz's, Ingrid seemed destined always to play the bridesmaid to her more illustrious countrywoman. Kristiansen had finished third to her in the Big Apple in 1980 and she knew that to prove her talent, to Norway and to herself, she had to beat Grete. Using psychological techniques she literally talked herself into it, dishing out defeat to Waitz in the 1984 Norwegian cross-country championships, her first defeat in fourteen years. That year Ingrid won London, the first of four wins. In the 1985 race she set the current world record of 2:21:06, a time that would have won every men's Olympic marathon up to 1960, a time faster than that of the immortal Emil Zatopek in 1952. Two years before her second London triumph she had run in the first women's championship marathon, the

European in Athens. It was particularly fitting that this first championship should be staged on the road supposedly run by the Greek, Philippides, bringing the news of the Persian defeat from the village of Marathon to Athens. It was the route run at the first modern Olympics, in 1896, a race won by the Greek shepherd, Spyros Louis. These marathon races ended in the marvellous setting of the marble stadium where those inaugural Games were held, floodlit, with a crowd full of expectancy as the runners, battling over the hills from Marathon, neared the finish.

Rosa Mota, just five feet two inches tall and weighing under seven stone, was as reluctant a débutante as Waitz had been in New York, four years earlier. As a native of Oporto in southern Portugal, she had, however, one enormous advantage; she revelled in the exhausting, humid heat that sapped the strength and will of her rivals. Earlier in the week Mota had run an unobtrusive twelfth in the 3000 metres and it was only at the insistence of her coach, Jose Pedrosa, that she took part.

She tagged along at the back of the field for the early part of the race, testing herself, determined to finish. As it unfolded she gained in confidence, moved to the front and battled it out with Kristiansen and the Italian, Laura Fogli. In the evening dusk the race approached the finish, the lead car and police escort with sirens and flashing lights heightening the drama. Hundreds of cyclists and motor cyclists wove in and out, adding to the chaos. The leader was Mota, on her way to her first major triumph. As she circled the black cinder track with its tight bends and inordinately long straights, she was drenched in sweat, her short black hair glinting in the floodlights, but her face was wreathed in a triumphant smile. A new running star had been born.

She was to repeat her triumph four years later in Stuttgart, win the Rome World Championship, the Olympic Games in Seoul and a third European in Split in 1990. Of the sextet it was Mota who ended the era in triumph. She was born in 1958, a year after the extraordinary running grandmother, Joyce Smith, made her international cross-country début.

When she took up road-running in 1976, Joyce Smith, a quiet, totally unassuming woman, was thirty-eight years of age and had, like Waitz and Kristiansen, a highly successful track and cross-country career behind her, stretching back over twenty-two years. She ran her first marathon three years later and won the second race in the Avon series, promoted by Kathy Switzer to attract women to the event. After winning the inaugural London, she returned in 1982 to win again, remarkable running for a forty-four-year-old. It would be her last major triumph, though many would point to her eleventh place in the 1984 Olympic race as a further example of an incredible running talent and an indomitable spirit, a spirit exemplified in that marathon by the winner, Joan Benoit.

I met Benoit at Boston University in the early eighties, when she was coaching there with David Hemery. A tiny, almost frail figure with a quiet, shy personality, she had already run a 2:30:16 marathon but her extraordinary moment of glory was to come three years later in the heat, smog and humidity that surrounded the Los Angeles Olympic Games. Benoit was lucky to be there at all. During the previous winter she trained assiduously for the US Olympic Trial race to be held at Olympia, Washington in May. Everyone in that race knew what they had to do to compete in Los Angeles. The first three would be automatically selected, regardless of injury or unusual circumstances. In March disaster struck with a painful right knee injury and with time so short there was only one drastic solution – surgery. On 25 April, eighteen days before the Trial race, orthopaedic surgeon Dr Stan James performed the necessary operation – an arthroscopic one to inspect the damage and then a cutting away of inflamed tissue induced by over-training. She left hospital the same day on crutches. Next morning she was swimming, five days later she was running twice a day. Despite further setbacks she won the Trial race by thirty-seven seconds and set about preparing herself for the first women's Olympic marathon.

It was a momentous occasion, an important milestone in women's sport. Finally women's running had become respectable. In the beginning it had been unacceptable and for them, embarrassing.

"When I first started running," Benoit said, "I was so embarrassed I'd walk when cars passed me. I'd pretend I was looking at the flowers."

Despite her problems, Benoit was ready. She had moved into Los Angeles some weeks before to acclimatise, to get used to the streets and heat and humidity. It was a mistake, for everyone recognised her. She moved north to Oregon and trained in the quiet of the countryside. To keep her mind off the race the week before, she indulged in an orgy of raspberry picking and canning.

In the end the race was an anti-climax. After ten minutes Benoit was away. No one chased her; everyone seemed mesmerised by Waitz, the World champion of the year before. Kristiansen became impatient but restrained herself. As mile after mile went by, Benoit went further ahead, but Waitz made no move. The American led by a minute at the half-way point. At fifteen miles Mota made a move that finally broke up the now despairing chasing pack. Benoit won by one minute and twenty-six seconds. Waitz was second, Mota third, Kristiansen fourth, waving her arms about in perplexity. As they stood in the middle of the vast Coliseum, Benoit said to Waitz: "I took a chance and lucked out." Women's running had come of age.

The men's story was really more of races than of personalities. Sure, the marathon had them in abundance, mostly concentrated at the beginning of the eighties. The Americans: Bill Rodgers, Alberto Salazar and Frank Shorter; the

New Zealander, Rod Dixon; Geoff Smith, Steve Jones, Charlie Spedding, Hugh Jones of Great Britain; the Japanese Toshihiko Seko; the Australian de Castella; the Ethiopians and the men from Djibouti. And the man who quietly began to dominate as the nineties were ushered in, Douglas Wakihuri of Kenya.

What became apparent too, was that there was a limit to what the body could take, if not the mind. There was a finite number of world-class marathons that even the very best could produce and as the years go by these very best are now rationing themselves, conserving their talent to reel off twenty-six miles at an average of four minutes and fifty-two seconds per mile. Thus pay days, as they are known amongst the fraternity, are few and far between and have to be lucrative. The winner of the New York Marathon has a good pay day but none deserved it more than the victor in the 1983 race, one of the greatest, a shoot-out as the Americans love to call it, between the Englishman Geoff Smith and the New Zealander, Rod Dixon. It epitomised the great marathon races of the eighties.

As dawn breaks on this October Sunday morning, black clouds hang over Manhattan, almost touching the tops of the giant skyscrapers. The rain falls vertically, not heavily but relentlessly. There is little wind. You know that the wet weather is set for the day.

All over the city groups of runners make their way to Lincoln Centre, to travel in their thousands to the great bridge out on the Verrazano Narrows, to encamp at Fort Wadsworth and await the start. I look at the digital clock by my bed in the Sheraton Tower Hotel on Fifth Avenue, the race headquarters. Rain spatters against the window. I am glad I have turned down an invitation to go and witness the start. I was there last year, in semi-earnest, wondering if I had made the right decision to take part. I hadn't. I had been reasonably fit when the chance came but nowhere near marathon fit.

I turn over and try to go back to sleep but now I am imagining what is happening out on Staten Island: the runners in multi-coloured track suits, mostly in marquees because it is wet, buying cups of coffee, keeping up the liquid intake, killing time, talking running. Last year the weather was dry, this year they wear green plastic garbage bags to keep out the rain. Except for Smith and Dixon, of course. They are the VIP runners, the élite, kept away from the running rabble.

The hours before the start seemed interminable. Loudspeakers blared music and issued instructions. We used the longest urinal in the world – because it was there. One of our party was the Running Dustman, who ran marathons with a dustbin tied to his back, collecting for charity. It had obviously given purpose to an otherwise mediocre life. He had been full of despair because Lebow had refused to let him run with his bin. Over the tannoy a voice said: "My name is

Fred Briggs. This is my fourth New York Marathon. I'm eighty-four years old. If I can do it, you can do it." The crowd roared applause. It was obviously what they needed to calm the jitters and fears now that the moment of truth was near. Then music blared and a lithe woman in a leotard led an aerobic warm-up in a harsh, Brooklyn accent that pierced the soul at eight o'clock on a Sunday morning.

As the start time approaches I turn on the television set, on the ABC channel. The weather is no different out by Verrazano, droplets of rain cover the camera lens. Last year there was a fierce headwind, this year it appears to be still. The runners are gathering at the head of the bridge, behind the markers that will indicate finish times. Last year I stood at the very back with a vague game-plan, slower than ten-minute miles to try and stop me "hitting the wall", which is what had happened to me at twenty-two miles in the Dublin marathon of the year before. It was a forlorn plan, doomed to failure.

The television cameras are homing in on the élite runners at the start. Geoff Smith is there, the former middle-distance runner from Liverpool, in his first marathon. So is Rod Dixon, in his second. His 2:11:21 in Auckland last year was the third-fastest-ever marathon début. The wet lens picks out Gidamis Shahanga, the unpredictable Tanzanian. At the other start is Grete Waitz, four-time winner of the race, now the world champion, looking, as always, cool and composed.

At 10:45 a.m. the great cannon booms to start the race and just over 15,000 runners move away slowly, like a great cobra stretching itself across the huge bridge. Last year I was amazed by the sight of hundreds of runners stopping, within a few hundred yards of the start, to urinate into the Verrazano Narrows, despite the earlier presence of the world's longest urinal. The cameras do not show this strange ritual in 1983, instead they concentrate on the early leaders as they spin off the bridge and on to Fourth Avenue. Already we are seeing shots taken by ABC's helicopters. We can see that there is a mixed bunch in the lead, O'Connor of Ireland, Villanueva of Mexico and as expected the fast-starting Shahanga. Suddenly the name Shahanga rings a bell but I feel disoriented here in this New York hotel bedroom and cannot remember what he has done. The opening mile, the commentator tells us, has taken five minutes and nine seconds.

Despite the rain crowds line the course, another ritual, an annual treat, something to look forward to, like the Tour de France *passing through your village.*

There were bigger crowds the year before, here in Brooklyn at about the five-mile mark. They shouted and cheered encouragement. "Right on! Don't stop! You can do it!" We were in a tough neighbourhood, near Sunset Park, the corner of Forty-fourth Street and Fourth Avenue, the home of a Hispanic community that had had more than its share of gang wars and deaths. Here at five miles, I had lost my initial nervousness, reaching it in a little over fifty minutes.

On my television screen people wave umbrellas, cheering Shahanga, who is timed at twenty-four minutes exactly according to the commentator, well ahead of the world record of Alberto Salazar. "If Shahanga can hold this pace," he says, "it will be a Beamonesque performance." He is referring to the great long jump world record set by Bob Beamon in Mexico City back in 1968. The Tanzanian looks comfortable, despite the rain; out on his own, going past the Williamsburg Savings Bank whose huge tower is shrouded in cloud. Then somewhere in my brain an index card slips into place and I remember who Shahanga is. Last year in Brisbane he won the Commonwealth 10,000 metres and then with his compatriot Juma Ikangaa, in the marathon, he set a pace similar to this in the early morning sunshine of a Queensland summer. I watched that on television, too, watched as Shahanga finally blew up and the race was won by the local boy, Robert de Castella, "Deek" for short.

We receive more pictures from the helicopter and a woman commentator extols the virtues of the cameras they are using. "They can," she asserts, "pick up a runner's eyelashes at five hundred feet."

Now the two great snakes merge, after eight miles, by the bank. Shahanga has gone, swerved left into Flatbush Avenue, an unprepossessing area, full of small shops and pawnbrokers. The cameras pick up Grete, surrounded by a small group of men runners; she has a clear lead in the women's race.

The race moves on to the half-way point on Pulaski Bridge, which connects Brooklyn with Long Island City. Shahanga is still leading, the rain glistening on his black face. He disappears down an underpass above which a sign reads: NYC Marathon, Perrier 13.1 – Runners Welcome to Queens. *The Tanzanian has arrived in 1:3:12, fifty-eight seconds ahead of the world-record schedule. If he keeps going at this pace he will make a 2:07 marathon.*

I remembered that sign from the previous year. I had reached it in two hours ten minutes, well after Salazar had reached the finish. As I plodded into Queens I thought, what a difference a year made. In 1981, to celebrate reaching fifty, I had elected to try and run a marathon. I had chosen Dublin and had set a target of four hours. At the half-way point there I had run for one hour fifty-eight minutes and was running at eight and a half minutes per mile pace. Now, in New York's Queens I was aiming just to finish. In Dublin at twenty-two miles I suddenly became transformed, in seconds it seemed, from a reasonable mover to, paraphrasing Chesterton, a parody of all two-footed things. Because I was less fit than the previous year I had run a slower pace, hoping to miss the perils of "hitting the wall".

New Zealander Rod Dixon rejoices after his victory in the most dramatic New York Marathon ever in 1983.

The news from the race is that Smith and Cummings of the USA, and then just Smith, are starting to close on Shahanga. Nine seconds separate them from Pulaski. Rod Dixon, another half-minute behind, is starting to emerge from the pack. The only real climb in the New York Marathon is on Queensboro Bridge. It is a crucial moment in the race and not only for the leaders. A green carpet covers the grille and leads up a steep slope, out of Queens, over East River and into Manhattan. There are few people to cheer you on, you have to drive yourself, realising there is still eleven miles to go. If seeds of doubt are going to creep in this is usually the place where they do it. Shahanga still leads here but the pace he has set is beginning to tell. He is labouring, his head is lolling and Geoff Smith is gaining stride by stride. The American Paul Cummings is third and Dixon fourth. The pattern of the race is beginning to show.

It is on Queensboro, half-way across East River, that the lead changes and Geoff Smith, now a student in the States, takes up the running and Shahanga fades and fades. I stand, don a wet-suit and prepare to go to the finish.

I began to fade, the year before, at around seventeen miles, after I had swung left on Fifty-ninth and left again into First Avenue. On the sidewalk, families of a strict Jewish sect, the Hasidim, stood and watched in silence, dressed so formally in black, the men with wide-brimmed hats, their curls dipping down the sides of their cheeks. Here it was that I became drained of energy; my legs stiffened, demanding to stop. Here it was that I remembered what Joyce Smith had once said to me, in a much higher context. "Your mind says Yes, your body says No." I staggered into the Bronx and Harlem and a big black man standing alone on the sidewalk said mournfully: "Hey, keep goin' there, Buddy." The appalling thing was there were still eight or nine miles to go.

I hurry down to Central Park. The rain, if anything, seems a little harder. As you enter the south side you can hear the beat music pounding out at the finish, see the crowds waiting under their umbrellas. Occasionally the throb of the music is interrupted by news of the race. Smith is leading, Dixon is second but is suffering from cramp in his hamstrings, caused by the slick road surface. I wonder who to support; Smith, the exiled, former fireman from Liverpool, or Rod, the likeable Kiwi whom I had met on a number of occasions. I plump for Rod. The music returns, someone singing appropriately about the moon and New York City. I am lucky, I sit in the stand next to a man with a tiny portable television. The rain runs down our faces as we crane forward to see what is happening. "Geoff is still leading," the man says as if he has known him all his life, "but Rod is closing." Now there are three miles to go. Dixon still keeps clutching at his thigh to try to ease the cramp. To catch Smith he needs to speed up considerably. Now they are passing the big hotels: the Plaza, Park Lane, Ritz Carlton. The commentator at the finish is becoming more excited, the music is interrupting him, rather than vice-versa. They enter the Park, Smith still leading but looking desperate, Dixon just behind him. They pass twenty-six miles and Rod, using all his track speed, strikes and sprints over the line, winning by nine seconds, in 2:08:59. He holds his arms aloft in triumph amidst the bedlam of noise. He turns and hugs Fred Lebow and as he does so Smith staggers in, his legs gone, and has to be carried away. It is the most exciting and dramatic New York Marathon ever. Gidamis Shahanga finishes over two minutes adrift in sixth place.

I walked and shuffled those last eight miles, the minutes ticking away embarrassingly on my digital watch. Central Park was almost deserted when I got there, the crowds had gone home. I finally finished in about four hours fifty minutes, forty minutes slower than my Dublin effort. In a post-race party given by Chris Brasher at our hotel afterwards I kept quiet amidst talk of personal bests and sub-three-hours triumphs.

I see Grete win again, hang around and then go back to the Sheraton, to change and bath. It is 2:15 and still raining and I realise that I would not have stayed to greet myself the year before. Interviewed on television Dixon is ecstatic, but Smith finds no consolation in the fact that he has run the fastest-ever début Marathon. A year later, though, he will prove himself by winning the Boston.

Whilst in New York I kept an appointment in an Irish bar on Fifth with Joe Concannon, a long-time sports reporter on the *Boston Globe*, a craggy, balding man straight from the stage of Hecht's *The Front Page*. We were there to talk about the Boston Marathon which in the early to mid-eighties was going through an identity crisis which in human terms was verging on the menopausal. Joe displayed an enthusiasm tinged with healthy cynicism for this time-honoured race, which had set Erich Segal on the road to a life-long passion that was cut short. Its problem, in a nutshell, was whether it could retain its pristine amateurism in the era of big bucks marathons (the Boston victor won a laurel wreath) and survive. Concannon, who had covered the race for over twenty years, thought not. Many others were convinced, with considerable passion, that it could.

"Come up to Boston," Joe said, "and see for yourself."

We agreed to meet the following week at the Eliot Lounge, on the corner of Commonwealth and Massachusetts, not far from where the great race ends. The Eliot Lounge is an institution for American runners. Flags of the leading running nations hang from the ceiling, pamphlets advertising races lie on tables. Its yellow walls are covered with photographs of famous runners, past and present, of famous Boston finishes, including a picture of a totally exhausted and bewildered Alberto Salazar, hanging on to a laurel wreath that looks more like a Christmas decoration, after having beaten Dick Beardsley by just two seconds in 1982. It had been a race that raised passions and brought tears to normally hardened, dry eyes. "You talk about a spectacle," Tommy Leonard, the Eliot Lounge manager is reported to have said, "that did it all! The good Lord can take me now."

He hadn't, and Tommy was behind the bar, washing it down in the way that barkeepers at slack times are wont to do. Dinah Washington's recording of *September in the Rain* played over a music system and as I waited for Joe it seemed an idyllic place to be. Tommy slapped a second pint of Bass down in front of me, waving away my attempt to pay. His photograph adorned the wall opposite, showing him sitting on a rock at Cape Cod, where he organised one of the country's top road-races, the Falmouth Ten. Next to him lounges Frank Shorter. The caption reads: "Frank Shorter with Boston's running guru, Tommy Leonard." The purists, Tommy said, pointed to the great history of the race, which was first run in 1897. He waved at the photographs. "They mean those guys," he said.

One of "those guys" was Clarence DeMar, who first ran in 1910 and last, at the age of sixty-three, in 1951. In between he won the race a record seven times, the last time in 1930, the year that a living legend of the marathon first completed the course, John A. Kelley. Old John, as he became known, was to complete over fifty Bostons, running the race well into his seventies. He had two wins and a number of epic races including the most quoted, that against a Narragansett Indian, Ellison (Tarzan) Brown. Brown set a seemingly suicidal pace for the first twenty miles until he reached the Newton Hills, when Kelley began to pull back the 900-yard gap that separated them. He closed on the final hill leading to Boston College and then made a fatal error, tapping the apparently flagging leader on the shoulder as he pulled out to pass. Brown jumped like a scalded cat, called upon some deep reserve and surged away. Kelley, broken in spirit, gave up the chase. The name and legend of Heartbreak Hill was born, a legend that is buried so deep in the souls of American runners that the 1983 winner Greg Meyer had said: "When I got to the top of Heartbreak … it sounds silly, I know … but I almost cried."

"Yes, I've run Boston," Tommy said, "twenty-four times." He went to a shelf behind the bar, shuffled through some magazines and finally emerged with an old *Sports Illustrated*. In it was a black and white photograph, browning now with age, which showed Leonard, younger, thinner, all alone on the course with not a spectator in sight. It typified, said the caption, the spirit of the race.

In 1983 it was this spirit of the race that the purists were determined to defend. Joe Concannon had joined us and over refilled glasses he told me that they felt that by allowing the race to go professional, allowing appearance money and prize money to be paid, they were somehow sullying the reputations of DeMar, Tarzan Brown and Old John Kelley. Bad money would replace good form. The opposite viewpoint, the pragmatic counter, was that either Boston must join the rest, the New York, London, Chicago, Los Angeles and Rotterdam, or die.

I asked Tommy how Eliot's had become a running bar. He told me that a decade ago he had persuaded the owners to allow him to convert it and since then its reputation had grown to such an extent that it had almost reached the status of a shrine for American runners. Although it was quiet on this particular Wednesday evening it filled to bursting on the day of the big races. It was where the *cognoscenti* of Boston's running world congregated most evenings.

A man in a dark, lightly pin-striped suit sidled on to the stool next to mine. His eyes and the aroma that emanated from him persuaded me that the gin and tonic in his hand was far from his first of the evening. He smiled unctuously.

"Better talk to this man," Tommy said as he went away to serve another customer. "He's with the sponsors." It was the man from the Pru.

The Boston Marathon was an institution, the Pru man said, that had started just over thirty years after the Civil War had ended. Not the least factor in this great tradition was that it was held on Patriots' Day. His unctuousness increased, and his red eyes smirked blearily at me over his glass of gin.

"I hope," he said, "that, as an Englishman, you don't mind me mentioning Patriots' Day?"

Patriots' Day was a public holiday, confined to Massachusetts, to commemorate the first battle of the American War of Independence, when the farmers of Lexington and Concord beat off the troops of General Gage. It and the race are always celebrated on a Monday. I made no comment. What he was saying was true. For many thousands, taking to the streets and cheering the runners on Patriots' Day had become a tradition; many of today's spectators could recall when their parents first took them to see the race. It was a day out, not only for those watching the leaders battling for the coveted laurel wreath but also for those who were running.

"As you may know," went on the man from the Pru, "the Marathon relies so heavily on this amateur effort that when the race went commercial last year we pulled out. If it happens again, the expense will be enormous; for one thing, the police will expect to be paid for their overtime."

What had happened the year before, in 1982, had had a deep and dividing effect on Bostonians. On the Saturday morning prior to the race the *Boston Globe* had scooped its rivals with a story of an extraordinary contract between Will Cloney and Marshall Medoff, a fast-talking, big-spending Boston attorney, straight out of a George V. Higgins novel. Cloney represented the Boston Athletic Association, organisers of the race. The contract made the lawyer exclusive race-handling agent and stipulated that Medoff could retain any sums accrued above the BAA's guarantee of $250,000. Medoff, according to the *Globe*, was reported to be making between a quarter of a million and three-quarters of a million dollars. Not only that – nationwide television were interested in covering the race in future, which would mean moving it to a Sunday.

"It was so incredible," Joe Concannon had told me in New York, "that I had to decide that Will Cloney, a man whom I have known and respected for many, many years was either a fool or a crook. I concluded that he must be a fool."

Shock waves divided Boston as effectively as any earthquake. "These thoughts make me weak at the knees," wrote Colman McCarthy in *The Runner* magazine. "The top runners need the Boston more than the Boston needs them." By the following year the race had reverted to its original form and a superior court judge in Boston had ruled Medoff's contract invalid. Everyone except Cloney seemed happy. He retired, hurt. The Pru resumed sponsorship.

Earlier in the week I had dined with a local advertising executive at the top of one of Boston's skyscrapers, gazing through the glass-panelled walls at the old Customs House and beyond to the planes landing at Logan Airport. A keen runner, he soon turned the *apéritif* chat to the Marathon. "We can do without the top runners," he said. "For people on Patriots' Day, it's the race that is the spectacle."

Back at Eliot's the man from the Pru was about to take his leave. "Commercialism in the race," he intoned, as if reading from a PR statement, "would no longer serve the goals of my public company's public service purpose." He gazed mournfully at the two lemon pips in the bottom of his glass and then noisily made his exit.

Half an hour later I too left, the sound of Dinah Washington singing *Cry Me a River* following me out through the door. The brisk October night air reminded me that I had not eaten much all day and that I was five Basses to the wind. Traffic moved over the Massachusetts Avenue overpass, which a former Mayor had designated the Tommy Leonard Bridge. I gave up on hailing taxis and decided to walk back to my hotel. The night-time runners and joggers were streaming along the towpaths that hug either side of the Charles River. Its still waters reflected the neon signs of the buildings that line the banks. On the Cambridge side the triangular Hyatt loomed up and then a bevy of churches that immediately let you know that this was New England. The runners, skaters, cyclists and land-skiers all flowed past on their way to Soldiers Field Road, to pass the stadium, shaped like the Coliseum, where the Crimsons, the Harvard football team, practise and play in their freakish outfits. On the river the still waters were suddenly disturbed as a college eight, in training, slipped silently by, the faint voice of the megaphoned cox coming across to the shore.

It was very idyllic. Perhaps, I thought, Boston is the running capital of the world but the problems it faces mirror those that face organisations and traditions the world over. Cloney's analysis of the race had been right, his solution horrendously wrong. If the new brooms of the Boston Athletic Association realised that, the race would survive. If not …

In 1986 the Boston Marathon, on the occasion of its ninetieth birthday, joined the ranks of professionialised, big-time marathons backed by a ten-year, $10 million sponsorship from John Hancock Financial Services. The race, until then a slap-dash, shoe-string affair but with much charm, was transformed. There was a new finish area in Copley Square, money for athletes, for clinics, for pre-race and post-race corporate entertainment, money for the police, for the volunteers. If it moved, you paid it. Rob de Castella was there, so was Kristiansen. And so was Old John Kelley, at seventy-eight, running for the fifty-fifth time.

"Thank God," some people said. "Some things never change."

What governs this particular passion? Over the past decade men and women in their millions have donned vests, shorts and shoes and gone out and pounded the roads of the world. Each has gained satisfaction in his own way, from the record breakers down to the loneliest faint-hearted jogger. Running has been accompanied by a fad for healthy living, a need to look good and feel good. It has been predominantly a middle-class activity. It has also been a medium for proving oneself. The organisers of the great marathons have provided that medium *in excelsis*. It is a well-worn cliché but nevertheless a truism that every finisher in a marathon is a winner, a person who has endured the hours of training, sometimes suffered like a thwarted lover for his passion, to emerge triumphant at the end. No matter that the winner of the London or Boston or New York could be on a plane home before the last runner crosses the line.

To try and understand it all we must return to England, to the heart of working-class Lancashire and to a man whose business, his sport, indeed his *raison d'être*, has been running. That man is Ron Hill, the Commonwealth marathon champion of 1970, a sub-2:10 performer but also a man who is much more. He was born in Accrington, a town spawned by the Industrial Revolution, a place of tiny back-to-back terrace houses that clustered round the great mills and factories that have long since gone. It was a town of cloth caps and stoical people, bound together by frequent hard times. These were Ron's roots and he has rarely strayed far from them. His early hero was "Alf Tupper, The Tough of the Track".

Tupper was a fictional runner in the comic *Rover*, a weekly fix for a whole generation of schoolboys in the days before television. Ron was attracted by identification with Alf's background – the northern town and Alf working on the railways. Ron's father had been an engine fireman and it all seemed to fit in.

The comic hero was quintessentially working-class, an assiduous trainer in all weathers who each week overcame some dreadful adversity and on a diet of fish and chips defeated the class-conscious Oxbridge athletes who dominated British athletics at that time. At the end of each episode Alf used to leap the rails at the White City at the last minute and beat the Varsity toffee-noses. This eminently satisfied the young grammar schoolboy wending his way to school each Friday morning.

I talked to Ron about this in the Tower Hotel in London, before a marathon. He had just set himself a new challenge. An avid collector of anything in his youth, he had allied this passion to another. A million miles run, over a hundred marathons completed, three-quarters in under two and a half hours, so many years without missing a day's training, so many years training twice a day without a break. Now he was aiming to run in fifty different countries before his fiftieth birthday (he achieved it in 1988).

In his youth running had not been enjoyable. "In those days," he said, "a harrier was a peculiar person, not like now. I used to run up all the narrow, cobbled, back alleys between the backyards of houses to the Oswaldtwistle Moors. I wouldn't dare run up the main streets in shorts because people would point and shout and the one thing that I didn't want from running was ridicule.

"I can't tell you why I used to race in those early days. I was quite happy to run the club runs but I used to get very, very scared the night before a major race like the Northern Cross-Country; then I could hardly sleep. I used to dread it on the day. I used to feel very uncomfortable in the race and finish quite well down. I hated every minute of it but something drew me back the following week. Don't ask me what it was. I knew that I had no chance of winning, I knew that it was going to hurt but something drew me back."

He pondered a moment and then said: "Someone once asked my old rival Mike Freary what he liked about racing. He said: 'It's the excitement of it', and maybe there is something in that. You're doing something that takes you out of the ruck, something that makes you different. The excitement of running and of racing becomes a drug."

Everything was and is written into his running log. Every step, every mile, every time, every emotion has been recorded and it formed the basis of his two volumes (self-published) of autobiography, *The Long Hard Run*. He ran in every major championship – the Olympics in Munich, the European in Belgrade, the Commonwealth in Kingston and Edinburgh. As he became more successful he drove himself, inexorably, along a road to fanaticism in both training and racing. He was to describe himself as like a moth circling a candle flame. I asked him what he meant by that, and he replied:

"It was because I was destroying myself, as I came to realise much too late. I was obsessed with collecting titles. I won the East Lancashire Cross-Country title nine times and the Pembroke Twenty Miles Road Race in nine successive years. I would not go on holiday if it was the Pembroke Twenty."

The dedication, the passion, the fanaticism took a social toll, imposing strains on his marriage and his family life. His wife May became depressed at times, and there were rows and arguments. Jim Peters, the great marathon runner of the fifties, reported exactly the same stresses; he bought his wife refrigerators and washing-machines to keep her sweet. I met Don Thompson, the Olympic 50 kilometre walk champion of 1960, late in the eighties. He had taken up ultra-distance running and trained before dawn every morning. "Nobody," he said, "can make demands on your time at four a.m." But still they kept on, running and running, so perhaps it was a drug. Ron used to carry his gear separately on his trips abroad and would run around airports to ensure that he could log in some training for the day. May, on the basis of "if you can't beat 'em, join 'em", took up running and when their family grew up and moved away, she travelled with him and they now live a rather serene existence.

He sat there, sipping a soft drink; a PhD, a successful man. "To me, it's a way of life, and the various motivations that keep me running are in a continual state of flux. There is one constant factor – I will never stop running. I'll run till I die."

"You'll run to your own funeral," I suggested.

"Yes," he said, "and when they head me towards the fire, you'll see a foot twitch a couple of times and I'll sit up and I'll shout, 'May! Get it in the log!'"

He roared with laughter, but we both knew that even for Ron Hill there has to be a final run.

5

TII-NA! TII-NA!

It was appropriate that the first time a women's javelin event gripped the public imagination, it should be in the Olympic Stadium in Helsinki. In the years between the two great wars the Finnish throwers, like the distance runners, had completely dominated their event. Legend has it that the architect who designed the great white tower that dominates the stadium had built it to the dimension of Matti Jarvinen's 1936 world javelin record of 77.23 metres. It is a nice legend, but totally apocryphal.

It was on the fourth afternoon of the inaugural World Championships that the women javelin throwers entered the arena for the final of their competition. A mighty roar went up as the spectators spied Tiina Lillak, their twenty-two-year-old world record holder, a tall blonde from the nearby town of Espoo. She had thrown furthest in the qualifying round and the great anticipation was that she would gain Finland's first gold medal of the championships. Twelve throwers had qualified, the last being Britain's Fatima Whitbread who had scraped in on her final attempt. Fatima had come a long way since she was found abandoned in a dingy north London flat twenty-two years before. The offspring of Cypriot parents, she became an angry foundling in numerous children's homes before she was adopted by Margaret Whitbread, one of Britain's leading javelin coaches. Now she was on the brink of greatness. She was very relaxed, better than the day before when her nerves had felt jangled. Because of her poor qualifying performance little was expected of her in this final round.

Her opening throw drew applause from the knowledgeable crowd as it sailed high out from the synthetic runway to land close to the seventy-metre line. It was measured at 69.14 metres, close to her personal best. Margaret, sitting in the stand behind her, felt a tingle of excitement. The throw could get Fatima a medal.

Tiina Lillak was under considerable pressure. The hopes of a whole nation rested upon her. Track and field is the Finnish national sport, the javelin *their* event. The fans knew their athletics and were realistic enough to appreciate that here was their only chance of a gold medal in the championships. We had

Finland's Tiina Lillak wins gold with her final throw of the first World Championships in Helsinki.

seen posters of Tiina all over Helsinki, smiling down on us like some inter-national pop star, along with the symbol of the meeting, a white rabbit.

Her opening throw was nearly two metres down on the British woman's effort. Fatima, however, had felt a jolt in her shoulder and knew that she had given her best. She threw only twice more in the competition, each a declining effort. All she could do was wait on Tiina.

Every time the tall blonde stepped forward to throw, a hush descended on the stadium. They watched as she stood poised, javelin held aloft, and then set off down the runway, slowly taking it back behind her, then jamming her front foot down and pulling, pulling against her taut front leg. She wasn't the great-est technician in the world but she had thrown further than any other woman. After each throw, a huge groan of dismay arose from the large crowd, for Tiina was not at her best form. Maybe the tension was getting to her; certainly there was little wind in the stadium and it was a good headwind that the javelin throwers liked best.

The stress was as bad for Fatima, *hors de combat* as she was. She paced around the javelin area, anxiously watching each throw. She felt a mixture of rising excitement and anxiety as five of the six rounds were completed and no one challenged her mark. She passed the final round and waited for Lillak's last effort.

The silence as Tiina stepped forward this last time was complete. She stood there, in her blue and white national kit, staring down to the end of the stadium, trying, perhaps, to absorb the crowd's collective will. Then she set off, unleashed the javelin and as it rose and rose a rumble turned into a mighty roar and even before it landed beyond the seventy-metre line, the crowd was on its feet in ecstasy and Tiina had leapt into the air, arms aloft in triumph. They knew, she knew, that she had won. Fatima went to the wall behind her and cried in the arms of Margaret. As Tiina set off on an extraordinarily fast lap of honour, the crowd around me celebrated, hugged each other in delight, punched fists into the air. I had mixed emotions: sadness for Fatima, but joy for these charming people who had welcomed us to their clean and healthy land and who had staged one of the greatest athletics meetings ever. They deserved this triumph.

The celebrations erupted once more at the award ceremony, as huge Finnish flags waved and people wept when the anthem was played and shouted "Tii-na, Tii-na!" The Finns, not noted for their sobriety, rejoiced in the bars and cafés of Helsinki well into the night. These scenes took my memory back twelve years to a warm, almost sultry evening, when another athlete had restored Finnish pride. For over thirty years their distance running had been in the doldrums; no medals, no records, just mediocrity. All they had were mem-ories. Then, at the first night of the European Championships, there stepped forward Juha Vaatainen to win the 10,000 metres. Raw emotion had erupted then, thousands of tapers had been lit and held aloft in the stadium under the floodlights and the thundering noise had gone on and on. Another British athlete had wept that night, too; David Bedford, with disappointment and despair, beneath the reverberating stands, his hopes and dreams shattered in a pulsating last lap.

Neither Vaatainen nor Lillak were to achieve such fame again. The pressure of it all made Juha turn into an alcoholic, from which he recovered to become a noted coach. Tiina threw on till the end of the decade, winning Olympic silver in 1984, but gained no further medals and failed to qualify for the final round of the Olympic javelin in Seoul. But maybe they had set themselves an impossible act to follow; perhaps their lives had climaxed on those two separate days of glory.

The women's javelin epitomised those first World Championships. They were full of drama, excitement, triumph and pathos and all the world was present – there were no boycotts. Ismail Mohamed Baraki of Afghanistan ran slower in the first round of the men's 100 metres than all but seven of the forty-seven women did in theirs, but he was there. It seemed a little ironic. Over the six days we marvelled at the enormous talent of Carl Lewis, who won three gold medals and vowed to go for four in the Olympics the following year; we shouted in despair for the American steeplechaser, Henry Marsh, who crashed into the final barrier when in the bronze medal position; we agonised with Alberto Juantorena as we listened to his shouts of frustration and anger as he was stretchered from the arena with torn ligaments, out of the championships, out of athletics; we celebrated with Eamonn Coghlan, wearing the green of Ireland, over the last 100 of a 5000 metres that he couldn't believe had been so tailor-made for him; we stood on the roads of Helsinki and applauded the cool, calculating marathon wins of de Castella and Waitz; we were impressed with the eight gold medals of the East German women but wondered about their institutionalised drug-taking, and we were embarrassed by the sheer masculinity of the double champion, Jarmila Kratochvilova.

Britain had to rely on two of its European champions to maintain its reputation. Daley Thompson battled again with the giant German, Jurgen Hingsen. As in the previous year Hingsen had snatched away Daley's world record, in the weeks leading up to the championships, by thirty-six points. But to prove himself the better man he had to beat the Briton, whose preparation had been hampered by a groin injury, in the head-to-head in Helsinki. As always, Daley threw down the gauntlet in the first event, clocking 10.60 for the 100 metres. That gave him the lead and he was not to relinquish it. By the end of the second day, as they lined up for the gruelling 1500 metres, Hingsen knew that he had to finish eighteen seconds ahead of the Olympic champion, which was more than the length of the home straight. He managed only eight and Daley, uniquely, had all four of the world's major titles.

It seemed at one time, early in the year, that we were going to witness once again the marvellous, nail-biting clashes between Coe and Ovett in Helsinki. Seb had been in action indoors with a new world best for 800 metres, a time of 1:44.91, set on the track at RAF Cosford. In June they both went to Bislett, Seb winning the 800 metres in 1:43.80, the fastest time by anyone for two years, while Steve took the 1500 metres in 3:33.81. They both seemed to be back in business.

In July, however, Seb began to show extraordinary fluctuations of form, losing to the Yugoslavian Dragan Zdravkovic over 800 metres at London's Crystal Palace and to the American Steve Scott over a mile. At the AAA Championships Ovett had stomach cramp for the second time that year and was unable to run the final. This allowed a young Rotherham joiner, Peter Elliott, to be selected for the 800 metres in Helsinki, a decision that caused some controversy. Coe, looking dreadful, was beaten into fourth place in an 800 metres race in Gateshead; he withdrew from the World Championships team and underwent urgent medical tests which diagnosed a lymph gland infection. All exercise was forbidden until he had a full hospital check-over. Seb came out in lumps and bumps all over his body, some of which were sliced open and sent away for diagnosis. In September, the results of his tests were announced. He was suffering from a rare infection, glandular toxoplasmosis.

"It was a deep worry," his father remembered, "because we didn't know what we were dealing with. All sorts of possible horrible diagnoses went through our minds. Seb was determined to carry on running and only the firmest persuasion kept him away from the track. He was on three different drugs at one time, plus a fourth to counteract the side-effect of one of the others. He was rattling like a pill-box. Did I think he would never run again? It did cross my mind but, you know, the stakes seemed higher than that."

In the end it was Cram, who had also had problems, and Ovett who went to Helsinki for the 1500 metres, with Elliott the main British contender in the 800 metres. Peter ran a gutsy race in the final, leading from the gun and fading only in the closing stages to fourth. He displayed a courage and demeanour here that were to be the hallmarks of his running for the next seven years. Sydney Maree, John Walker and the hare turned greyhound, Tom Byers, all made their exits in the semi-finals of the 1500 metres. John Walker said of the final: "It's got to be between Scott, Cram and Ovett with maybe Aouita as an outsider. Ovett is not his usual self. He's looked susceptible to me these past few days. Cram is going to be very, very tough. It will probably be a kicker's race and 3:39 could do it."

The race, in reality, was a dismal affair enlivened in the end only by the courage of Cram and the amazing tactical ineptitude of Steve Ovett. The opening lap was slower than that run in the women's final and the field remained bunched until the Moroccan, Said Aouita, a man who would make his true mark in later years, took up the running. Cram made his bid with half a lap to go and stormed into a three-metre lead which the runner-up, Scott, was never able to close. Aouita won the bronze. Ovett was badly boxed at the bell, in eighth place. He finished fast but fourth. Afterwards he said: "It was the worst race of my life ... I ran like a goon." Cram now held three of the world's four major titles. How close Ovett might have come was shown in the last British meeting of the season, when only inches separated him from Cram in an epic mile race. But he ended the year happier than in 1982. Sydney Maree had redeemed his Helsinki performance by setting a new world 1500-metre record at Cologne but Ovett seized it back on a windy evening in Rieti exactly a week later.

Mary Decker was running's Shirley Temple, a young woman of precocious talent whose tempestuous life surely should have made the movies. She started running at the age of eleven when her family moved to California from New Jersey. There she joined the Long Beach Comets Track Club. Its coach, Don DeNoon, a graduate, it seemed, of the Zatopek School of Human Destruction, had the frail youngster undertaking track training sessions where she ran forty quarter-miles in eighty seconds each with a short rest in between. She attained the dubious honour of running the fastest-ever half-mile by a twelve-year-old and then in seven days ran a marathon, in just over three hours, and races at 440 yards, half-mile, one and two miles. At the end of the week she was rushed to hospital for an emergency appendectomy, the result of extreme stress. Nobody, it appears, thought to ask why. At thirteen she began to suffer from the spate of injuries that were to blight her running life, hobbling around for a while with plasters on both feet to cure ankle and heel damage. A year later she was one of history's youngest-ever internationals when she ran for the USA indoors against the Soviet Union at Minsk; a spindly girl, with buck teeth in a brace, who blew bubble-gum at presentation ceremonies.

Not before time DeNoon bowed out of her life and her parents divorced. Over twelve months in 1973 to 1974 she grew five inches and increased her weight by almost a third to 111 pounds, but no one changed her training programme. She was running now with great pain, particularly in the shins, and the mentors of this sixteen-year-old tried every cure they could think of: orthotics, acupuncture, drugs (some illegal – these made her hair fall out). All to no avail. It was the end of a reel in the *Perils of Decker* story. Would she ever run again? At the invitation of Frank Shorter she went to work in one of his

Mary Decker on her way to a 3000 metres gold, shadowed by Britain's
Wendy Sly (188).

running shops in Boulder, Colorado, where to deal with her stress fractures she lived in plaster casts for ten weeks. Again there was no improvement, but salvation was at hand in the presence of twenty-nine-year-old Dick Quax, on a visit from New Zealand. He had had the same problem, he told her; it was compartment syndrome. An operation would cure it. She had turned down such a solution before but now in desperation she agreed to surgery. Within a few weeks she was cured and running again. In 1978 she made a successful return to the track, though further operations were to follow.

She was now close to Quax who was also coaching her, mostly by mail from New Zealand. She moved to Eugene, Oregon, home of the Nike shoe company and ran on the Pre Trail, named after the American distance runner Steve Prefontaine who had died in a car crash in 1975. The paths were soft and smooth, ideal for Mary's troubled legs. She made the American team for the 1980 Olympics but like the rest of them, never boarded the plane. That year Quax made his exit from her athletic and emotional life and for a while she was coached by one of America's greatest, Bill Bowerman. In 1981 Mary, whom a friend once described as being caught between being a woman and a girl, put her life through more emotional upheaval, getting engaged in January, breaking it off in the spring, getting engaged again in May. The second engagement was to Ron Tabb, a marathon runner. They were married in September and spent their wedding night on a plane flying to Montreal for a marathon. Her next coach was Dick Brown, a physiologist, who said that from the knees up she was world-class, from the knees down they lived from day to day. It all held together in 1982 and she set world records for a mile and 5000 metres.

As she boarded the plane for Helsinki, Mary's two-year marriage to Ron Tabb was in ruins and she had become friendly with the English discus thrower, Richard Slaney. Her ambitions were extreme: to win the 1500 and 3000 metres titles at the World Championships. Such a challenge meant a total of four distance races. First came the 3000 metres. The opposition was formidable, including the world record holder, Ulmasova, and Tatyana Kazankina, winner of three Olympic titles. A born front-runner, Mary duly led for seven laps with long, smooth strides. Shadowing her were the two Soviet runners, together with Brigitte Kraus of West Germany and Britain's Wendy Sly. Mary looked vulnerable to attack all through the last lap as everyone upped the pace in the run for the line. Kazankina drew level with the American down the home straight but Decker accelerated again. The Russian's challenge crumbled so much that Kraus ran by her to take the silver.

"It was great," Mary said, "having someone on your shoulder on the last bend. I just gritted my teeth, lengthened my stride and moved away again."

In the 1500 metres Decker set a fierce pace and only the Soviet runner Zaytseva was in a challenging position as they entered the home straight. She

"It's so easy!" says
Mary Decker's expression
after her Helsinki victory...

...but *Perils of Decker* had
another reel to run. Husband-
to-be Richard Slaney comforts
Mary after her ignominious
exit from the Los Angeles
Olympics in 1984.

went past on the inside and we thought that Mary's chances had gone but she dug deep into her thirteen years' reserve of training and challenged again, passing Zaytseva with ten metres to go. As she tried to respond the Soviet champion overbalanced and crashed to the track but she was over the finish line, second. Mary Decker had won an amazing double.

"What you've got to understand about Mary," one of her former coaches, Tracy Sundlun told *Newsweek* magazine, "is that she judges her worth as a person solely by what she accomplishes on the track. It's scary to contemplate but the competitive nature that we so admire in this woman is actually a huge personality flaw."

Flawed or not the Americans loved her, watching at home on their television sets, as she effectively demolished the representatives of the Communist sports machine. They waited in great anticipation for her to do it all over again at the Los Angeles Olympics the following year. At long last *Perils of Decker* seemed an obsolete movie. Fate had a trump card to play, however. Five days into Olympic year, at Stellenbosch in South Africa, a seventeen-year-old girl called Zola Budd, looking equally as frail and fragile, ran over six seconds faster than Mary Decker's world record for 5000 metres. It could not be recognised because South Africa was banned from world athletics. But her grandfather, Frank George Budd, had been an Englishman.

6

WHO INVENTED ZOLA BUDD?

Neil Wilson sat in the train taking him to London, gazing out at the Sussex countryside, budding into spring. He had had a leisurely start to the day and planned to keep it that way. His main task was to submit his expenses at the offices of the *Daily Mail.* As athletics correspondent for his paper he was not expecting any major developments; the indoor season was practically over and so when he had bid farewell to his wife that morning he had promised to be back by mid-afternoon. He was not to see her again for five weeks, for unbeknown to him, his editor, Sir David English, had unleashed a storm of activity at the paper's offices. Jan Wilson had been telephoned and instructed to pack a suitcase "for four or five days" and transport it by taxi to Fleet Street, together with Neil's passport. Brian Vine, the *Mail*'s special correspondent, had also been alerted. When Vine was with the *Daily Express*, he had master-minded that paper's sensational "capture" of escaped train-robber Ronald Biggs. Both Wilson and Vine were to fly to South Africa that evening.

The reason for all this activity was a tiny South African teenager, Zola Budd, the youngest daughter of an extraordinary mismatched marriage between Frank and Tossie, he of English descent, she an Afrikaner, which had nevertheless produced six children. Zola Budd had first come to the attention of the *Mail*'s features editor, John Bryant, through the pages of the American magazine, *Runners' World.* Her running exploits – she had come close to and finally broken Mary Decker's world record for 5000 metres – had made an imprint in his mind and so when the paper's South African correspondent, Peter Younghusband, submitted a story that included a couple of paragraphs on Zola's world record and the fact that her father was investigating her eligibility to compete for Britain, Bryant immediately went into English's office.

"This is a better story than the one Peter's written," he said. "It's worth a feature."

"The best story of all," said the highly perceptive English, "is to get the

71

girl a passport. Let's investigate if she is eligible."

Wilson was instructed by English to ascertain, whilst he was at the European Indoor Championships in Gothenburg, the exact ruling; he approached John Holt, the General Secretary of the IAAF, a Council member, Emmanuel Rose, and Marea Hartman, the long-serving secretary of the English women's association. All agreed with Hartman's definitive statement: "The day she walks into my office and shows me a British passport, she's a British athlete."

After an afternoon of frenetic activity, which included two and a half hours getting visas and a telephone call from David English to delay briefly the South African Airways flight to Johannesburg, the two journalists travelled by underground to Heathrow. They were rushed through formalities, on to the jumbo jet, the doors immediately closed behind them and the plane climbed into the air. It had been quite a day. The Budds were expecting them. Vine had telephoned the father to clarify the situation. Frank, who had been investigating for himself and had contacted McCormack's International Management Group, had arrived at a state of distrusting everyone. "Nothing has been decided," he had said, "but I'm not going to come to any agreement with the *Mail* over the telephone. You'll have to come and see us."

Zola was running at Port Elizabeth on the Wednesday; this was Tuesday evening. It was necessary for the *Mail* to check the veracity of the claims being made for the sensational seventeen-year-old, so Wilson and Vine were to attend the meeting. As Wilson finally dozed off, exhausted, and the plane crossed the Sahara, English's instructions rang in his ears: "Get to Port Elizabeth and phone me back immediately after she's run to say whether she's worth bothering with or not. Find out if she really is as good as they say she is, or whether it's just hype."

One other Englishman was wise to the plans of Frank Budd and that was the top sports photographer, Mark Shearman. Earlier in the year Mark had contacted him to set up a photo assignment, which Budd had agreed to, providing that Shearman would perform a service in return. He was to visit St Catherine's House in London and obtain a copy of the birth certificate of his father, Frank George Budd. He was also asked to contact various government departments to find out if Zola, the granddaughter of the Englishman, could obtain a British passport quickly. He was told flatly: no chance. Shearman was also the first to notice and feel the stressed and strained atmosphere at the family smallholding not far from Bloemfontein. He photographed Zola running amongst wild ostriches and feeding them at the zoo and then asked to take some shots of her running barefoot, for which she was well-known. Frank Budd drove them to an army grass track but when they arrived Zola refused to leave the car, despite the orders of her father. In the end Frank gave up. "She won't do anything for me," he said, and walked away. Shearman went to the car and told her that he had come a long way for this assignment and asked if she would do it for him. She shrugged her shoulders, then burst into tears. "My father always tries to interfere with my life," she said between sobs. She recovered her composure and Shearman got his pictures, including one of her bedroom, where a picture of Mary Decker hung on the wall.

Frank Budd had three dreams in his life: one was to have a million pounds in the bank; another was to have tea with the Queen, and the third was to divorce his wife, Tossie and thus be able to indulge himself freely with the young men and boys that were his fancy. In the phenomenal running talent of his daughter this bisexual man saw a way to achieve all three. The household had always been a strange mix of culture. The parents conversed in English but the children spoke Afrikaans to their mother, English to their father. Zola spoke only Afrikaans to everybody. That she would be a very great runner emerged early in life at junior school, where she was winning not only short sprint races but 1200-metre races as well. She continued into senior school, met the man who was to become her controversial coach, Pieter Labuschagne, and won the South African Schools cross-country championship. The turning point in her career, maybe even her life, when running became a reason for living, rather than just an activity, came with the death of her eldest sister, Jenny.

Different relationships build up in large families and Zola was closest to her strong-minded sister. It was to Jenny that Zola turned for guidance, security, even love, when she was very young. So when her sister died, a year into her marriage, after an operation for a tumour on her arm, Zola was grief-stricken. At just thirteen years of age, a major prop had been taken from her life. She turned to her running for solace. With her parents' marriage in turmoil she also turned more to Labuschagne, a Svengali-like figure now, whose every whim or command was Zola's to obey. She indulged in a volume of training that approached Decker's, 100 kilometres a week at fifteen. She improved and improved and finally set a world record that would never be recognised.

Wilson and Vine landed at Jan Smuts airport, bleary from their overnight flight, travelled to Port Elizabeth and immediately contacted the Budds at their hotel, to let them know that the *Daily Mail* had arrived. They went to the evening meeting and watched Zola run a time for 5000 metres that only she, Waitz and Decker had beaten. Wilson, crouched behind a desk in a little room that served as the stadium Press-box, as far away from local reporters as possible, telephoned David English, call-collect on his private line, to tell him that she was the greatest talent he had seen since the young Sebastian Coe. It was this statement that set in train the series of events that would culminate in the second most sensational athletics story of the decade.

The next day they went to Bloemfontein, in the Orange Free State, high up on the veldt and began negotiations with the Budds, which almost immediately became stalled.

"I'm not signing anything until you can guarantee me that my daughter will get a passport if she comes to Britain," Frank Budd said. "Otherwise there is no point in us talking like this."

He was adamant. It was final. They reported back to the *Daily Mail.*

They booked into the President Hotel in Bloemfontein and began a cloak-and-dagger operation worthy of the CIA. Vine, a reporter of the old school, was paranoid about secrecy. Before he left, he even told his wife, who worked in public relations, to spread a rumour that he was following a tip-off that Lord Lucan had been found in Botswana. Wilson had left no such instruction and so when another athletics reporter telephoned to find out which train he would be taking to Cosford for an indoor match, Jan told him that Neil would be absent, because he was in South Africa. They tried to keep their profession a secret but after a week the manager of the hotel, who was English, passed Wilson in the corridor and said: "Ah, Mr Wilson, if you'd like to leave your Press cards at reception you can have our special rate."

"How did you know we are Pressmen?" asked a dumbfounded Wilson.

The manager smiled. "Well," he said, "you've been making about six calls a day to a Fleet Street number."

When Wilson told Vine, he became very edgy. "We mustn't keep staying here," he said, "we must keep moving around."

They toured the area endeavouring to put up a smokescreen. They spent a day visiting the Kimberley Gold Mines, telling its public relations woman that they were working on a major feature.

Zola kept running, but she was ambivalent about testing her talent on the international scene. On the one hand she loved her home, her pets, her family, the warmth and tranquillity of white South Africa; on the other, she hated her life at the University of Orange Free State and going to Britain would relieve her of that. She knew also that unless she left South Africa she would never know how good a runner she was. One man had made the move before her, the black athlete, Sydney Maree. Frank Budd and Pieter Labuschagne had no reservations. Frank saw international running tracks as a yellow brick road to glory and fortune for him and his daughter; Pieter saw fame beckon him as the coach to the world's most outstanding distance runner.

The *Daily Mail* viewed it all as an enormous scoop, a sporting equivalent of the Falklands war, ending with Zola winning a gold medal for Great Britain in Los Angeles. Each had their own motive, independent of the others, except that everything focused on the success of one frail teenager. If she failed they would all be just mundane South Africans again. If Mary Decker was running's

Shirley Temple, Zola was its Judy Garland. Nobody thought any further ahead than the Olympic Games.

What surprised Neil Wilson was the fame of Zola Budd in her own country. Her picture appeared on the front page of every newspaper, except perhaps *The Sowetan,* at least once a week. Her breaking of the world record had given pride to a beleaguered sporting nation and she became a very marketable property. Frank Budd became involved in a series of sponsorship deals, recruiting another businessman, Bill Muirhead, to help him. Zola kept running, training in the thin air of the veldt, like the Kenyans and Ethopians thousands of miles to the north. The only person (apart from Zola, perhaps) who was not excited by all this was Tossie Budd. The prospect of losing her darling youngest daughter depressed her immensely. Wilson and Vine could not help noticing the acute difference between the photographs around the house of a thin, very attractive woman, and the large lady who sat around the homestead, knitting furiously, like Madame Defarge counting dropping heads at the guillotine. It was Frank who, repellingly, gave the explanation. As he drove them one day he told them that two years before she had been severely ill with a blood disease and a complication of it had been a considerable weight increase.

"The doctors told me, at the time," he told the two shocked reporters, "that she could drop dead at any moment. I've been waiting for it ever since."

Zola appeared to the two Englishmen as a spoilt teenager, who only thought of herself. Of course, such self-centredness is the hallmark of most great champions but in Zola's case it was combined with acute shyness. At dinners at the President she spoke only monosyllabically. Vine would look at her uncertainly and ask: "You do want to run for Britain, don't you, Zola?" "Yes, yes," she would reply in her heavy Afrikaans accent, and then look away.

Finally a way was found around the impasse concerning her passport. David Waddington, the Minister at the Home Office in charge of immigration, telephoned Sir David English in his office. The editor put it on a conference call and rang Zola Budd in Bloemfontein. Zola was then able to communicate with Waddington without speaking directly to him. It was important to the Budds that they could hear what the Minister was saying. Her family did not trust the *Mail* to provide a passport. Zola asked David English if she would receive a passport if she came to Britain. Waddington told the editor that such an application would be considered very sympathetically. The final big discussions were held at the smallholding. Frank Budd and Zola, with Muirhead, faced Vine and Wilson. Tossie sat knitting in another room. They argued about the passport, about how long they were willing to stay in England to get it, about money. Zola sat unhappily by, finally getting up and leaving the room. She went away to cry.

The pace now quickened. Smokescreens were set up. Frank Budd told

Rob Hughes of the *Sunday Times*: "We have no plans to come to England at all. I can't see anything happening, certainly not until after the Olympic Games. She's not ready to move to a completely new set-up. We would be like the first guy going to the moon, not knowing what he might come across or how it might affect him. We are not yet looking for recognition from the Home Office. She's a good athlete but it's too early to be talking about moving into world competition."

Frank was talking sound sense but he wasn't listening to himself. The South African AAU held a dinner in Zola's honour a few days before she left, but no hint was given of her imminent departure from the country. She honoured a commitment to run in a two-kilometre fun run in the Free State town of Welkom and then, heavily loaded with luggage, the family drove to Johannesburg. They stayed with relations overnight and using influence he had with the Interior Ministry, Frank had the whole family driven straight to the KLM airliner in a BOSS car. They were on their way, Business Class.

The Budds travelled incognito, under the name of Hamilton. Frank was travelling with the British passport that he had collected from the British Consul the previous day; Zola, as a minor, was on it as well. Her fame prevented secrecy and people on the flight kept coming up and asking for her autograph and enquiring how she was. Brian Vine, in Economy Class, fretted the flight away. The cover story was that she was travelling to meet representatives of a European shoe company with a view to signing a contract. At Schipol Airport, just outside Amsterdam, they transferred to a private plane, chartered by the *Mail*, and flew to Southampton airport. All the while Neil Wilson took pictures with a Canon Sureshot. When they landed at Southampton the sky was leaden and it was pouring with rain. "Welcome to Britain," said the *Daily Mail* men. Zola thought of the warm, sultry weather she had left behind and became more depressed. The Home Office sent a man down to the airport to deal with immigration, but they had to go through customs and there was a leak. Next day the *News of the World* carried a story with the headline "Zola Budd Arrives in Britain." There then followed a cat and mouse game, *Daily Mail* versus the rest of the British media. They went from an apartment in the New Forest to an hotel in Haslemere, and then to rented accommodation in Guildford. The *Daily Mail* carried the headline "Mail brings Wonder Girl Zola to Britain". The "Wonder Girl" did not think it so wonderful.

Zola's first competition was to be at Dartford, Kent, on 14 April in a Southern League match. The *Mail* non-athletics reporters had some idea that they could helicopter her in to the centre of the arena, that she would step out on to the track, run a world record and then be helicoptered out again. That was Plan A, making her a kind of female Alf Tupper. When put to Labuschagne, who with his wife Carin had now joined the Budds in England, there was, unsurprisingly, some foot-stamping and threats to leave for home. John Bryant, an experienced runner, who was always to have considerable empathy with Zola, was called in by English to produce a Plan B. He did, arranging warm-up and toilet facilities for her away from the assembling media hordes.

Central Park, Dartford has never seen anything like it before or since. A cinder track in the middle of a field seemed an inappropriate place for Wonder Girl to show her paces but it was away from the mainstream of British athletics. Zola had joined the Aldershot, Farnham and District club and was running as a guest in the League event. The host club could hardly believe their good fortune and officials were up nearly all the previous night making cakes and sandwiches. Their initiative was rewarded when 5000 people turned up the next day, fifty times more than at any Southern League match before or since. The race was shown live on BBC's *Grandstand* and broadcast on Radio Two. The club made a four-figure profit.

Zola, bemused, as she was to be for most of her British running career, ran a solo race, set a new British Junior Record and Olympic qualifying time for 3000 metres of 9:02.6, mutely disregarded questions from the media who thronged around her and Labuschagne and was driven away by Neil Wilson. David Emery of the *Daily Express* (who didn't witness her departure) wrote that she was escorted by her "minders". Wilson telephoned him to say that he must be the smallest "minder" the world had ever seen. As the crowd left a club official shouted despairingly: "We're here every week, you know!"

By now she had been granted a passport and Tossie had not smiled since the news came through. She loudly pined for the homestead, saying she didn't want to die in England. Frank gave her a finger-wagging, lengthy rebuke in Afrikaans. He was having the time of his life, and felt he was back home. The Labuschagnes had burnt their boats to come to England. He had bought a new house at Bloemfontein and was expecting to be offered a lectureship at the local university. He also had a Master's thesis to finish – yet here he was, in an alien country, drawn by the possibility of Olympic fame.

All relationships have their breaking-point and events in England quickly moved to that stage in the Budd family. The cause was the father's greed. The *Mail* had agreed to pay the Budds £100,000. £20,000 went in Zola's Trust Fund – there had been a ceremonial handing-over at lunch at the Hurlingham Club: £20,000 went to the Labuschagnes, £15,000 to the other sons and daughters and £45,000 to Frank. Then Zola learned that in the negotiations with Brooks' shoes her father was asking for an agent's fee of thirty-five per cent. He refused to give her money to rent a flat in Guildford so that she could be on her own. It was almost the final straw. After a bust-up over Labus-chagne's control over her she slammed out of the house and left, writing

The arrival in Britain of tiny South African teenager Zola Budd, pictured here in Lisbon in 1985, created a furore which continued throughout the 1980s.

Zola's ill-matched parents, the unsmiling Tossie, who pined for home, and the avaricious Frank (right).

to tell her father she did not want him in Los Angeles.

Once the initial surprise of Zola's arrival in Britain and the speedy award of a British passport had been absorbed, the protests began. Anti-apartheid groups, relishing the prospect of such good publicity on their own doorstep, began gearing themselves up for demonstrations. The Joint Council for the Welfare of Immigrants pointed out the discrepancy between the thirteen days that she had waited and the twenty-four months that other applicants, mainly black, had to endure. The Labour Party added its voice in protest. In truth their memories were short for in the past athletes of every colour had been given preferential treatment in citizenship applications. Britain's women distance runners were unhappy too. They regarded Zola as a cuckoo in their rather complacent nest. Some even wrote to the British Board urging them not to forget those who had trained hard for years to make the Olympic team. With one or two exceptions, notably Wendy Sly and Chrissie Boxer, they knew that Zola's arrival was going to bring the spotlight to bear on the poor standards in Britain. In later years she would be recognised as the catalyst for a revival of standards that would produce Yvonne Murray and Liz McColgan as Olympic medallists.

On the track Zola made triumphant progress and the crowds flocked to see her. She set European Junior Records at 1500 and 3000 metres. The protesters had arrived and at the Crystal Palace she had to endure cries of "Go home South African white trash" and "Fascist bitch", which upset her, but it was something she was going to have to live with for most of her stay in Britain. She was duly selected for the Olympic team and the family, minus Frank Budd, who would have to watch it all on television, decamped to Los Angeles together with the Labuschagnes. Zola's date with destiny was near.

The English-speaking media were having a collective orgasm over the prospect of the meeting between Mary Decker and Zola Budd in the Olympic 3000 metres. The hype was the equal of any world heavyweight title fight and American television led the way. Each was quoted *ad nauseam* in the weeks and days leading up to the final. Nobody talked to Romania's Maricicia Puica, or to Canada's Lynn Williams, or to Zola's friend, the South African-born Swiss, Cornelia Burki. Certainly the other British runner, Wendy Sly, was of absolutely no interest. The reason was not hard to find. Following her victories in the Helsinki World Championships America waited impatiently for Decker to repeat the performance in Los Angeles, to defeat again, this time on home soil, the sporting representatives of what their President had called the "Evil Empire". When the Soviets and most of their East European satellites disobliged by staging a boycott, the media were stuck for a story. Mary Decker had no obvious protagonist. Then along came Zola, this eighteen-going-on-twelve-year-old, as one British journalist described her, complete with her own controversy. She looked and acted like Little Orphan Annie and ran in bare feet; what more could anyone want?

Decker was angry with the media. When she was asked at a pre-Games press conference about Zola Budd she snapped, "Zola who?" The journalists smiled; it was all boiling up nicely. Decker, though, had had her usual traumatic lead-in to a major championship. At the American trials a thirty-five-minute delay to the start of a 1500 metres semi-final made her tendon tighten up and though she ran and qualified for the team it proved to be costly. Four days later when she tried to run the pain was too much. She thought it was the end of her Olympic aspirations, but a most painful injection followed by a week in a pool, strapped into a harness that ensured that her feet couldn't touch the bottom when she ran in water, did the trick. She was ready for LA.

Zola flew in with the British team and travelled on with them to a Holding Camp at Point Loma in San Diego, where Labuschagne awaited her. After their acclimatising sojourn there the team moved into the Olympic Village where her coach had no access and where her over-reliance on him became apparent. She felt homesick and just wanted out. In truth, Zola was never ready for these Olympic Games. Her inexperience showed like a sore thumb. As American writer Eric Olsen was to comment after the 3000 metres, Budd had not paid her dues as Decker had, as Puica had. They were hardened, experienced competitors; the Romanian especially had had a marvellous competitive run-in to Los Angeles. Budd's whole approach was wrong. She felt that the Olympic Games were something to be endured, a kind of penance before salvation, which for her was to be a return to South Africa immediately afterwards.

All the leading contenders qualified safely for the final and after a day's rest the athletes assembled again and America sat back to await the coronation of its distance-running queen. But *Perils of Decker* had another reel to run.

Decker went into the lead immediately in the final and completed the first two laps inside world-record pace, with Budd and Puica in attendance. It was a repeat of Helsinki, the only way, it seemed, that Mary knew to run. Another lap went by and the position remained the same, the pace still fast. After the fourth circuit the pattern changed when Budd moved alongside Decker as they entered the back straight, and then edged into the lead. Around they came into the home straight, the crowd intrigued that someone had had the effrontery to overtake their heroine at such a stage. Budd in the lead – but when Decker brushed against her, each faltered and then resumed running. Five strides later they brushed again; Budd was thrown off balance, her leg swung inside in front of Decker who tripped in avoiding it and crashed out of the race, out of the Olympics, out of the money.

Now the scenes were pure melodrama, the race continuing and building to its climax; on each lap the runners passed the stricken Decker lying trackside with a damaged hip, being tended by medics, her shouts and cries of anguish and frustration so loud that some feared they might open the San Andreas Fault. The crowd, most of whom had taken time out from their picnics to watch the race, now began booing. A lap and a half after the incident Budd faltered and slowed, the realisation of what had happened dawning on her. Sly went into the lead, a woman inspired, Puica her shadow. With 300 metres to go the Romanian made her effort and sprinted ahead, her blonde hair streaking behind her, power and grace personified. She would not be challenged and won in an Olympic record time. Wendy Sly finished second, well clear of Canada's Lynn Williams, one of the least-publicised silver medals in history. No one was watching, no one was caring, all eyes were on the tiny figure in red, still crumpled alongside the home straight and about to find solace in the arms of her fiancé, Richard Slaney.

Zola finished seventh. She was grief-stricken as she left the track with Burki. She passed Decker in the tunnel that led from the track and went across to her. Their worlds had fallen apart, they had ended with nothing except, perhaps, notoriety. Zola said she was sorry. Mary's face contorted with rage. "Don't bother!" she spat back. Budd went sadly away. Mary Peters, a former Olympic champion and one of Britain's top team managers, comforted Zola and then went to find John Bryant, who was in Los Angeles for the *Mail.* He gained access to the track, where he found Zola weeping. The priority was to get her back to the Village, away from the cauldron of the Coliseum. Labuschagne, in a state of shock, drove her to her mother's flat.

The post mortems went on *ad infinitum* on television around the world: in slow motion, in still-frame sequence, backwards, forwards. Coaches, runners and officials gave opinions. Everyone had a field day. It was like being at a well-loved Shakespearean play; you know that Ophelia is going to die but you just hope, this one time, that it won't happen. Zola was disqualified, then reinstated. Decker blamed Budd; Budd, hiding away in downtown LA, made no comment. The best judgement came from the German runner, Thomas Wessinghage.

"Whoever is in the lead in lane one is not to be blamed for anything that happens behind him or her," he said. "There is really nobody you can blame it on, except maybe Mary, because she got a little too close on the inside."

In the end, that was the consensus except, perhaps, that everybody was to blame. Eric Olsen wrote in *Runner* magazine: "Ultimately, we all created the race, in our fervent desire for spectacle. What we created was not an honest contest that grew naturally out of the competition between two women of equal talent and desire contending for the same prize, but something distorted by media hype, thrust unwanted on both of them."

Seconds before the fall: Zola Budd hot on the heels of Mary Decker in the Olympic 3000 metres in 1984.

Ron Brown, Mary Decker's coach, approached Labuschagne with regard to a proposal by ABC television. It was that Mary and Zola should sit in a studio and analyse the incident between them. Pieter thought this a good idea but pointed out that Zola was contracted to the *Daily Mail* and they would have to be asked. Brown went to see John Bryant. Bryant was horrified on three counts. One, it wasn't a good idea. Two, the *Mail* would have done its collective nut, and three, Zola didn't want to do it. Mary Decker, articulate, thrusting, media-experienced, would have, figuratively, eaten the shy inarticulate Zola, whose English was still hesitant. He said "No" and, feeling like Andrei Gromyko, kept saying "No". Finally Brown brought the US team psychologist to see Bryant. What this man basically said was that it would be a very good thing for the two girls to expiate the guilt that existed in them, to cleanse their souls in front of the great American public. Bryant said "No". Rebuffed at last, the man, a fine example of the Californian school of psychology, left with the parting shot that he felt Bryant was taking too much on himself making decisions for an eighteen-year-old.

A few hours later Bryant received an urgent telephone call from Mary Peters. "This is very confidential," she said, "but I've got a man here from the Los Angeles Anti-Terrorist group. Death threats have been made against Zola – that she'll be shot, either at the stadium or at the airport when she leaves. They are taking it very seriously. Zola should get the next plane out."

Hasty arrangements were made. There was a flight out in a few hours. Bryant hurried round to the Budds' apartment. As he entered, the first thing he saw was Tossie knitting. There was an air of doom and gloom. He told them the good news but that they had to be packed within forty-five minutes. There was a flurry of activity and in the middle of it the door burst open and a bevy of LA policemen, heavily armed, crashed in. The Budds looked startled. Bryant smiled weakly. It was, he said, just a police escort. With sirens wailing and with a massive escort they drove to the airport, straight out to the jumbo jet. Bryant had settled in his seat when a man approached. Their luggage hadn't been checked, he said, and in the circumstances it was vital that it was. Bryant and a team scrambled over the hold until the luggage was found.

Zola stayed only two days in England, just time enough to pack. She was impatient now to get the nightmare over, to get home to Bloemfontein, to the smallholding and her pets. The family flew out, landed at Jan Smuts, successfully negotiated the mob of reporters that greeted them and drove home. She immediately went up to her bedroom and tore down the picture of Mary Decker from the wall.

7

EIGHT DAYS OF SCHMALTZ

Just before Christmas 1983, as Sebastian Coe drove past the Pooterish houses which abound in north London and along the more genteel part of White Hart Lane to Haringey's New River Stadium to resume training following his illness, he must have had ambivalent feelings about the Olympic Games, then just over six months away. On the one hand, in his debilitated condition, the Games must have seemed perilously close; on the other the long, dark, chilly nights and the lack of any immediate competitive motivation probably made the warm sunshine of California seem light years away. The training, when he started it, was tough. Even the fourteen-year-olds, he said, were giving him a hard time. But meticulous planning by Peter Coe brought the Olympic champion through to a peak, with perhaps one hiccup, in the right place and at the right time. The highlight was a superb run in Oslo in June where he won the 800 metres in 1:43.84; the low point was a defeat by Peter Elliott in the AAA Championships 1500 metres. There was one place vacant in the Olympic squad – Ovett and Cram had already been pre-selected – and there was a media clamour for Elliott to be awarded it. Fortunately, wiser heads prevailed at selection and Coe was picked to defend his Olympic title. At 800 metres, Ovett, Elliott and Seb would make the British challenge. Coe, however, was not supremely confident of his chances. Over the years he had been used to winning, now there was some doubt.

"The minute you start losing," his father said, "even though you can rationalise such losses with illnesses or injuries, it does get to you and you start to wonder. I said to Seb, 'All these problems have compounded themselves in your mind. There is only one person who can get them out and that's you.'"

For father and son Los Angeles was the second bite at the cherry. Both were more experienced now and knew what the Games had in store for them. In Moscow they emphatically did not. The most important question was whether they should travel to the Olympics together; whether, as Peter said, he should "be there valeting". Moscow had been a traumatic, emotionally draining experience for both, and the team management had tried to keep Peter and Seb apart in the interval between the 800 and 1500 metres. Seb had travelled to Oslo solo and run successfully. Now, through mutual telepathy almost, both decided that he should proceed alone to California, armed with the weekly schedules.

He travelled via Chicago, staying with a coaching friend of his father's, and then went straight into the Olympic Village, missing the Holding Camp that the British team had set up near San Diego. Peter arrived only a few days before the Games were due to start, checked his son's progress, was highly satisfied and withdrew again.

The two Steves, Cram and Ovett, had had fluctuating seasons, plagued by illness and injury. Ovett had nearly drowned while swimming off Bondi beach in Australia, where he had gone seeking sunshine to accompany his winter training. Cram had suffered a knee injury in New Zealand and had run a humiliating ninth in a 1500-metre race. With less than a month to go before the Games he was doubtful he would be competing, because of calf and ankle injuries. Only a secret time trial at the Gateshead Stadium, with wind and rain sweeping in off the North Sea, convinced him he could acquit himself well in Los Angeles. Ovett and his wife stayed in a house off Wilshire Boulevard, Cram in a hotel and Coe in the Village, contrasting approaches and styles. Many were convinced that the three could give Britain a clean sweep of the medals in the 1500 metres, a fitting climax to our eight years of domination of the event. But first Coe and Ovett had to face each other in the 800 metres, as well as a young Brazilian, Joachim Cruz.

Cruz was an ex-shoeshine boy from the city of Taguatinga, in the heart of Brazil, who had made good athletically thanks mainly to his coach, Luiz de Oliveira. His height and immense stride cast him in the mould of Alberto Juantorena, the double Olympic champion of 1976 and had taken him on a scholarship to Oregon University. In Helsinki he had won the World Championship bronze medal, just ahead of Peter Elliott. In Los Angeles he was to put on an exhibition of 800-metre running such as the world had never before seen.

It was clear that the defending champion, Steve Ovett, was mentally unprepared for the change that had come over the event since he had won in Moscow. In describing the sequence of Olympic races that led to the final he constantly bemoaned the fact that they were too fast. He also had the misfortune to face Cruz in each of the four rounds. But the sad truth was that he just wasn't fast enough. He had never run faster than 1:44 and his best time had been set all of six years previously. In three of his four races in Los Angeles, Cruz ran faster than Steve's winning time in Moscow. Ovett should have given the 800 metres a wide berth.

There were other worrying signs for Steve as he moved up from Point Loma College, the British Holding Camp near San Diego. He had noticed that the air was smog-ridden; his eyes smarted, his breath rasped and the intense heat was also beginning to affect him, as it had done in Moscow. After his first-round race his fingers and arms tingled and despite taking in gallons of fluid he was dehydrating. The same symptoms appeared after the second round, but with greater intensity. Foolishly he told only Rachel and his friend and training partner, Matt Patterson, about the problem. He only made the final with a desperate lunge in fourth place, collapsing on to the track. He said he found the pace "absurd". The truth was he was out of his depth. He took some medical advice that evening and used a spray to fight his breathing problems. The next day he stepped forward, along with five men who had all run faster than he, to toe the line for the final.

Cruz was clearly the man to beat. He had run faster each round, setting a personal best in the semi-final. The Kenyan, Koech, led for the first lap and for half of the second. Cruz shadowed him, Coe likewise in third place. On the last bend Cruz shot into the lead and was never headed, Coe chasing him manfully down the home straight to gain his second Olympic silver medal. Still a major 800-metre title eluded the world record holder. Cruz set a new Olympic record of 1:43.00, the third-fastest time ever. Earl Jones of the USA won the bronze medal. Ovett said later that when they hit the bell it was as if somebody had pulled the plug out of his system. He finished last. Seb went up to him, put a consoling arm round his shoulder and said: "I guess we're a bit too old to be playing with fire like that." He gave Steve a drink; he vomited immediately and collapsed in the tunnel that led from the track. He was stretchered out of the stadium in a semi-conscious state and whisked away to the Los Angeles Orthopedic Hospital and most thought he was out of the Games.

Sebastian Coe, meanwhile, had walked away with a smile on his face, totally content with his silver medal, in sharp contrast to the histrionics of four years before. In addition to being a more mature person there was another reason for the change of spirit. In Moscow he felt he had lost the gold medal, in Los Angeles he felt he had won the silver. He knew that he could not have beaten Cruz on that day. He also realised, and his father–coach sitting in the stands knew, that the speed he had displayed in the 800 metres would make him almost unbeatable in the 1500.

In the days between the two middle-distance races considerable efforts were made by almost everyone concerned to persuade Steve Ovett not to compete in the 1500 metres. Indeed, the only person who felt that he had to run the event, which had three rounds, was Steve himself. Whilst in hospital he felt that he was in some dream world, hardly conscious of what was going on around him. Rachel was adamant that he should not run, frightened of the

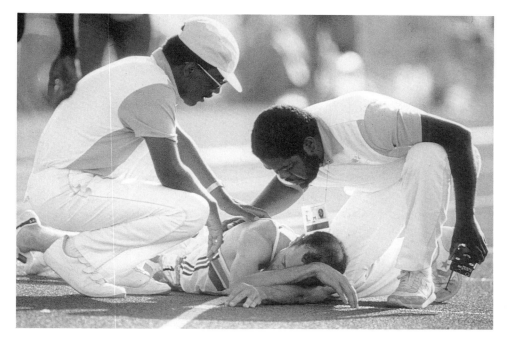

The old rivals find contrasting fortunes in Los Angeles. An exhausted Steve Ovett receives medical attention after collapsing on the track . . .

. . .while Seb Coe takes silver in the 800 metres and gold in the 1500 metres. "Thanks, Dad."

long-term consequences of a recurrence of his problem. After a whole battery of tests, the medical people could not say whether his problem would recur. On the other hand, they did not believe that he would do himself any lasting harm by running. He was visited by the British Olympic Association's Doctor Archibald, who hinted that he should not run, and by the British athletics team manager, Nick Whitehead, who agreed. He left hospital after two days and announced that he was running the 1500 metres. He had arrived in California in the best athletic condition of his life and still felt that he could win a medal. All three British runners reached the final. After his semi Ovett had again suffered from breathing problems, witnessed by Rachel and there was, as Ovett described it, an appalling atmosphere in the house that night, which was a sleepless one. But it was a situation caused solely by his own insensitivity and intransigence.

Everyone was hoping for a great final but not expecting one. The Olympic record was still that of Kenyan, Kip Keino, set at altitude in Mexico City in 1968. Subsequent races were likened by the American writer, Hal Higdon, to the cyclist's five-lap sprint event where, for four laps two cyclists pedal leisurely around the track, weaving about, looking over their shoulders, until the final lap when one catches the other napping and wins the race. What Higdon and many others were hoping for was a classic race where the winner makes a commitment, throws down the gauntlet and wins in record time. They wanted a revival of the spirit of Herb Elliott, Peter Snell and Kip Keino. Another man who said he wanted a classic race was the American record holder, Steve Scott, a runner who mostly flattered to deceive in the big events. He was the second-fastest miler alive. He had duly made the final, along with his conqueror of the year before, Steve Cram, the defending champion Sebastian Coe and the world record holder, Steve Ovett. The day was as usual hot and sunny, as the runners set off on their three and three-quarter laps. Omar Khalifa of Sudan took on the early pace and then came something of a shock when the renowned "kicker" Scott took the lead. The rest of the field mentally reacted in different ways.

"What on earth is Steve doing?" thought Cram. "Crikey, we're going to run quick here," Coe said to himself. Jim Spivey, Scott's fellow-American, thought that Steve had taken the race by the scruff of the neck. "If he keeps this up, he's got it won," he muttered to himself as he kept pace.

What had made the man who normally waits until the closing stages suddenly change tactic? Was it a sudden rush of blood to the head? Did he feel the partisan American crowd would sustain him to victory? In fact it was a move he had been considering for months. He had been outsmarted by Cram in Helsinki, he had been out-kicked by Spivey in the American trials. His only chance of victory was a sustained long run for home. The crowd yelled him on but it was a tactic doomed to failure. Scott would eventually finish tenth.

Up in the thick of the battle at the half-way mark was Steve Ovett, clearly not yet suffering the hyperventilation problems of his previous races. After 900 metres Spain's José Abascal took the lead; Scott went back and back. He was to describe the moment graphically: "An elephant, a giraffe and a monkey all jumped on my back," Scott said, meaning that his legs had gone. Abascal led as the bell tolled impending defeat for eleven of the twelve runners. Coe, Cram and Ovett followed and for one fleeting moment it seemed as if a British clean sweep of the medals was possible. Then Ovett dramatically left the track as the pain in his chest and arms returned. Abascal had taken on the pace, gambling all for a medal, as did Straub in 1980. He too succeeded, winning the bronze. Cram went to move into the lead but he was too late. Coe was in front and for Cram it was over. "I knew," he said afterwards, "that unless his legs went to jelly he had won."

And so it was. Coe won in majestic fashion, in a new Olympic record of 3:32.53. Cram won the silver medal. It was a moment of Olympic history. No one had ever won two 1500-metre titles. It was Renaissance man at his very best. But then, at this moment of his greatest triumph, Coe did a very strange thing. His face contorted in anger, he turned to the Press area and shoved his arms fiercely towards them, pointing with his forefingers. He shouted at them and then marched angrily around for a few moments before calming completely. Simon Barnes of *The Times* wrote that he was "drunk on adrenalin". Reports differed on what he shouted at the British Press that day. Some said he shouted, "Don't write me off!" but the more likely version was "*Now* believe in me!" Perhaps that had been the motivation Coe had needed to spur him to greatness, that dismissal of his chances by the British media following his defeat by Elliott. Maybe the facile, hurtful words, written by uncomprehending head-line writers over columns written by journalists who should have known better, had lit a fuse deep inside him that had burned to this day, to this moment of triumph and anger.

Peter Coe, who had, of course, known him all of his twenty-seven years said: "Seb is a gentle person but he is also steely and has within him a deep streak of aggression which doesn't normally show. When he is able to channel it into that single endeavour then the adrenalin really flows."

Coe said: "Where's my old man?" They met and shared this moment of mutual triumph before he took a Union Jack and went off on a lap of honour. He had been a man with a mission that day and that had made him virtually unbeatable. Most of the field recognised and accepted it. That night cele-brations were held in one of those revolving restaurants that puncture the Los Angeles skyline. It was a good night, a relaxing night, the adrenalin had receded, the mission was over. Seb didn't tell his family till later that he

"*Now* believe in me!"

had booked it all well in advance of the final, an act not of bravado but of supreme confidence.

In Jurgen Hingsen's house in Krefeld, Germany, hang five silver medals and three world record plaques – a succinct commentary on the decathlon career of a man who never really quite made it, never, as his main protagonist over the decade, Daley Thompson, would put it, won a Big G. Frustratingly, as Daley's star waned through injury in the latter years of the eighties, so did Jurgen's. Younger, fitter, more ambitious men were mounting the podia. An only child, Jurgen had grown up in the Ruhr steel town of Duisburg, where his parents enrolled him in a track club to enable the tall, gangly youth to make friends. He had excelled at a whole range of events and in 1977 had competed in the European Junior Championships, finishing third. The winner had been Daley Thompson.

Jurgen arrived in Los Angeles as the world record holder. Two months previously in Mannheim he had won the Federal Republic's Olympic Trial with 8798 points, nineteen better than his own previous mark. *Now*, he thought, *at last I've got him*, though in his mind there must have been a constant, lurking doubt. He had arrived in both Athens and Helsinki in exactly the same position. It might only have been a minute percentage of doubt but it is all that is required to bring about failure on the crucial day. Many athletes will tell you that there is at least one rival that they are always confident of beating. They know it, and more importantly their opponent knows it. It is nothing to do with training and physical competitive fitness but all to do with the mind, a psychological advantage, often established early on. So it was with Hingsen and Thompson. The preliminary verbal skirmishing would have done a world boxing title fight proud. It was pure Ali and Foreman.

"The only way Hingsen is going to get a gold medal here is to do another event," Daley said: "or steal mine." The German, who had been training for weeks in Santa Barbara, said: "Daley may be the better talker but I'm the better decathlete."

Thompson threw down the gauntlet in the first event, running a 10.44 100 metres. It was his fastest sprint in a decathlon, an ominous sign for his rivals. Throughout the first day he streaked ahead, jumping further than anyone previously in a decathlon long jump, 8.01 metres (which only five British long-jumpers have ever beaten), and setting a decathlon personal best in the shot put of 15.77 metres. At the close he took tired limbs around the track once in 46.97 seconds and ended 114 points ahead. No man had ever bettered his first-day score of 4633 points.

"Ah," Jurgen Hingsen said to the contingent of German journalists, "remember that Day Two is my day."

In most decathlons there is a pivotal moment in one of the events when those competing and those watching know that it is then that the competition will be won or lost. In Los Angeles this moment came in the pole vault. Up until then, on the second day, Hingsen had been as good as his word, reducing Daley's lead dramatically to just thirty-two points, a fraction of time or a few centimetres in one of the remaining competitions. He had achieved this with exemplary performances in the hurdles and discus.

"I'm ready to win now," Jurgen thought to himself as he prepared mentally for the pole vault. "I can match his vault and javelin and I am the better man at 1500 metres. *This* is my moment at last."

The sun beat down relentlessly on the Coliseum stadium and suddenly Jurgen began to feel nauseous, a little dizzy. His vision became blurred. He could not see the crossbar clearly. He felt desperate and only just managed to clear 4.50 metres on his third attempt, sixty centimetres below his best. He went off to the stadium tunnel and vomited. He failed to clear the next height. The battle was over, and the war. Jurgen knew it, Daley knew it. The champion cleared 5 metres and the rest was a formality. Daley had lost his motivation and failed by one point to match Hingsen's world record. Five months later, a close inspection of the photo-finish film of the 110 metres hurdles gained him that extra point. In 1985 the scoring tables for the decathlon were revised and Daley's total score became a world record in its own right.

In many ways a decathlon is like a round of golf, full of ifs and buts, especially for the losers. Hingsen brooded and half listened to his wisecracking conqueror holding court in the interview tent. Around him were a group of German journalists, the only ones who wanted to listen to the silver medallist. "If we had been level going into the 1500 metres I would have blown him away," he reflected sadly, "because I am a very good runner." The journalists nodded but looked embarrassed, already planning the phrases they would use to explain another Hingsen failure.

Daley Thompson had become only the second man in history to win two Olympic decathlons. The first was Bob Mathias, who had triumphed in London in 1948 and Helsinki in 1952. Bob was in Los Angeles to see the battle between the German and the Englishman and Daley promised him that he would go one better. Up in heaven Jim Thorpe was smiling too. In 1912, in Stockholm, he had won the gold medal but was later disqualified for "professionalism". In 1984 he was posthumously reinstated to his rightful place by both the IAAF and IOC, his name back on the medal and record lists. Who knows, perhaps he had influence with those Greek gods that mythology tells us control these things and recognised in the now double Olympic champion a kindred soul. How else to explain Jurgen Hingsen's sudden attack of nausea at a crucial moment in the Olympic decathlon?

When Allan Wells arrived in California he was out of sorts with the world and with himself. If he was a carefully-programmed sprinter then a hacker had been infiltrating him. Los Angeles was not his kind of town. He began to fret. Before the Games he had sustained a not very serious injury but now he had a toe that was hurting. He didn't like the crowded rooms in the Village, he hated the hype and the heat. The team management, Nick Whitehead in particular, seemed more "Establishment" than before. He longed for the orderliness of Moscow and felt that Olympic values were being let down. Margot tried to soothe him.

"Everything's there," she said. "You're running well. I don't know what's wrong with you."

He became irritated at small incidents. On the first morning of the athletic events he came across some piece of officiousness at the reporting area and strong words ensued. Basically, in his heart, he knew that he should not have come to LA to defend his title. He ran in the first two rounds of the competition but still wasn't happy. As he prepared for the semi-final his foot seemed worse. He told Margot his feelings.

"You look fine," she said.

"But I'm only ninety-nine per cent," he said testily. "I'm not going out there one hundred per cent." To a man to whom meticulous preparation was a credo this was a total disaster. "I'm just going to go down there and do what I can," he said. In Moscow he had said that he would do everything that he could to win.

He carried all this out with him to the start of the race. The adrenalin was pumping away, but for the wrong reason – he was frightened. Afterwards he was to say that he acted like a man who knew that he was only going to make the semi-final. He really felt that he was marching out to face the firing squad. His toe was killing him, his foot felt red-hot. Carl Lewis, the world champion, was in his semi-final. Allan had run fourth in both sprints in Helsinki and should have been a certainty to make the last eight here. They went to their marks; the gun fired and the semi-final was under way. He felt lethargic, and couldn't get up on his toes. Towards the end his eyes felt bloodshot. "I felt for a moment that I was running through red ink," he said. He came in last.

Though his foot was burning he vowed that he would not take his spikes off until he was back at the start. He walked there on the grass infield. Lewis, who had won, was jogging back, waving at the cheering spectators. Like Coe in Moscow all Allan wanted to do was leave the arena as soon as possible. He left the track through the tunnel under the stand. Lewis was in front of him and he saw the irony of the moment. Lewis the prospective Olympic champion coming in; Wells, the old champion, going out. He met Margot, who looked at him quizzically, but before they could speak Nick Whitehead passed by.

"Well, it wasn't physical anyway," he said.

Allan felt pole-axed and slumped down. The tears started to roll down his cheeks. He already felt humiliated that people had seen "the iron man of sprinting" appearing so weak. Now he knew what people would feel, would say; that somehow he had been chicken-hearted. He wept and Margot wept too. It was the worst moment of his life. His first reaction was to leave Los Angeles at the earliest possible moment. He was gently talked out of this idea and he went for a medical diagnosis which told him that his toe had been pushed too far back. Then he remembered that prior to the Olympics, in his quest for perfection, he had had the mechanics of his spikes changed with an inlaid sponge placed in them in a certain way. He had been told that it would give him half an inch on each stride. All it had given him was total indignity.

A few days before the Games were to begin Rafer Johnson, the 1960 decathlon champion, sat in the office of Peter Ueberroth, the President of the Organising Committee, and wondered what he was doing there. Outside the yachts in the marina bobbed quietly in the late afternoon sun. Opposite him sat David Wolper, the man in charge of the opening ceremony, and Ueberroth, who suddenly told him that he would like him to be the final torchbearer, the man to light the Olympic flame. Johnson was stunned but accepted the honour. Wolper came straight in.

"It's a bitch," he said. "We're talking a lot of stairs, Rafer. You've got to run a lap around the Coliseum track, climb the stairs leading up from the floor of the stadium and then the real back-breaker – ninety-six steps by the hydraulic slip stair to the top, where you'll face the crowd and light the flame."

This encounter seemed to encapsulate the American approach to staging their third Olympic Games. Everything had to be bigger, better and noisier than ever before. It certainly had to be better than Moscow.

The Soviets were not present. Nor were most of the Eastern bloc countries. They stayed away in a tit-for-tat boycott for Moscow. The Romanians arrived and were wooed and fêted. Their president Ceausescu was hailed as a great man for his defiance of the Soviet Union. It all seems very ironic now. The Chinese too were there and received a standing ovation at the opening cere-mony. This was pure schmaltz, and set the tone for the sixteen days of the Games. The Americans thought that it was Hollywood at its best but for many it embodied all the worst aspects of show-biz: glitz and glitter without substance. A thousand-voiced choir sang; a man with a jet-pack flew through the air to land on the track; an eight-hundred-strong Olympic marching band blew their way into the Coliseum and eighty-four white baby-grand pianos played Cole Porter. It was "Welcome back, Busby Berkeley".

Tessa Sanderson wins the women's javelin for Britain...

...and proudly displays her gold medal for photographers.

The athletics events took up eight days of the celebration. Live in the Coliseum or on ABC television it was strictly an American party. There was never a mention that the winning of medals had been devalued by the boycott, especially in the women's events. There were some very great athletes absent – Marlies Gohr, Marita Koch, Heike Daute and Petra Felke from the German Democratic Republic; Yuriy Sedykt, Tatyana Kazankina and Olga Bondarenko from the Soviet Union and Lyudmila Andonova from Bulgaria – each would have expected to win a medal. All this was ignored in the glorious hype that surrounded the American successes – Carl Lewis emulating Jesse Owens with four gold medals; Edwin Moses repeating his 1976 Olympic win; Evelyn Ashford at last shrugging off her anger at not being in Moscow. The pictures being flashed around the world by the host broadcaster were of Americans winning in front of Americans cheering. Even the International Olympic Committee, who had gratefully received $225 million from the US network felt the need to make critical remarks which they soon, however, retracted. What the Games of the XXIII Olympiad lacked, as John Rodda reported in the *Guardian,* was dignity. Requests by the IOC to return to more traditional ways were not just ignored, they were turned down. The Americans were running the show. As the Games ended in another sugar-soaked ceremony, many feared for the future of the Olympic movement.

For British athletes the Games were eminently successful. It was here that the seeds of future triumphs were being sown. As well as the middle distances, where we still tended to look upon success as a God-given right, excellent performances were achieved in both the javelin events. Tessa Sanderson won a gold medal, David Ottley a silver and Fatima Whitbread a bronze. In the hurdles Shirley Strong won silver and Kathy Cook won two bronze medals to become the first (and to date, only) British woman to run below fifty seconds for 400 metres. Mike McFarlane and Donovan Reid reached the final of the men's sprint. Some athletes were now full-time, thanks to the new subvention system payments, but what Britain now needed was substantial funding to consolidate on and improve its position as a world athletic power. In 1984, with negotiations for a new television contract concluded in Independent Television's favour, such an opportunity arose.

Kathy Cook battles away towards her bronze medal before a packed stadium.

8

WINNING THE POOLS

The BBC had been covering domestic athletics since 1953 but the real break-through came a year later when two events of major importance occurred. One of the commentators, Norris McWhirter, telephoned and said that an event of world-wide impact might take place at the Iffley Road track the following week and he felt that the BBC should have a presence. It was Bannister's four-minute mile. Later that year Chris Chataway beat the Russian, Vladimir Kuts, over 5000 metres at a packed White City in London and it was obvious that athletics could become a major televised sport. David Coleman joined the commentary team in 1960, replacing Peter Dimmock, and it was further strengthened a few years later by the ex-National Coach, Ron Pickering. This team, later augmented by Stuart Storey and Brendan Foster, was the one that presented British athletics to the public right up until the mid-eighties. The popular profile of the sport in this country is almost certainly down to the BBC, its commentators and its production teams.

Independent Television battled valiantly against the exclusive contract which the BBC signed every four or five years. They covered the enormously popular end-of-season Coca-Cola meeting, which was promoted by the International Athletes Club, and early overseas events, including the major championships. Their commentary team in the seventies and early eighties had been Adrian Metcalfe and Alan Pascoe, both former Olympic athletes and the latter a Commonwealth and European champion. Every time the contract came up for renewal ITV made a bid, and each time they were unsuccessful – until 1984. John Bromley, who then headed ITV Sport, was determined to wrench athletics from the BBC and made a bid of £10.5 million for the five-year contract, well in excess of the BBC's offer. Athletics officials were in a quandary: should they stick with the tried and trusted formula that the BBC offered for another five years? Or should they accept the ITV bid, with all the wealth and excitement and uncertainty that it would bring? A group of men were tasked with the problem including the two chairmen of the most important organisations, Arthur McAllister of the AAA and Bill Evans of the BAAB.

There was an additional factor for the sport to consider; its decision to appoint a marketing company to handle sponsorships. In the past athletics had found itself having to deal with a welter of agencies representing various clients, whose techniques and approach were often entirely different. The sport's record with sponsors over the years was appalling and they had come and gone like leaves on an oak tree. Arthur McAllister and his team pondered long and hard and finally, though the BBC had upped their offer, they decided to accept the Independent Television bid. A major factor was that they felt that ITV would give any marketing contract a better chance to work. It was ironic that at the moment of the announcement ITV was hidebound by union problems that were to prevent them covering the Olympic Games. The clincher had been the eleventh-hour withdrawal of the International Athletes Club from the main contract negotiations. McAllister went to both companies with the news, which could take around £750,000 from either bid. It was Bromley, for ITV, who said that their offer still stood. The BBC said that their bid must be reduced by that amount. A thirty-year association with the Corporation had been broken and there are those in the BBC who carry to this day their bitterness at what they saw as a betrayal.

Now the search began for a marketing agency that would seek sponsors and service them on behalf of the sport. A number of companies showed interest: the powerful International Management Group of Mark McCormack: the Keith Prowse Agency; West Nally, another international sponsorship agency, and MSW, a smaller company that was soon to change its name to that of the man who had become its Chairman and Managing Director, Alan Pascoe. I had first met Alan many years before when as a junior he came from Portsmouth to compete in Buckinghamshire for the Southern Counties on a wet grass track. Tall and lanky, there was no sign then that he would become a major international athlete, European and Commonwealth title holder at 400 metres hurdles, and later a highly successful businessman, running a marketing and sponsorship agency with a world-wide reputation. Whilst he was still competing he had dabbled in sports promotion, directing the Philips Night of Athletics at the Crystal Palace in London for his physical education college. On his retirement he also became involved with the Nationwide sponsorship of the AAA Championships. This was really the sum total of his commercial experience in athletics when the idea was being strongly mooted that with its new-found television coverage the sport was looking for an agency to handle its commercial affairs.

What Alan brought to the business world from his athletics career was his capacity for sustained hard work and the drive and motivation to succeed. He wanted to be as successful in business as he had been in track and field. Luckily he was in Los Angeles for the Olympic Games with ITV, and having time on his hands he was able to gather the background to their bid and to gain some insight into the way they intended to tackle future coverage of the sport. He lobbied hard, and athletics recognised that here was a man who knew the sport intimately, and they were inclined towards him mainly on the principle of better the devil that you know than the one you don't. They were asking for sponsorship guarantees and to obtain them he had to go to banks, and most particularly to Len Hatton, a wealthy businessman who had been involved with club athletics for a long time.

There were bad moments in this drive to make the great breakthrough that his new company needed. One night, whilst in Oslo for ITV, one of his colleagues breezed into the hotel and chirpily announced that IMG had won the contract. It was a Friday night and no one was available to talk to in England. He felt pole-axed, let-down, depressed and angry all at once. He had been talking to the officers of the sport only the day before and they had mentioned nothing. He went to his room to brood. "If there had been a bottle of whisky there," he recalled, "I would have drunk the lot." British officials arrived in the Norwegian capital late that night and confirmed that though IMG had made an official bid no deal had been signed. On the Monday, Alan was back in England again lobbying hard. There should have been some sense of urgency in the deliberations, for ITV were to begin transmitting the following April and the sport needed to have sponsors in place ready for the spring road-races. But at every level athletics is notorious for an unspoken maxim – why take one week when six will do? It was not until November that they finally decided that Alan Pascoe Associates should be their marketing agent.

The package that was put together was – and remains – an attractive one. ITV would be covering eighteen major meetings and these would be divided between five major sponsors, each of whom would have a title event. They would also, and this was the attractiveness of the scheme, have their company boards at all the events, which gave them year-round coverage. In addition they were encouraged to sponsor much non-televised activity as part of their package. The idea for this came from Alan Pascoe.

"It was based on Andy Norman's ideas in the late seventies and early eighties," he said. "Much of our up-and-coming talent obtained races at Oslo and other meetings in Europe on the backs of Foster, Ovett, Coe and Moor-croft. If you want these top stars, Andy told them, you have to take these other athletes as well. I applied the same principle to the sponsorship deals."

Immediately three companies, Kodak, Pearl Assurance and Peugeot Talbot signed on; then there was a worrying gap of quite a few months before McVitie's and Dairy Crest joined the package. At the end of 1990 three of the five are still there, now joined by a host of others. As Chris Brasher said at the AAA Annual General Meeting that year, "athletics has won the pools". Indeed

Alan Pascoe, pictured in Birmingham in 1989 bearing a tankard presented to him as a past Commonwealth champion.

it had, and the stage was set for an amazing transformation that would take Great Britain to even higher levels of success than its distance runners had already achieved. But there was one man who was crucial to all this, the man both Independent Television and Alan Pascoe insisted must be part of their deals with the sport. He was the larger-than-life character who had been running British promotions for a decade or more, dragging the sport in Britain into the modern era, a tough, no-nonsense man who was revered and feared in turns by most athletes. He was Andy Norman.

9

EVENING ALL, IT'S ANDY NORMAN

If Andy Norman has nightmares they must be about empty seats. For this ex-copper of twenty-two years' standing has the job of filling athletic stadia around the country, not only with athletes of international calibre but with crowds as well. He also has to satisfy the ever-avaricious television moguls, their eyes always on the ratings. Upon his ample shoulders lie the present and future of British and, he believes, European athletics. Ninety-five per cent of British athletics' income comes from television and sponsorship. In 1990 that was running at something in the order of £6 million a year, a turnover probably exceeded only by the wealthy IAAF itself. Many adjectives have been used to describe this charismatic man, not all of them polite or supportive. He certainly has more enemies than friends, bluntness and bullying being the key elements in his personality. But underneath this hard exterior lies a gentler, kinder soul that will never make its escape. Andy has been well and truly hoisted with his own petard as the hard man of British athletics.

Life began for him in Ipswich in Suffolk and as a youth he ran capably at middle distances. Then he joined the Metropolitan Police as a cadet and gradually became administratively involved with its athletics club. As team manager and captain he spent hours each week trying to assemble a team from policemen on shift work all over London. Late in the sixties he became involved on a wider basis and in 1974 he accepted an invitation to become Director of the Coca-Cola televised end-of-season meeting. The credentials he brought to the job were all from the police. He had served as a desk sergeant at both Chelsea and Notting Hill police stations, liaising at the latter with Michael X, the black activist, and with the early carnival committees. So he was streetwise and like every policeman saw everything in clear-cut terms. Andy would not suffer fools gladly; in fact, he would not suffer them at all.

Before his first Coca-Cola he flew to Oslo to see how they ran things at the Bislett meetings. Arne Haukvik was the director there, a man who had been bringing world-class athletes to the track for years. Andy savoured the special atmosphere and saw how the Norwegian promoter dealt with the globe-trotting stars who could make or break his meeting. He remembered watching Arne walking up and down the track negotiating with Dwight Stones about the bonus for a world high-jump record whilst the large crowd sat silently and waited. He also met and became friends with John Walker and Rod Dixon, the world-class New Zealand runners, who spent every summer in Europe.

"From them," Andy said in his oft-mimicked voice, "I had an education. I found out very quickly how the world really worked and I was amazed that thousands and thousands of pounds were pumped into the sport on the backs of half a dozen athletes. I found out that you don't sell the sport as a package – you sell individuals."

In those days he had two trump cards, Steve Ovett and Brendan Foster, and these combined with the New Zealanders made up a package that he could sell. His early meetings were built around these stars and they were successful. In 1978 he went to a European Fixtures Congress in Rhodes to obtain one fixture for England and came back with a series. These were the days of the "brown envelopes" and queues of uncomfortable-looking athletes standing outside fashionable hotel bedrooms. It was nothing new – back in the fifties all the great middle-distance stars received money for running. In the twenties even Harold Abrahams sold some of the trophies he had won. The one thing that Andy insisted on with British athletes was that they paid their taxes. He helped with the creation of the Nice and Brussels meetings and in 1981 sat on the working party to decide the future of the amateur status. They met in Rome, and Samaranch, the IOC President, came to see them.

"I asked him one question," Andy said. "'If Sebastian Coe were to receive payment for competing and it was paid into a Trust Fund would you object?' Samaranch said, 'No.'"

It was with this concept that he faced the IAAF Congress in Athens. He looked around and saw many ex-athletes, now administrators, who had received illegal payments in the past. He told them bluntly that if they failed the sport at this crucial time chaos would follow. He hinted that if they voted against the working party's scheme a top meeting might publish, just before a major championship, a list of athletes who had received payment. Such an action, of course, would have thrown the sport into confusion. They took the hint and voted for appearance money and trust funds, even finding support from the East European nations, still ideologically hidebound by hard-line Communism.

Throughout the seventies and early eighties this Falstaffian character built up his connections with the other European promoters – Sven-Arne Hansen in Oslo, Andreas Bruger in Zurich, Wilfred Meert in Brussels and Sandro

Entry of the gladiator: Andy Norman in typical pose at Crystal Palace.

Giovanelli in Rieti. They formed the Euromeister organisation, a forum for all the meeting directors in Europe. The era of the European athletics circus had dawned, a circus that was to be the progenitor of the international Grand Prix series. During this time Andy did not forget his athletics roots, the winter and spring nights at Crystal Palace, where he staged meetings for all who wanted to compete, regardless of standard, and the big open meetings at the Imber Court police ground in Surrey. Even today he will hurtle around the country to Grimsby, Wrexham, Horsham and other tracks where decathlons or junior internationals are being staged, making sure that the arrangements for the athletes are right. The athletes, first and foremost, are his major concern.

"One thing that I learnt from Walker, Quax and Dixon," he said, "was that athletics is all about competing. They trained like hell for nine months of the year and ran their bloody legs off for three."

He was rarely challenged at home and became an all-powerful figure within the AAA. His England promotions, slick two-and-a-half-hour meetings, presented with flair and razzamatazz, were making the organisation a lot of money. Perhaps, though, he became too powerful.

"Everyone is happy for someone else to do the job," he said. "If you succeed then they say 'Well, didn't we do well'. If you fail, then they say 'Where did you go wrong?'"

Most athletes have had a love-hate relationship with him but very few would doubt that he has brought competitive opportunities for promising athletes that were totally missing before, opportunities that have been the lynch-pin of Britain's great successes in the decade. Few would deny either that he has been the one man who has had the vision to shape the future. He went into Europe, liked what he saw and came back and implemented it. His concept in those days was a simple one. You had to give everybody a chance. You threw them in the deep end and they swam or nearly drowned. If they nearly drowned, well, you dragged them out and threw them in a second time. If they went down again, they drowned. He has always deprecated the shilly-shallying that goes on within the sport, the prevaricating, the failure to be truthful.

"You can't keep people dangling on a string," he said. "You owe it to athletes to tell them the truth. You're dealing with their lives, for God's sake."

So, if they are not good enough, he will tell them so. Sometimes it hurts. Linford Christie, in his early days, nearly cried when Andy telephoned to tell him, just as he was leaving for Crystal Palace, that he had given his lane away. Yet it was Andy who had recognised the talent latent in the great sprinter and jerked him out of his happy-go-lucky attitude to the sport. When Joachim Cruz turned up for a meeting at Crystal Palace and demanded more money than Andy was prepared to pay, he was summarily told to pack his bags.

This, then, was the man, who was crucial, in the eyes of television and of the marketing agency, to the success of the sponsorship and television package and indeed, to the whole future of the sport. The job would be full-time and would take over his life and consume on the way his marriage. Through the years he would bring the sport success, wealth, glory, controversy, anger, envy. As athletics grew in profile so did he, and his enemies have multiplied. Indeed, they were in action even before he became British athletics' Promotions Officer. One day in 1984 he received a telephone call from an equally ambitious, equally hard man in athletics. The threat, tersely made, made it clear that there were those who were out to destroy him. He survived, but had no doubt that they would try again. They did, and so athletics in Britain, the machinery and the people in place, embarked on a bumpy ride to glory.

10

ZOLA'S YEAR, CRAMMY'S GLORY

Life on the Budd farm at Bloemfontein was certainly strange and as Zola viewed the bare backside of her favourite dog, Fraaier (shaved for a hip operation), her thoughts must have dwelt on the crazy months that she had just endured. Frank Budd had returned home in October and Zola had moved out into a small rented flat. His avaricious attitude towards her in England had done irreparable damage. The family was divided. Quintus, Zola's brother, who on just a few weeks' training annually ran the 52-mile Comrades Marathon, fiercely defended his father and blamed the rest of the parasites who had gathered around the Budd phenomenon. There were tears and recriminations. In the end Frank converted the garage into a flat and with a good deal of false bonhomie moved into it. When Zola spent time with Tossie and when she and her father met there were awkward glances and embarrassment. She was back running again, under Labuschagne, freely and without inhibition, the sunshine on her back, across the veldt where she wanted to be. She had seen the future and it frightened her. It could not be ignored, however, and if she refused to contemplate it, then others would think it through for her.

Two men now entered her life. One was a millionaire vineyard owner, Jannie Momberg, an influential figure in South African athletics circles, administrator and promoter. The other was Graham Boonzaier, another wine-grower and industrialist, a man with a profusion of black hair, including a beard. He was a friend of Momberg and both were to support Dennis Worrall, the former ambassador in London, in his bid for the South African parliament.

One alternative for Zola was to compete again in South Africa. In so doing she would burn her boats completely as far as international athletics was concerned. Such a race was even contemplated, a 3000 metres at a Momberg promotion at Stellenbosch in November. However, the news somehow leaked out and rumours spread like wildfire. Momberg, realising that he could be labelled for life as the man who terminated Zola Budd's international career, quickly dampened his ardour for the event and began to investigate ways in which she could continue to run internationally. John Bryant flew to Stellenbosch to discuss the matter. He wanted to know, on behalf of the *Daily Mail,* if Zola wished to continue her association with the newspaper. There was considerable relief at the offices when they were given a negative response. Then, winging his way in on a South African airways jumbo jet, came Nigel Cooper, then the British Board General Secretary. His mission was to discover Zola's intentions.

Nigel had replaced the Board's first General Secretary, the progressive but ultimately disillusioned David Shaw, in 1982. He first came to the notice of the British public in Athens that year by appearing on BBC television in a pair of long khaki shorts and sandals, waving a crumpled telex, crucial to Sebastian Coe's entry, which had been lost but ultimately found in a waste-paper basket. Such things happened, he had assured a bemused David Coleman, in the best-run offices. Nigel was a very likeable fellow but he always reminded me of Mr Magoo, both in personality and gait, and in his six years at the Board I felt that he never really grasped the complexities of the sport. Cooperisms abounded in athletics as much as Colemanballs, *Private Eye*'s list of commentators' gaffes, did generally. Many of course were apocryphal, and it was difficult to separate fact from fiction. Did he really ask a hammer-thrower if his throw was wind-assisted? In any case he was, with hindsight, the wrong man to fly into the Zola Budd situation. Certainly, if he did not connive at the arrangement that Momberg and Boonzaier finally came up with, that Zola race internationally but spend considerable time living in South Africa, he did not protest firmly enough either. When I spoke to him about it in 1985 he prevaricated.

"The only sanction that the British Board has," he said, "is not to select this little girl for major championships or the team. Apart from that we cannot dictate where a citizen lives." He added that many British internationals spent a good deal of time abroad training in the sunshine, indicating to me, anyway, that he was missing the entire point.

In November the Zola Budd Trust was formed to handle her affairs. The three trustees were Momberg, Boonzaier and Labuschagne. She was being dragged back into international competition. Her first assignment was to be a road-race in Zurich two days before the end of the year. As she again left Jan Smuts airport Zola's main thought was to get the race over with and be back in the protective ambience of South Africa as soon as possible. In Switzerland she met and raced against Cornelia Burki, a former South African athlete, now Swiss by marriage. The eight-kilometre race around the streets of old Zurich was held in zero temperatures and Zola wore black tights to keep out the cold. The pace of the race soon warmed everything, except for her ears, and she outsprinted Burki for victory and then met the world's Press. Momberg answered most of the questions.

Rejuvenated by Zola's win they went on to an Austrian resort to celebrate the New Year. As she sat and gazed at the unfamiliar snow-capped mountains, Zola must have thought back twelve months, when at the celebrations in Bloemfontein the family had been, on the surface anyway, united. There had been little talk of the Olympic Games – she was still four days away from unofficially breaking Decker's record – and the greed and temptations that were to assail her father and coach, and later many others, had not yet surfaced. Now the family was split and she had finally seen her father for what he was. She had suffered disapprobation, she had been hounded by the media, her life was a shambles. And now they wanted her back into that turmoil. Her only problem was, what alternative had she? A life as a nobody on the home-stead farm with her mother? She vacillated, exasperated her friends and advisers and then finally, like a reluctant bride, boarded the plane for London to announce her return to the international arena. The year was now 1985, the greatest of her short-lived career.

In London the Trust members met with Andy Norman to finalise their plans. It was agreed that Les Jones, the Northern Ireland promoter, recently appointed Great Britain assistant team manager, would "help guide her career". Les had been summoned to London at a few hours' notice for a meeting with Andy and the South African trio to agree such an arrangement. Zola's state-ment, which she says she did not see before it was given to the media, announced her intention to continue competing for Great Britain and gave her 1985 racing plans. Once it was issued she returned to South Africa.

A month later she was back in England, living in Guildford. Her first competition was in the RAF hangar at Cosford, Britain's only indoor arena. She won the 1500 metres national title and a few weeks later won an international 3000 metres. Then she travelled to Liverpool for the English cross-country championships; the weather, for her, was bitterly cold.

She had been told there might be demonstrations from anti-apartheid groups, thirsting for her blood and for publicity. The difficulty was policing a cross-country course. The hatred of the demonstrators was visible to all as they hurled abuse, waved banners and tried to encroach upon the runners. The race got under way with Angela Tooby in the lead but half-way round the first lap the demonstrators invaded the course, yelling and shouting. Zola ran off, surrounded by the jeering crowd, and crashed into bushes to avoid them. She seemed a sad and pitiful sight. Despite not finishing the race she was selected for the World Cross-Country Championships in Lisbon. She returned to South Africa to train and recuperate in the sunshine.

Lisbon was warm and sunny as the city welcomed the world's greatest runners

Anti-apartheid demonstrators were an ever-present feature of Zola Budd's races.

at the end of March. Carlos Lopes won the men's race, defeating a formidable African challenge, but for once the main interest centred on the women's event in which Zola would face Ingrid Kristiansen, Cornelia Burki and Rosa Mota, among others. After a training run around the course the eighteen-year-old decided to run barefoot, much to the chagrin of Mel Batty of Brooks, the shoe company she had signed with, who had begun to contemplate painting his logo on her feet. Kristiansen was a narrow favourite, mainly because Zola had been beaten a few weeks previously by Wendy Sly in a road-race in Phoenix, Arizona. Both started fast but after a quarter of a mile Zola went into the lead and then moved further and further ahead to win by twenty-three seconds, one of the biggest victory margins in the history of the race. Kristiansen tired at the end and finished third.

It was a great triumph and underlined the enormous talent that the tiny frame of Zola Budd encompassed. The question now was, would that talent be able to express itself freely? Would Zola come to terms with the commitment to the country that her possession of a British passport required? The signs were not propitious when in the grandstand in Lisbon, Momberg and Boonzaier, her self-styled "loving uncles", danced and shouted in strong South African accents within earshot of the IAAF President, Primo Nebiolo. For their pains they received an earful of unambiguous comment from Andy Norman.

Already, though, the Press was becoming aware of the fact that Zola was commuting to Britain from South Africa, rather than the other way round. Adverse comment was starting to appear, led by *The Times* correspondent, Pat Butcher, a journalist of left-wing propensities. Others were to follow. But that was for the future; for a while Zola could bask in the glory of being the world champion. Labuschagne and his wife were now in a state of limbo. Although they were living with Zola in England he could not, of course, seek employment here. At the end of the year he would have to return to South Africa and resume teaching. Meanwhile he continued to train her, both at Stellenbosch and in Surrey.

On her return to England Zola ran at Belfast in a Les Jones promotion, and then won at Gateshead against France and Czechoslovakia. But controversy was never far away from this young woman and it broke again as she was re-matched against Mary Decker-Slaney at the Peugeot-Talbot Grand Prix meeting at Crystal Palace in July. The pressure for the re-match came, originally, from American television. John Bromley of ITV approached Andy Norman and said that there was considerable interest in a race between the two women.

"You want it," said Andy, "you pay for it. It's as simple as that."

Negotiations took place; Boonzaier, on behalf of Zola, struck a hard deal, extracting £90,000 from the television companies for her participation. Slaney

Zola's great victory in the World Cross-Country Championships in Lisbon underlined her enormous talent.

was to receive £60,000. The money was to be paid into the coffers of the Southern Counties AA, acting as a holding house, who would then transfer the money on to the women's Trust Funds. There was just one snag – and it came late in the day – American television wanted the race live. The Peugeot-Talbot Games was on a Friday evening and so, in the week of the meeting, a second day's events was added. The move created anger and chaos. The pre-publicity and hype for the race were unprecedented in Britain and, thankfully, have never been repeated. It was billed as a grudge match and ITV and American television milked the situation for all it was worth. The Press conference at London's Waldorf Hotel was full of noise and babble and television lights and we looked for the weighing machines, so much like a boxing promotion were the proceedings.

In the end the race was, almost inevitably, a disappointing anti-climax. Slaney won in 8:32.91. Burki was second, Kristiansen third and Budd fourth. Eleven million people watched on ITV, the biggest-ever athletics audience in Britain. Burki and Kristiansen received £2000 apiece. When these sums were leaked, some weeks later, there was a predictable outcry and those who had opposed the television and marketing deals had a field day. Zola was crestfallen and dejected and tended to blame Labuschagne and the other members of the Trust but perhaps, in the end, it was good that the re-match had happened so soon. The media had purged itself of a desperate longing and athletics could get on with its normal activity.

The following Tuesday there was further controversy, this time at Edinburgh's Meadowbank Stadium. The left-wing city council insisted on displaying their banners above the scoreboard in contravention of ITV's contract with the sport. The banners read "Edinburgh – Against Apartheid". All day long protracted, noisy and ultimately angry negotiations failed to solve the impasse. I was undertaking the public address commentary that night and it was difficult to concentrate as angry representatives of television, APA and the sport kept coming in, demanding that statements be made to the crowd. Finally, exasperated, Richard Russell of ITV on behalf of Channel 4 pulled the plug on an hour's live coverage. He issued a statement that said: "ITV/ Channel 4's contract with the BAAB/AAA – in accordance with the regulations of the Independent Broadcasting Authority – very specifically prohibits political advertising. Requests that the offending banners be removed and/or covered up proved unsuccessful. Therefore, the programme was not transmitted."

I read it to a bemused crowd of 10,000 who, despite the incessant rain, had come to see Zola Budd run. She duly obliged and won the mile, side-stepping on the way a skin-headed demonstrator who rushed on to the track and sat in the path of the runners. Zola won, amidst great cheers from the damp assembly, beating the Soviet runner Nikitina and Yvonne Murray, who was finding the presence of Budd in Britain an inspiration and a challenge, which is more than could be said for a number of our other women distance runners.

Zola was now running into form and she produced a series of scintillating performances. Despite Soviet protests she was included in the British team to compete in the European Cup finals in Moscow. Sir Arthur Gold, President of the European Athletic Association, had made it very clear that if they attempted to ban Zola the meeting would be transferred. Always a stickler for the rules, Sir Arthur stuck by them firmly, even though he had opposed Zola Budd's selection for Britain the year before. She led the 3000 metres from the gun, beating Zaytseva of the USSR and Bruns of the GDR in a new British record of 8:35.32. In Zurich she set a new British mile record behind Slaney and Puica: in London she again beat Kristiansen and set a new world record for 5000 metres; in Brussels she was again third to Slaney but went under four minutes for 1500 metres for the first time and in Rome, at the first Grand Prix final, she set her fifth Commonwealth record of the season, clocking under 8:30 for 3000 metres. It had been a magnificent twenty-one days of record-breaking; she was only nineteen, and the world was her oyster. After the season she flew back immediately to South Africa.

If it was Zola's year it was also Steve Cram's, as he set three magnificent world records. The spree began on a balmy evening in Nice at the Nikaia Grand Prix meeting where he was to face the Moroccan, Said Aouita, the Olympic 5000-metre champion. Aouita was the most versatile of distance runners, being able to set world-class times from 800 to 10,000 metres. The race was billed as a world-record attempt and it lived up to its reputation. The pacemaker, Niang of Senegal, ran the opening lap in 54.36 with Cram, striding well, about ten metres behind. Though he faded, Niang reached 800 metres in 1:53.68 before the new pacemaker, Omar Khalifa, took over and immediately raised the pace, reaching the bell in 2:36.18 with Cram still in close attendance. Gonzalez and Aouita were just a few metres adrift. Ovett's world record was now under threat. With just over 350 metres to go Cram went into the lead, committed to a long run for home. His effort had put him six metres ahead and it was Aouita who set off in pursuit, steadily closing the gap down the home straight; the crowd, with one eye on the race and one eye on the clock, were also reaching a crescendo of excitement. Cram held on, inches ahead of Aouita, and made history by becoming the first man to run under 3:30 for the distance. Aouita also broke the barrier and behind them Gonzalez of Spain and Scott of the USA set new national records.

Ten days later, in the Dream Mile in Oslo, he beat another world-class field, including his conqueror in Los Angeles, Sebastian Coe, for a new world record of 3:46.32. Finally, nineteen days after Nice, he set a new world best of

Steve Cram became the first man to run under 3:30 in the 1500 metres in the 1985 Nice Grand Prix.

4:51.39 for 2000 metres, erasing John Walker's nine-year-old time from the lists. It had been a magnificent winning streak, the tall Geordie on a running high, reminiscent of both Coe and Ovett in their record-breaking heydays. John Walker, still a world-class miler, had a rear view of Cram's record at the Bislett Stadium, finishing in sixth place. Earlier in 1985, aged thirty-three, he had made history for the second time in his long career by running, in Auckland's Mount Smart stadium, his hundredth sub-four-minute mile. It had taken him eleven and a half years and in that time he had become the first man to run under 3:50 for the mile and had won the Olympic 1500-metre title in Montreal in 1976. Still running – and clocking more sub-four-minute miles – in 1990, John has endeared himself to crowds all over the world by his demeanour and by the fact that he has almost always given of his very best, even when, as in the latter years, he has finished down the field. Now he has a new target, to become the first veteran athlete to run a sub-four-minute mile. On or after 12 January 1992 he will be able to attempt it.

At the very end of the season, at the Olympic Stadium in Berlin, Said Aouita erased Steve Cram's world 1500-metre mark from the record books. It had lasted just five weeks. In an interview with Mel Watman, then of *Athletics Weekly*, Steve had talked in heady terms of a 3:42 mile being a possibility and of "Said and I being capable of 3:44 now." Five years on the world records of the two athletes are still there and as the years have gone by the challenges to them have become fewer and fewer. The halcyon period of middle-distance running had, perhaps, just one more year left. The question that British athletics might be facing in the next few years was: would the closing of the Coe, Cram, Ovett era also mean a premature ending of its new-found wealth? The answer lay in the East German town of Cottbus.

The European Junior Championships are very often the starting point of many fine careers in international athletics. Steve Cram had been a champion in 1979; Steve Ovett, Daley Thompson and Fatima Whitbread amongst many others had also taken titles. Late in the 1960s the British Board, in a moment of inspiration, had set up a Junior Commission, specifically tasked to nurture our junior talent. Over the years British teams not only competed in every European meeting but also in a series of internationals against other European countries, which they have invariably won. In 1985, as part of their sponsorship, Dairy Crest Foods supported the Junior Commission, its executives getting enthusiastically involved. In the Cottbus Championships young British athletes won ten titles plus eight other medals, excelling in the sprints and hurdles. Amongst the medal winners were those who were to play a prominent part in the next five years of British athletics – John Regis, Roger Black, Jonathon Ridgeon and Colin Jackson.

Back in Britain, another athlete was contemplating his future. For years he had been promising much, but a lackadaisical approach to life and training had always meant that he had been unable to produce the sustained effort that was needed to project him into international class. He had received a shock in not being selected for the British European Cup relay squad and had protested vehemently to the Director of Coaching, Frank Dick. But in his heart he knew that he had not been putting the work in. One autumn morning he received a letter from Andy Norman. It told him that, if he trained hard, cut out the good life (and the rum and blackcurrant) he could be Europe's number one sprinter. He had enormous talent, Andy wrote, why was he wasting it? If a sod like Andy Norman thinks I can make it, the athlete thought, it must be true. He decided to give it a go this coming winter. He would stop playing dominoes instead of training these forthcoming cold winter nights at West London Stadium and get down to it. Linford Christie was on his way.

11

CHILLY WINDS AND CHILLED HEARTS

At the beginning of 1986 I had become a consultant to British athletics, acting as their Public Relations Officer. The sport's relations with the media had always been distant and wary, except during the tenure of David Shaw. With its new high profile it needed someone to handle the Press on a day-to-day basis. Within weeks we were embroiled in the ongoing saga of Zola Budd, which was fast becoming a soap opera in its own right. Why were we so obsessed with the future of this young woman, who was taking up hours of everybody's time? Clearly we all recognised the enormous talent that she possessed and we were anxious that it should reach total fulfilment, but there was more to it than that. Her physical frailty, which hid a steely heart, made everyone feel protective, the public included. *Newsweek* magazine in 1983 had written: "The sight of Mary Decker in action generates the kind of delicious anxiety that once came from a new Alfred Hitchcock film." It was the same with Zola; even Andy Norman succumbed, not to the charm, because there was little of that, but to the vulnerability, and he became a Dutch Uncle. He joined a large club.

The problem was that Zola had been a spoilt child all her life. The youngest in a large family, she was the only object of affection in an estranged household, her every whim was everyone's command. Where the British Board and everybody connected with her made an error was in continuing that overindulgence. They had the opportunity, before her arrival, to lay down strict criteria for her to be selected as a British athlete, including more or less continuous residence in the country. They failed to do so. Once they had agreed, by default, to the Momberg and Boonzaier plan of competing in Europe and living in South Africa, the international career of Zola Budd was doomed.

In South Africa, following her successful 1985 season, she trained hard under Labuschagne, often running a hundred miles a week, and began to suffer niggles of injury that were to plague her in the coming months. When she told the man she always addressed as *Meneer* (Afrikaans for "Sir") of her pains, he dismissed them as being psychosomatic.

Early in 1986 she flew to Britain, this time without Labuschagne, left behind in Stellenbosch, a reluctant teacher. It was an enormous personal break – an important prop was gone from her life. Just what role her coach fulfilled in her own mind only Zola knew. It was, she said, a love-hate relationship. On her arrival in Guildford she found a letter from Marea Hartman spelling out the conditions for competing in the Commonwealth Games. These included a clause stipulating that competitors must have resided in a country for six months of the previous twelve or have their normal place of residence or "permanent home" in that country. Zola replied that there would be no problem.

Indoors she ran a world record for 3000 metres but moped after Labuschagne and his paternal presence. Mel Batty met her at the airport and tried to keep her spirits up. Andy Norman warned her that her frequent journeys to and from Africa were beginning to aggravate a lot of people. She listened but did not hear. She longed for the warmth of her homeland, her family, her animals. She was exiled from everything she had known and loved for almost twenty years and she hated the cold, damp British climate. Various friends flew in from South Africa to keep her company, but they did not satisfy her longing to be back on the veldt.

Before every race Zola prevaricated, telling anyone who would listen that she didn't want to run. Then she ran and set records and the crowds cheered till the rafters of Cosford echoed. It was a strange ambivalent existence. She returned to South Africa for a few weeks and was happy. She bought a house in Guildford; finally in Neuchatel, in Switzerland, she successfully defended her World Cross-Country title, despite running barefoot in wet, squelchy conditions. At the award ceremony there was a highly significant action by Lamine Diack, the IAAF Vice-President from Senegal, who refused to present Zola with her gold medal.

"As far as I am concerned," he said, "she is a South African. I have nothing against Miss Budd, but I cannot give a prize which will be seen as propaganda for South Africa."

In March, with international pressure mounting, a group of us met quietly in an Italian restaurant in Wandsworth. From the British Olympic Association and England Commonwealth Games Federation was Dick Palmer. From the sport were Andy Norman, Les Jones and myself. Diaries were closely studied and days totted up. It was evident that if Zola was to meet the six-month residential criterion she would have to return from South Africa within the next week or so. Les was deputed to contact her immediately.

In South Africa she was suffering from a hamstring injury that was to severely affect the rest of her season. She failed to return in time to satisfy the required six months' residency. All would now rest on the legal nicety of what constituted "domicile" – would her house in Guildford suffice? She won the WAAA 1500-metre title in Birmingham and was duly selected by them for the Commonwealth Games.

Another man now entered Zola Budd's life, although they never met. He was Sam Ramsamy, the executive chairman of SANROC (South African Non-Racial Olympic Committee), a tireless sporting campaigner against apartheid. Budd represented a wonderful public target for his organisation. He determined that she would not run in Edinburgh. "A house is not a home," he said. "Many people have homes in the Costa del Sol in Spain but that does not give them domicile there." Whilst I supported the anti-apartheid movement very strongly, I could not help noticing the hypocrisy surrounding the SANROC position and also that of Peter Hain, the well-known anti-apartheid campaigner. Zola was targeted whilst they allowed tennis players, golfers and other individual sporting celebrities to play with impunity. It seemed to me that this inconsistency weakened their case. However, African countries were now joining in the protests and there were threats of a boycott if either Zola or swimmer Annette Cowley, also born in South Africa but with an English mother, competed.

In the end neither arrived in Edinburgh. The Amateur Swimming Association did not pick Cowley, the Commonwealth Games Federation banned Zola. She ran dismally in the European Championships, owing to her hamstring problem; fourth in the 3000 metres and ninth in the 1500. Yvonne Murray had beaten her to take the bronze in the former event. In times of stress and unhappiness she did what she always did – she flew back to South Africa.

The Edinburgh Commonwealth Games were bleak in all senses of the word, a parody of the highly successful gathering in the same city sixteen years before. In the end there was a massive boycott, called not because of Zola Budd but on account of the projected New Zealand rugby tour of South Africa and disenchantment with Margaret Thatcher's views on economic sanctions on the country. Of the African nations, only Botswana arrived in Edinburgh. The Asian and Caribbean countries stayed away. Had it not been for the preponderance of black athletes in the English and Canadian teams, these would have been an all-white Games. They hit a financial crisis as well, and at one time the organising committee was insolvent. It looked touch-and-go as to whether the Games would take place at all. The government found themselves facing a dilemma: ideologically they could not pump money into the beleaguered organisation; but if the Games were cancelled, Britain's and Scotland's reputations around the world would be besmirched. Frantic activity took place behind the scenes and finally a saviour arrived, avuncular Robert Maxwell of the *Daily Mirror*. When his men investigated the organisation they found it a shambles. There is a story that when the Duke of Edinburgh visited the Games' headquarters some months before, officials proudly showed him a huge chart depicting the plethora of committees that were in charge. When he suggested that perhaps a small team of professionals would be more efficient they looked at him as if he were mad. Maxwell put up the cash, pulled things round and on 24 July, the Duke declared the unlucky thirteenth Commonwealth Games open.

The worst thing about the week was the weather. Constant chill winds blew straight from the Arctic and most of the time they brought rain. I was working on public address commentary so I kept warm, but Gwenda my wife sat and shivered in the makeshift stands and like so many others, once the day's events were over, literally ran from our car to take a hot bath in the flat that we had rented. Because of the lack of competitors the heats of the athletics were a drag, with long gaps between events. The organisation had not moved on from 1970. It was a sad, sad week. But not all was disaster and gloom. There was Ben Johnson, the muscular sprinter from Canada.

Johnson, born in Jamaica, like so many Canadian and British athletes, had emigrated to Canada in 1976. In 1982 he had won a silver medal over 100 metres behind Allan Wells in the Brisbane Commonwealth Games, and in 1984 a bronze at the Los Angeles Olympics, behind the man who was to be his greatest adversary, Carl Lewis. In 1985 he had won the World Cup and in Commonwealth year he came to Edinburgh with a formidable reputation – he had twice beaten Lewis and had run 9.95. In the 100 metres he duly won from Britain's new top sprinter, Linford Christie. Linford, injured, withdrew from the 200 metres to concentrate on the forthcoming European Championships.

Roger Black's story was almost a fairy tale. He had dabbled in athletics at school, running perhaps three times a year, ending up at the English Schools Championships. His aim was to be a medical student but his A-levels let him down. He decided to resit them, and for some reason, which he is not very clear about, he decided to discover how good he could be at athletics. He joined Mike Smith's training group at Southampton and within three months was running indoors for Great Britain. In 1985 he won the European Junior title and now here he was, at just 20 years of age, aiming at his first major championship. His main opposition was Darren Clark of Australia, who had also shown a precocious talent. In the final Roger had the advantage; he was in lane six with Clark in lane eight. By the half-way mark he had caught up the stagger on the Australian and entering the home straight had a big lead. The race was virtually over as Black hung on to win by almost four metres in 45.57.

The truncated Games continued with titles and records falling to British athletes like leaves in autumn. There was some magnificent running, jumping and throwing: Cram did a magnificent double at 800 and 1500 metres, Daley

A delighted Kirsty Wade waves the Welsh flag after her success in the 1500 metres at the 1986 Commonwealth Games.

won again, Ovett revived memories by winning the 5000 metres and Kirsty Wade won twice for Wales. The Scots were able to express their intense chauvinism when a new, waiflike figure, deep in concentration until she finally crossed the line, won the first-ever women's major championship 10,000 metres. Then, Liz Lynch's face was wreathed in smiles. A new running talent had been born. But many of the victories were hollow, for likely challengers were deep in gloom back in Kenya and Jamaica. The Games ended, as they had begun, in wind and rain. The Queen came and Robert Maxwell made an awful speech. The pipes swirled, the athletes celebrated, the crowd cheered; but it was more like an Irish wake.

The athletics circus moved south to Gateshead International Stadium. It was a big meeting, Great Britain versus the Commonwealth, and it enabled those who had not competed in Edinburgh to challenge some of the champions. Among those was Allan Wells and he had the bitter memory of Los Angeles to purge from his life. He was now thirty-four years of age. After the Olympics he had had an operation to deal with his foot problem, but because of further injuries he didn't sprint again for nearly two years. The Scottish selectors hadn't picked him for the Commonwealth Games, mainly because he hadn't shown fitness. So he had something to prove, not only to them but to himself. He went up to Scotland, where his soul really lay, and trained at Glenrothes in Fife. Whilst the Games were proceeding at the Meadowbank Stadium he ran one of his favourite time trials, with the qualified timekeepers present, and clocked a gale-assisted 19.8 for 200 metres. He asked Andy Norman if he could get him a run at the Gateshead meeting. Andy placed him in the Commonwealth team. Allan wanted to do something different, he told Margot, to give himself a psychological boost. He hit upon the idea of wearing black cycling shorts, not only for effect but to protect his hamstrings against the North Sea winds.

The stadium was packed; everyone wanted to see Ben Johnson and Atlee Mahorn and a host of other champions. It was good to see Allan Wells back again, even though his time had gone. When he appeared in his black cycling shorts a buzz went round the crowd. Linford Christie, sitting injured in the grandstand, looked totally amazed and immediately vowed to go one better. The gun went and Allan blasted off his blocks and was never headed. Johnson came in fourth. There was a stunned silence and then enormous applause. He was to repeat his remarkable performance later in the evening, as an addition to the 200-metre field, beating Commonwealth champion Atlee Mahorn.

Andy Norman had promised to pay him well if he beat Johnson and did so with good grace; after all, like Tom Byers' win in Oslo five years before, it had been magnificent entertainment. Later that week Allan Wells was selected for the European Championships in Stuttgart.

Thirty-four-year-old Allan Wells, sporting new "go-faster" shorts, blasts to victory at Gateshead in 1986.

12

"LIKE THREE SPITFIRES COMING OUT OF THE SUN"

It was a cold, damp morning. Grey clouds overhung the huge Neckar Stadium in Stuttgart. It was early, just after nine local time. Back home in Britain men were studying eight o'clock shadows in bathroom mirrors and mothers were preparing breakfasts. The stadium was almost deserted; a few souls hung around, mostly in the media area, discussing the previous night's events in these 1986 European Championships. For those television stations that were carrying the meeting live, a lone commentator sat in his booth. A few odd journalists milled around their monitors, held telephone conversations with their offices, scratched and yawned, their furry tongues a legacy of an evening spent in intellectual debate.

The only colour to enliven this drab scene came from the centre of the arena where the women javelin-throwers, still heavily track-suited against the morning chill, threw their implements in warm-up. They too seemed struck with some lethargy. They formed the first pool of the qualifying round of the competition. The distance they had to attain was sixty-two metres. World champion Tiina Lillak was there, and Anna Verouli, the burly Greek thrower, the defending champion. Local hopes rested on Ingrid Thyssen. For Britain there was Fatima Whitbread. Since Helsinki she had maintained a steady progress. She had won the European Cup competition in 1983, gained bronze behind Tessa Sanderson at the Los Angeles Olympics and thrown second in Moscow's European Cup the year before. The winner there had been the young blonde from the German Democratic Republic, Petra Felke, now the world record holder. Despite this competitive record there was just a tiny modicum of doubt in Fatima's mind, placed there by her performance in the Commonwealth Games in Edinburgh a few weeks previously, when she had inexplicably lost her form and, unfortunately in the end, her composure. Tessa won and Fatima had collapsed on to the synthetic surface in tears, whilst her great rival performed a triumphant dance around her. Their long-standing rivalry would have done justice to the American television series *Dynasty*.

Andy Norman had watched these histrionics with some anguish – he was already a close friend, a friendship that would develop and blossom over the ensuing years – and tried to get Les Jones, a member of the Jury of Appeal, to intervene. Les, wisely, demurred. Later Margaret Whitbread had taken a firm grip on her charge, who was beginning to feel jinxed. "Stop whingeing and whining," she advised her.

Fatima moved around the Neckar infield, staying loose, thinking about Edinburgh, knowing this should be easy. She was hoping to qualify on her first throw and get back to the warmth of her hotel room in the city as quickly as possible. Thyssen threw and landed the javelin well beyond the single arc that marked the qualifying distance. Next it was Fatima's turn. She concentrated, ran down the runway, smoothly transferred the javelin to its throwing position and then released it, sending it winging away over the grass infield. She felt, knew, that everything had been just right. She watched it as it soared away, up and up, over the yellow qualifying arc, felt a millisecond's satisfaction as it did that, and then began to get excited as it sailed on and on. Others in the stadium stopped yawning and sat up and took notice. It was a very long throw, but with only the qualifying arc marked out it was difficult to gauge how far.

There was an agonising wait until the measurement appeared on the event scoreboard. When it did flash on it showed 77.44 metres, a new world record. Panic ensued in hotels all around Stuttgart as word of the performance spread among the media. Taxis hurriedly transported bedraggled men to the stadium. Commentators appeared, as if by magic, to describe a replay of the throw, hyping themselves up to sound as if they had been there at the great moment. When Fatima left doping control the media were ready for her, mostly with inane questions – was she happy, was she pleased, what did she think? She answered them all with the charm that had become her trademark.

For the final the following day the world record was history; all the competitors were equal again, and there was still a title to be won. Fatima knew that athletics had been full of javelin-throwers who had been magnificent in qualifying and utterly mediocre in the main competition. On every inter-national javelin-thrower's mind the name of Yelena Gorchakova was clearly etched. In 1964, at the Tokyo Olympics, the Soviet thrower had also achieved a world record in the qualifying round, only to throw dismally in the final the next day.

Felke led from the first round until the fourth and tension was starting to grow in the British camp, not least with Margaret Whitbread. She knew that Fatima had wrenched her arm with the world-record throw the previous day.

Heavy rain was falling and it was often the case that the early throws were the ones that finally counted in such conditions. But then the gods that she thought had deserted her came to Fatima's aid. The rain eased for the fourth round and she unleashed a throw of 72.68 metres to take the lead. Felke could not respond; Fatima crowned her triumph with 76.32 metres in the final round, the second-longest throw ever. For her it had been a perfect championships. "Now I know I'm the best in Britain," she said pointedly. Sanderson, reported injured, watched on television back in Britain and could only agree.

It was Linford Christie who had given the team the magnificent start that they needed to boost morale. He had emerged from the rigours of winter training under his coach Ron Roddan a totally different sprinter to the one who had entered it the previous October. Feeling fitter, stronger, faster than he had ever felt before he had won the European Indoor 200-metre title in Madrid, set a new British 100-metre record of 10.04 in Seville and gained silver behind the Canadian, Ben Johnson, in the Commonwealth. Now he was here in Stuttgart, psyching himself up to be the first British sprinter to win the 100 metres since Jack Archer in 1946. He had been helped by his annoyance at the media for their eulogising of Allan Wells. For the Press it would be nice for Linford to win – it would be a sensational fairy story if Allan Wells did. The gun went on the clear, dark night and under the intense floodlights, Linford showed ahead at fifty metres and then surged away to his first major title. Bringmann was second, Marie-Rose third. Wells came in fifth (a position he was to repeat in the 200 metres). Afterwards Linford landed Wells with a new epithet.

"He's the Godfather of British sprinting," he said graciously to reporters. "He showed that it was possible to take on the Americans and beat them."

Linford went on to the medal rostrum swathed in a Union Jack (and earned a reprimand from the European Athletics Association). In an extraordinary championships seven others were to follow him as the week went on.

When he arrived in Stuttgart Sebastian Coe knew that this was his final chance to erase a blemish on his exceptional competitive record. For though he had been the 800 metres world record holder since 1979 he had failed in five attempts to win a major title and people were starting to notice. In the Europeans he had won two silver medals, in Prague and Athens; likewise in the Olympics, in Moscow and Los Angeles. Illness had prevented him from running the Commonwealth final in Edinburgh. After witnessing the speed and strength of Cruz in Los Angeles he had felt it was time to leave the event to the younger fellows. He had meant what he had said to Ovett after the Olympic final; they were too old to be playing with such fire. Yet here he was back again, doubling up once more. The disconcerting thing was that his main opposition would come from his British team-mates, Cram and Tom McKean.

Linford Christie celebrates his 100 metres win in Stuttgart — and is admonished for wearing the Union flag on the podium.

McKean had emerged from Scotland the year before to achieve a surprise win in the European Cup. This year he gained a silver medal in the Commonwealth Games behind Steve Cram and it was Steve that Seb was really concerned about. Coming into the championships, Cram was the fastest man in the world, a time he had achieved in Edinburgh. All three qualified safely for the final, held on a damp cool evening. Of the rest Rod Druppers of Holland looked the best, and although this time there were no East Germans in the final to spoil the chances of a British celebration, there was a West German, Peter Braun, running on home territory.

It was Braun who led them off their lanes at the start of the back straight and through a first lap at a respectable 51.98. The British runners were all tracking the leader, content not to make any move. Then Cram and McKean were leading with 200 metres to go and as they came off the last bend the three British athletes were together. It was a marvellous sight and Ian Wooldridge of the *Daily Mail* was to write lyrically, if a little chauvinistically given the circumstances, that they were "like three Spitfires coming out of the sun". The young McKean was running the race of his life, leading Cram into the home straight and increasing pace when the Geordie came up to his shoulder. Could Tom win it and defeat all the predictions? The answer was no, for here came Coe in top gear, roaring past Cram and finally edging past McKean. At last he had done it, won a title that now meant so much to him. McKean won silver, Cram bronze. It was a clean sweep.

Coe said that this time he was in the right shape. "Sometimes when you put your foot down, it's there and sometimes it isn't. This time it was and it's hard to fault it as a race, though no doubt my old man will. This victory was more important to me than any other."

McKean said: "I looked to my right and there was that little sod Coe on my shoulder, excuse my French."

Cram said later: "I've never been so depressed in running terms than after that race. I was just so disappointed that I couldn't run at my best. It wasn't the real Steve Cram out there."

Both Coe and Cram now had to turn their attention to the 1500 metres and the situation was interesting, for both athletes were, psychologically, in new territory. In his three attempts at the double Seb had never gone into the second race with a win under his belt. For Steve, this was the first time that he would have to pick himself up from defeat in a race that he had expected to win. He let the race get to him. He brooded in his hotel room. His wife Karen knew his moods well but this was a new experience. "We were all there if he needed us," she said, "but it was down to him to sort himself out."

What worried him was that he didn't know why he had lost, so he didn't feel in charge of his destiny. Had he reached a peak with those brilliant runs in

"Like three spitfires coming out of the sun": Seb Coe (first), Steve Cram (third) and Tom McKean (second) make a clean sweep of the 1986 European Championships 800 metres.

Edinburgh and was he now heading for a trough? Was Coe to be a jinx in his career? Who knew? The man who could give him sound advice on these matters was the one he couldn't turn to, Sebastian Coe.

"We sat and suffered," Karen said, "but we carried on in the usual championship routine."

Both qualified easily from the heats along with a third Briton, John Gladwin, who had won bronze in the Commonwealth Games. Also there were the two Irishmen, O'Sullivan and O'Mara, Gonzalez of Spain and Kulker of the Netherlands. José Abascal, the fastest man in the world to date that year, failed to qualify. The final was a crawl, back to the bad old days before Los Angeles. Cram and Carreira of Spain were reluctant leaders who didn't want to be martyrs. The first lap was covered in a funereal 63.85. The second lap was no better and everyone felt that the race was now tailor-made for Coe, especially after his win in the 800 metres. Then Gladwin went to the front and increased the pace, but with 300 metres to go Cram shot into the lead on a long run for home. With half a lap left he shifted into top gear but Coe was coming with his attack. Round the final bend Coe looked threatening but Cram kicked again and again fifty metres from home, just holding off the Olympic champion. He had successfully defended his title and run a last lap close to fifty seconds. He said: "I was very, very determined to win this one."

Karen knew from early in the day that her husband was going to be successful. "This morning when I woke up," she said, "I just knew he was going to win when I heard him singing in the shower. From then on I never had any doubts. He'd sorted himself out."

Coe said that he had been critical of Ovett in Moscow for being unable to raise the necessary motivation for the 1500 metres but now he understood. He had attained his main aim in coming to Stuttgart, and it had been difficult to raise himself again. Before he left for home Peter Coe looked at his son. "If you run the distance in Rieti," he said, "give us the definitive 1500 metres." Coe went to the Italian resort and ran just that, the fastest time in the world that year, just four metres short of Aouita's world record with 3:29.77, his only excursion under 3:30. Cram went too and ran the fastest 800 metres of the year, 1:43.19. None of us realised that the runs were something of a last hurrah. The era of British domination of world middle-distance running had come to an end.

The team had been on a high all week. Roger Black had defeated the world champion, Thomas Schonlebe, at 400 metres to win his second Championship of the year and then over the central two days came Daley Thompson's bid to retain his title. This time he was up against his old rivals Hingsen and Wentz, whom he knew would get tremendous local support. It was the sort of challenge that the double Olympic champion relished. As usual he threw down the gauntlet in the opening event, this time clocking 10.26 – a world best for a decathlon 100 metres. But over the next three or four events Hingsen, urged on by the crowd, clawed back the points deficit and by the high jump, Daley was lying third behind Hingsen and Voss, of the GDR. It was a new situation for him but he came back in the final event of the first day, the 400 metres, and ran 47.02 to retake the lead by twenty-eight points. Was it enough to hold off Hingsen, backed by a highly biased crowd who were at times abusive to Thompson? Daley had a fight on his hands. There followed a sleepless night.

He set a personal best in the hurdles the next morning to increase his lead considerably but in the discus he immediately squandered all his hard-earned points. The crowd yelled and shouted abuse every time Daley went into the circle. Though he had steady throws, Hingsen threw much further and regained the lead.

The crowd now sensed that the moment of truth might be near for either Hingsen or Wentz and that Daley might be vulnerable. As in Los Angeles the critical event was the pole vault. If Hingsen could keep with Thompson he would win. The tension visibly rose. Daley prowled the area like a panther ready to pounce. The first to crack was Hingsen, who only cleared 4.60 metres, so the gold medal was again out of his grasp. Wentz cleared 5.00 metres but Thompson went ten centimetres higher. The javelin went evenly and in the rain that had hampered the championships all week they ran the 1500 metres. Hingsen finished ahead of Thompson but not by enough to gain the necessary points and Daley won by eighty-one. It had been, probably, his finest hour. Everyone knew that it would be a tough task to defeat the Germans on their home soil but Daley's unrivalled competitiveness had won through. He took his usual lap of honour, relishing the moment. If he had known what was to come in the next two years, perhaps he would have relished it more.

On the last day, when Cram successfully defended his title, Jack Buckner took his courage in his hands and stormed away over the last lap of the 5000 metres to hold off the Italian Stefano Mei and win the gold medal. Tim Hutchings gained bronze. In the men's sprint relay an extraordinary last leg by Linford Christie also won bronze. It had been that sort of season. Could Britain crown everything by winning the final event, the 4 x 400 metres relay? They were the favourites. They had the first and fourth men in the individual 400 metres, who would be backed up by a strong squad. An hour before the race Frank Dick, the Director of Coaching, dropped the man who had been a stalwart of British and English teams for years, Phil Brown. He had been showing indifferent form all season. Redmond led the team off magnificently, held a lead and passed the baton to Kriss Akabusi. The army sergeant kept ahead, just holding off the challenge of the Soviet Union, West Germany and

Spikeless in Stuttgart: Brian Whittle is about to lose his shoe, but goes on to run the race of his life without it.

Les Jones, now Great Britain's team manager, poses for the camera before the 1988 Seoul Olympics.

Italy. He came in to hand the baton over to Brian Whittle and in so doing trod on the Scotsman's spike, sending it flying across the track! For a moment there was consternation, but, undeterred, Whittle ran the race of his life, probably a world record for someone in one spiked shoe, and handed over to Black, who nursed the opposition to the home straight and then pulled away. It was an extraordinary victory.

Les Jones stood next to the British team manager, Mike Turner, his arms folded, surveying the scene. "You know, Mike," he said, "we'll never see a week like this again."

13

STEVE'S ROSICKY BLUES

No one in Prague looked you in the eye. People you saw in cafés near the hotel, or in the street or even at the stadium, would glance away if they thought there was any danger of contact. Other writers have described foreigners' glances as a "violation of internal exile" and have written of the Czechoslovaks as suffering from a collective schizophrenia. It was easy to see what they meant as people made the best they could of their lives under the harsh Stalinist régime of Gustav Husak. Prague was staging the 1987 European Cup final and we were there hoping to perform better than we had done two years previously in Moscow, when the men's team had finished fourth, beaten by the Soviet Union and the two Germanies. The British women had finished third then and were hoping to match that this year.

It was my first trip away with the team. Our hotel was plain but the food was adequate. It was good to see that there were some entrepreneurial skills still left in this oppressed place. John Brown, our Administrative Officer, conducted all currency negotiations with the hotel porter, at a black-market rate, travelling for considerable periods of time in one of the lifts. We sat drinking coffee, watching the lift's light travel up, down, up, down, without stopping on any floors, until the deal was done.

The team manager was Mike Turner, a Cambridge don, a former international cross-country runner and a very affable fellow. I shared with Les Jones, his assistant, and found it strange that every time we passed his room, which was next to ours, he would be fast asleep on his bed, no matter what time of day. Les explained quietly, as we crept past, that Mike was an ardent veteran distance runner and still trained twice a day, requiring an equal amount of sleep for recovery. Mike's other propensity, at team meetings, was to make really quite unfunny risqué remarks at people's expense, which were not always appreciated, to say the least. Still, he was what we had until the Seoul Olympics, a man more suited to the world of C.P. Snow than to that of modern athletics.

The team was a strong one. We had four of our European champions there, albeit two of them reluctantly. Pressure had been put on Roger Black and Steve Cram to compete, and the carrot of selection for the World Championships in Rome had been dangled for those who achieved a place in the first two in the Cup events. Steve's problem had been calf injuries sustained during the previous winter. There had been much chopping and changing about in the selection leading up to the event and he was very much a last-minute call-up. He had added two or three track sessions to his normal training programme in the previous week but it was hardly ideal preparation for facing men like Jens-Peter Herold of East Germany and José Luis Gonzalez of Spain. Black too was coming into a major meeting without the necessary speed training, another late call-up.

Steve had felt the pressure. He had initially turned down selection; Coe then withdrew through injury, Gladwin developed a back problem and Ovett said that his training could not be adjusted in the time available. So the selectors returned to Cram. "I got slagged off in the Press," he said later, "with people accusing me of running for money instead of my country. Total nonsense. It almost looked as if I turned it down there and then, not months in advance. That got me riled. You shouldn't let things like that get to you but it did. I said I would run."

The Rosicky Stadium was well-filled as the opening ceremonies took place. I had agreed with the Press that I would collect for interview athletes who finished in the top four of their event. As the weekend wore on that was reduced to the first three, first two and then only winners. It was a long trail down to the tunnel under the grandstand, along to the presentation area and back up again. The interview facilities were non-existent, athletes answering questions in a small archway at the back of the stand, often pinned to the wall by a scrum of scribbling scribes.

The British message to the rest of Europe was maintained, on the track at least. Linford Christie re-emphasised his sprinting superiority, taking not only the 100 metres on the first day but the 200 metres on the second. It was the first time that a British sprinter had achieved the double in the Cup. Tom McKean won his second 800 metres and Kirsty Wade won the women's 1500 metres in magnificent style. Roger Black lost to Thomas Schonlebe of the GDR in the 400 metres by just three-hundredths of a second but he went below forty-five seconds for the second time in his relatively short career. Talking to the Press afterwards he seemed happy with the result. "I had trained hard on Monday and Tuesday," he said, "and I did not have that feeling I normally get before a big race." Shortly afterwards injury problems began to beset him and he would not be fully fit again for three years.

The 1500 metres was the usual European Cup affair, a three-lap jog and then a race over one lap. The runners reached two laps in a time that old Walter George would have sniffed at and they were tightly bunched together. Cram made his move and shot into the lead down the home straight. Only one athlete attempted to stay with him, the Spaniard, Gonzalez, but Steve had a five-metre lead and the race seemed over. Steve's last lap was a magnificent 50.2 but it had not been good enough, for Gonzalez ran 49.9 and won in the last metre. It was Steve Cram's first defeat at the distance since he had lost to Coe in the Los Angeles Olympics. Steve was never the same athlete after that defeat. Indeed, to date he has not won a major race since. Was it a pivotal moment in his career? There are some who believe that it was. Three years on I talked to his friend and mentor, Brendan Foster.

"He was going to be brilliant that year," Brendan said, "but he was talked into a race that he should never have been in. He lost it, but he lost it in a way that he didn't think he could – on the last lap. In a race like that, he thought, if I run fifty-one seconds then no one will beat me. Well, Gonzalez did, by running faster. So suddenly he sees that his big weapon, his last lap rush, is vulnerable. So all kinds of doubts came into his mind. It was purely a case of him not being fully prepared for his first major race on the track."

"So was it a turning-point?" I asked.

"I believe that it was," replied Brendan. "Believe it or not, Steve's greatest asset was his confidence. Look at his world-record run against Aouita in Nice. To take on Aouita from the front with 300 metres to go on a catch-me-if-you-can basis took supreme confidence. After Prague he thought: My God! I can lose."

Three years later, in Split and in Sheffield, the old Cram returned, not winning, mainly because of early-season injury but running again with purpose. It had taken a long time.

If Britain's track men had done well, our field-event athletes did abysmally. They were last in four of the eight events and no higher than fourth in the others. Heike Dreschler, the tall, attractive East German long-jumper had jumped 7.45 metres the week before coming to Prague, for a new women's world record. This distance was four centimetres in excess of the effort of Derrick Brown in the men's Cup competition. Indeed in Prague itself Heike was just 15 centimetres down on Brown's best effort. I was walking past the ITV commentary point after that result and a fiercely angry face appeared over a monitor. It belonged to Ian Hodge, their statistician, one of the best in the world. Ian can get very incensed over athletes' performances.

"Did you see that Brown," he shouted, "did you see that? They ought to lock him up here and throw away the key!" Hushing sounds arose from colleagues and he was pulled gently down to his seat again, totally unmollified.

I hoped they weren't on live transmission to Britain.

Britain came third in the men's match, a one-place improvement on Moscow. Of our points total of ninety-nine, seventy-eight came from the track athletes. The women's team slumped to fifth place in their competition. Only three athletes made the top three – Wade, Yvonne Murray and Angela Tooby, all in the distance running events. These were areas that would need dramatic attention if Britain was to improve its standing as a European athletics power. The euphoria of Stuttgart had waned a little.

Travelling back to the hotel we passed the splendid architecture of the old city and that night had a meal in a restaurant just off Wenceslas Square, scene of momentous happenings two and a half years later. When we left, the square was empty and quiet and beautiful. It seemed a tragedy that such a magnificent city and its people should be under a blanket of fear. The next morning we boarded the plane for home, our thoughts now turning to Rome and the World Championships.

14

ROMAN PRESSURE COOKER

A huge sign hung over the main grandstand entrance to the *Stadio Olimpico* in Rome – "Welcome to the Athletics Family". We laughed and made connotations with the *mafiosi*. Any athlete who beat the Italian hero, Francesco Panetta, we said, would find a dead horse's head in his bed the next morning. It was all very amusing and light-hearted but the humour went sour some months later, when we found that the Italians had been cheating to gain their man a medal in the long jump.

Our contingent flew into Rome's Leonardo da Vinci airport late on the Tuesday evening before the World Championships began. We travelled Club Class on Alitalia, courtesy of the IAAF, though in truth it was the last luxury they were to give us. Immediately after landing the plane was surrounded by Kalashnikov-toting guards, an indication of the tight security to come. Our advance party came to meet us, which was just as well, for some, including me, were not on the accreditation list. This was of vital importance if you were to move freely around the various stadium areas and the Village. The officials were not helpful. Their mouths turned down, shoulders rose, heads were tilted, their hands spread. "Tomorrow?" they suggested. We persevered. Les Jones whispered, "Do we make them an offer they can't refuse?" We finally made it and were driven to the two hotels that were to house all the competitors and team officials, Ergriffe Palace and Princess.

We had flown into a problem that had been festering for some weeks. In Prague the men's sprint relay team had been a disaster, breaking down at the first change-over between the newcomer David Kirton and Linford Christie. Linford, on a high after the 100 metres, went away too quickly and this combined with the difference in height – Linford was ten inches taller – led to the baton being exchanged outside the area. Britain were disqualified. It was the first time that Linford had run the second leg. In Stuttgart, he had run the anchor and though Britain had come third he had clocked the fastest time on that stage. Now he wanted to return to the last leg of the relay. Frank Dick firmly believed that he should remain on the second or third stage – in which the sprinters cover the greatest ground. Technically, Frank was right; emotionally, Linford was.

In the weeks leading up to the World Championships Linford brooded and brooded on this until the problem grew out of all proportion. Instead of concentrating his mind solely on the 100 metres, where he would meet Carl Lewis and Ben Johnson, he fretted about the running order of the relay. The arguments continued and all sorts of irrelevancies were brought into the discussion (for instance, Frank's training association with Boris Becker), and it became very messy. In a sport like athletics, where the officials and coaches are just as competitive as the athletes, there are often considerable leaks to the Press. At a Crystal Palace meeting just before we left for Rome, Linford expressed his opinions at a post-race Press conference. Neil Allen carried the story in the *Evening Standard* the day we left. An impasse had been reached.

It is in the days leading up to a championship that a team has to be at its most wary, for this is when the reporters are searching for stories and when their sports editors, back in London, are often most demanding. We try to help as much as possible in this situation by calling daily Press conferences with leading athletes present, but the Christie versus Dick confrontation in Rome was too good a story for us to combat. On the Thursday I was just closing the conference, held in the "mixed zone" between the two hotels, the only place the journalists were allowed to infiltrate, when the news came through that there had been a major row at a relay practice, not only between Frank and Linford but between Linford and the mass of photographers who had somehow assembled at this remote training track. The row began as soon as they had gathered, with the other sprinters joining in. The photographers, not quite believing their luck, were clicking away merrily. Suddenly, incensed by the noise of the camera shutters, Linford cracked and stormed over to them, cursing and shouting, with four-letter words in abundance. The photographers continued shooting. The most awful pictures appeared on some of the tabloids' front pages the next day. Linford left the practice, trained on his own and then returned to the hotel.

The situation, of course, should never have been allowed to reach this critical stage. It had been obvious for some weeks that a problem had arisen and that there was genuine disagreement between Britain's Director of Coaching and the number one sprinter. It should have been sorted out well beforehand; discussions held, decisions arrived at. It needed an arbitrator and one wasn't available. In short, it was bad team management. Linford asserted that his running was not affected by the rows but I am not so sure. The tensions before a major championships are enormous, especially for those who are expected to do well. He was at his first World Championships, akin to an actor playing Lear at Stratford for the first time. It was essential that he be kept away from all distractions, let alone emotional boil-overs. He wasn't.

Coaches have their tensions too. Frank was now advising Daley Thompson and must have known of the problems that the defending decathlon champion would be facing come Thursday.

It is early morning, still grey and misty outside. The telephone rings. It is Radio Leeds wanting to talk to Angie Pain, who is running the marathon. "Ring back at nine," I say. I find Angie but she can't make it, she is due to go for a femininity test at that time.

Radio Leeds phone back. "Sorry," I say, "Angie's not here. She's gone for a virginity test." There is a brief silence. Horror dawns. "No, no," I say, "I mean femininity test. Jesus, are we on the air? My God, did I say Jesus?" Not a good start to the day.

The Friday Press conference is over and the athletes have departed but the Press have requested the management to stay on.

"Now," asks Colin Hart of the Sun, *a broad grin on his face, "what about Linford?"*

"Linford's fine," I say.

"Yes," says Les, "we went to Linford in friendship . . ."

I wish he wouldn't keep doing that. Somebody might be listening.

The *Stadio Olimpico* came alive on the Saturday morning. As usual we all spent considerable time discovering the logistics of the place and learning which pass could get you where. Which was the quickest way from the warm-up track to the stadium? There wasn't one. How do athletes get to the call-up area? In the Press section of the main stand – *La Stampa* – the daily correspondents put their feet up, whilst the Sunday men looked a little feverish. Their deadlines would come early.

The physiotherapists were in a room deep under the stand, alongside the warm-up track. It reminded me of a nuclear bomb shelter. There was just one light bulb shining down on their ministrations, which somehow had a ritualistic, almost religious feel about them. The athlete, silent and brooding, mostly uncommunicative; the expert hands bringing comfort and sometimes, after a defeat, solace. They are some of the unsung heroes of track and field for they rarely see much of the action, as they unfailingly respond to the insatiable, sometimes manic demands of their highly-strung charges.

On the first day of the meeting the mixed area, where the athletes and media were supposed to mingle, was a hell on earth, a faithful reconstruction of the Bedlam asylum. Situated in a dark cavern beneath the main stand, seemingly carved out of rock, it was a cross between the Black Hole of Calcutta and the Wig and Pen. The Latin temperaments of the officials and the reporters rose in direct proportion to the frustration. Arms were raised, bodies were pushed, vituperation was uttered in many languages and when the athletes came in, boiling from the pressure cooker of the track, most of them frustrated and angry at losing, the temperature in there rose accordingly. Pete Nichols, a freelance, and I, collecting quotes for the British reporters, overheated as well.

Panetta did lose the 10,000 metres and thousands of Italians metaphorically threw themselves into the Tiber in despair. The race was brilliantly won by Peter Koech and we knew that the Kenyans were back.

I looked Les in the eye. "Don't even think about saying it," I said.

Jon Solly finished seventeenth and though he had run with a broken bone in his foot, he had in that half an hour or so destroyed the concept of pre-selection for major championships, for it had been obvious all season, except apparently to him and his coach, that he was not in the physical shape to warrant selection.

At a major championships, where there are heats in the sprints, psychology can play a great part in the proceedings. The expected confrontation was between Carl Lewis and Ben Johnson. Both considered Linford to be an inexperienced upstart. Coming into the meeting, Johnson had the five fastest times of the year, including three under ten seconds. Linford was faster than Lewis at this time with his British record of 10.03 in Budapest. Most significantly Johnson had beaten Lewis by just one-hundredth of a second in Seville in May. The odds seemed stacked in Johnson's favour.

In the sixth heat of the opening round, however, Carl threw down the gauntlet, setting a new championship record of 10.05. It was clearly intended to make Ben edgy. He had cruised through in 10.24 in the previous heat. In the second round Lewis won ahead of Linford, clocking 10.38 into a strong head-wind. Johnson lost to Ray Stewart in the last sprint of the day, though by the narrowest of margins. The general consensus was that Carl Lewis was back. On the second day, Johnson and Lewis both won their semi-finals but Carl seemed to have the edge, setting another new championship record of 10.03 into a stronger headwind than that suffered by Ben. The pre-race ballyhoo had been enormous. Swaggering around Rome was Charlie Francis, Johnson's extrovert coach, an ex-sprinter himself. "Ben is number one," Charlie said. "Lewis has got to prove it otherwise on the track. Lewis always comes back with the same story – 'I'm the best' – but Ben always beats him."

So to the final. The stadium was hushed and packed when the sprinters went to their marks. Lewis had said that he thought that Ben had panicked in their close race in Seville and believed that the Canadian was vulnerable if someone was with him at sixty metres. That obviously was Lewis's game plan but on the day it didn't materialise. As the gun went Johnson was away with an enormously fast start that left the field, including Lewis, floundering. After ten metres he was clear, at half-way he was nearly two metres ahead. Lewis closed but only by a metre. Johnson was the world champion, and not only that the new world record holder with an amazing 9.83. Pandemonium broke loose, the two protagonists shook hands perfunctorily and Johnson took his lap of honour. Television commentators and interviewers went into overdrive. When the times were shown they indicated that Lewis had equalled the previous world record with 9.93. In all that bedlam, almost unnoticed, just ten minutes or so after Ben had won, the Bulgarian Stefka Kostadinova cleared 2.09 metres for a world record in the high jump. It was, in the circumstances, a truly remarkable achievement. Linford finished fourth, behind Ray Stewart of Jamaica, suffering a slight pulled muscle five metres from the line. He said that he was disappointed not to win a medal but that he felt privileged to have taken part in such a race. He would not race again in the championships. Three Jamaican-born athletes had finished in the top four.

After the day was over I sat in the packed bus that would take us back to the hotel and talked to Don Quarrie, former Olympic champion and now one of the world's most respected sprint coaches. Outside, the crowds still milled about, shouting and waving at the athletes, thrusting autograph books forward. I asked him how he had seen the confrontation. He was succinct:

"Carl Lewis was ready, but Ben was more ready." I guessed that about summed it up.

Everyone enjoys the early-morning coach-ride to the main stadium from the two hotels. We proceed like royalty through Rome. Two obviously experienced carabinieri *on motor cycles lead the way, whistles in mouths, sirens wailing. Woe betide the commuter who ignores the procession and does not mount the pavement to clear our way. Traffic lights are ignored – but that, as I remember, is nothing new. Rumour has it that there is an early morning curfew on old ladies but no one will confirm it. We bundle out of the coaches at the stadium feeling very important indeed.*

It was obvious that Tom McKean had a great talent and when he won his semi-final of the 800 metres in 1:44.86, over a second faster than Billy Konchellah in the other race, many, including large numbers of the British Press, thought that our first gold medal of the championships was just around the corner. It seemed incidental that Peter Elliott, the man who had come fourth four years previously, had also qualified. There was much hype accompanying Tom's arrival in Rome – his employers had provided him with his own personal transport – and as he proceeded so well through the heats, the expectations of millions of Scots back home were fully massaged by their media. Some of us, however, remembered "Ally's Army" in a previous soccer World Cup and worried about Tom's relative inexperience. He had been shrouded in cotton wool in Glasgow by his coach Tommy Boyle.

In the event such fears were justified. Peter Elliott ran brilliantly, McKean performed like a novice and suffered the acrid taste of a bad defeat. The Brazilian Barbosa set a fast pace and reached the bell in 50.59, Elliott in close attendance. McKean was trapped on the inside as they entered the penultimate bend and remained there as they proceeded down the back straight. In desperation he tried to barge his way out of trouble, caught a heel, stumbled on the kerb, lost all rhythm and heart and jogged in a painful last.

Meanwhile, Peter Elliott was having the race of his life. Konchellah led with half a lap to go with Barbosa second but down the home straight Peter dug into his reserves and battled past the Brazilian for the silver medal. As he said afterwards, his 1500-metre training had been a significant help, as sheer strength pulled him through.

Peter is one of the nicest men in athletics and has never personally criticised anybody. He has a straightforward Yorkshire way of assessing everything, without the rude bluntness that sometimes accompanies that trait. He has earned himself the soubriquet "The Tough of the Track", after Alf Tupper, that comic fictional hero, and the silver medal that he won in Rome was a reward for many years of perseverance and overcoming of injury.

Tom McKean was mortified and left the stadium in tears. In later years he would look back on Rome and acknowledge his total naivety, but for now he had to suffer the indignities of failure, including a crucifying the next morning by the Scottish Press. The morning after, Tommy Boyle, his coach, rushed into our room. He was distraught. What was he to do? Should the lad go home? Yes, we said, he should go home, better to face the music and get it over with.

"He needs more experience," Les told him, "he's got to learn his trade. Get him a lot more races next year."

"You're right, you're right," Tommy said and rushed out again.

Edwin Moses did it again but only just, mere inches separating him from Danny Harris and the German, Harald Schmid. Two Olympics and two World titles now, but his invincibility was surely fading. The great encouragement for Britain was the run of Kriss Akabusi in the final. This run-of-the-mill 400-metre runner transferred to hurdling and in one year became world class. The change of event seemed to have acted as the elixir of life for him.

"Kriss has improved a hell of a lot," Moses told the man from BBC radio, in front of the stony faces of two guards in the TV interview area; "he could be the next British record holder."

Andy Norman arrives at the Village and his progress through the two hotels is akin to the Pope's procession, with Les and I as accompanying papal nuncios. His reputation as one of the world's leading promoters has preceded him, along with the fact that he has a hefty budget in Britain. Athletes and coaches don't quite kiss his hand and he doesn't quite touch their bowed heads, but that is the general impression. It takes an hour to travel two hundred yards. Above the babble that surrounds him he first of all asks about the food, which we tell him is so awful that we do not eat there. This is bad news for Andy. Then in a loud voice he complains about the adverse publicity back home. We know what is coming and hold our breaths in anticipation. We are right.

"I suppose," he says and our silent lips accompany him, "they're whacking me for Linford?" No one, in fact, has.

At night, presumably to deter the Red Brigades, a wartime Italian searchlight is added to our defence armoury at the back of the hotel. It cranks into action on a noisy generator, designed to penetrate the deepest slumbers. We complain. The charmingly compliant Italians promise to deal with it but nothing happens.

Thursday was significant for Britain. We won three medals and came to realise that Daley Thompson was mortal after all. The medals were won by three athletes just out of the junior ranks. In the hurdles Jon Ridgeon and Colin Jackson battled behind Greg Foster for the silver and bronze. Ridgeon finished ahead. Their rivalry had revitalised British hurdling. In 1985 Jon was in the ascendancy, winning the European Junior title ahead of Colin. A year later, in the inaugural World Junior Championships, the places were reversed and Colin won the gold medal. Now, in Rome, Ridgeon snatched the silver and equalled the British record.

In the 200 metres John Regis, at twenty the same age as the two hurdlers, was ahead of the field with three metres to go and all of us in the Press area rose to our feet. But then the American Calvin Smith and Queneherve of France eased past and John had to be content with the bronze. It was, though, a magnificent run.

Daley was defending his world title and his unbeaten record since 1978 when he stepped out into the sunshine on the first morning of the decathlon. We waited with some anxiety for his performance in the 100 metres. Rumours had abounded about his fitness following injury, but assurances had been given that he was "as fit as he was in LA". Daley won his race but only in 10.67 with a minimal headwind. It was one of his slowest runs ever and the pundits looked gloomy. It was the fastest time of all the competitors, though, and he led after the first event. After that he was not the man we had known; four men ahead of him in the long jump, eight in the shot put, ten in the high jump. At lunch-time I watched him speed away in a black Mercedes, courtesy of the BBC, to a secret resting-place. Frank Dick was with him but their faces were drawn and grim. Frank said later that Daley's lack of competitive fitness had come as just as much of a shock to them as it had to everyone else. In the end he had just run out of time.

Three medals means two visits to the interview room in an eyrie at the top of the grandstand, which with the waving of arms, the shouting in Italian, the escorting of the bemused-looking medallists by armed guards, makes these World Champion-ships more and more like a Marvin Hagler title fight. Staying cool amongst the steamy chaos that stands for organisation in Italy, sits the interpreter, the lovely Anna Legnani – perfect in English and French but with "just a little German" which turns out to be exceptionally fluent. We first came across her at Crammy's Press conference late last week and the way she rattled off the questions and his answers means that she can add Geordie to her repertoire. But how does she stand the daily grind, the endless, often inane, questions and the always articulate answers. "No problem," says Anna, "I love track and field." Jon speaks of his dis-located toe and of his delight at his silver. Colin, more reserved, says it is the best race of his life. Greg Foster says that he won it for his mother who had died in a car crash two years ago.

John Regis tells us that a smile flickered on his lips momentarily after the 200 metres when he thought he had won, but the instant replay on the scoreboard and the scurry of photographers away from him to Calvin Smith told otherwise. "My greatest run," says John, "a British record and everything has been a bonus follow-ing my injury." He thinks of his coach John Isaacs back in Hackney. "He'll be jumping around the room right now."

Outside a huge electrical storm empties its waters and floods Rome. As the sheet lightning flickers around the surrounding hills Daley goes to his marks for the final event of the day. He needs a great run but clearly the gods have deserted their favourite son, the elements are against him. The water pours off the athletes as they struggle around the track. Daley finishes fourth in a poor time. The British suppor-ters cheer and wave their flags as he walks off disconsolately. He is third behind the East German Voss and the Frenchman Plaziat.

I go to the other side of the stand to see if the sky is clearing and there, emerging from a doorway below, stripped to the waist, is the magnificently massive figure of Eddie Kulikundis, shipping magnate, theatre impresario and athletics fanatic and benefactor. Eddie thunders off to the car park to his Mercedes.

As I leave the stadium I meet his wife, the actress Susan Hampshire. "I felt the earth move," I say of Eddie's run.

"I'm sending him to a health farm," she says, "if he wants to do that sort of thing."

On the Friday, Ingrid Kristiansen hypnotised the rest of the field in the 10,000 metres with a second lap of 69.15 and a third equally as fast, to establish a huge lead which she increased gradually, and though the field eventually closed dramatically she had done enough to win. Everyone else battled for the lesser medals and Liz Lynch lost out, coming fifth, though setting a British record. She had learnt a valuable lesson and summed up her effort succinctly: "Perfect preparation, pathetic performance." It sounded even better in her Dundee accent.

For the rest of the day we watched, painfully, the end of an era. Mid-morning, the air cooler now after the storms of the night before; I went over to the open part of the stadium, behind the moat, beside the pole vault and sat with Auntie Doreen again. Behind her sat Daley's wife Trish, in the early months of pregnancy. Daley was battling away in the vault. He had begun the second day disastrously, finishing last in his heat of the hurdles and we began to realise that his mission to retain his title was impossible. He finally cleared 4.80 metres, ninth overall, and plunged another place. The man who was making all the running was Torsten Voss of East Germany. In the afternoon, after his vault, Daley seemed to be just going through the motions in both the javelin and the 1500 metres. He finished ninth. Auntie Doreen didn't say much; there wasn't much to say. She just thought that this would probably be her last trip. A quieter life beckoned her and she had done her job. Many thought that he might have quit, but to think that is not to know the man. As Frank Dick said: "Lesser men would have walked away." The truth was that he knew he owed it to the event that he loved to complete it. The irony was that the two men who had battled with Daley over the years and never defeated him, were not able to take advantage of his lack of fitness. Hingsen had no-heighted in the high jump and had withdrawn injured and Wentz collected the silver medal. The medallists indulged in a lap of honour and took Daley with them. At the end they raised his arms and he looked embarrassed – but they knew what he had done, not only for the event but for them as well.

Saturday, the penultimate day, proved to be a great one for Italy, but as it later turned out, a black one for athletics. Francesco Panetta, the darling of the crowd, easily won the steeplechase to make up for not winning the 10,000 metres and 68,000 fans sang and celebrated. Over at the long jump, where Carl Lewis won his fifty-second consecutive competition and Robert Emmiyan came second, the real battle was for the bronze medal, between Larry Myricks of the USA and the Italian, Giovanni Evangelisti. The crowd were considerably

Christie, Johnson and Italy's Pavoni contest the 100 metres semi-final in Rome.
Johnson went on to take the final in an amazing world record 9.83 seconds.

A jubilant Fatima Whitbread – Britain's only gold medal-winner of the
World Championships.

biased, whistling and jeering the American's efforts. I remembered similar behaviour back in 1974 when the East German Rosie Ackermann battled with Italy's Sara Simeoni in the high jump. Perhaps the judges remembered that Ackermann won that day. First Evangelisti, then Myricks, held the third position. In the fifth round the American consolidated himself in third place by jumping 8.33 metres, but in the last round Evangelisti was credited with 8.38 and the crowd broke into a frenzy of cheering.

Later investigation (in Italy) proved without any shadow of doubt that the Italian had not jumped that far, that cheating by the judges (unknown to Evangelisti, it must be said) had gained him the bronze medal. The IAAF was slow to move to acknowledge this wrongdoing but in the end reversed the result and awarded Myricks his rightful medal. Resignations were called for and accepted, including, as they say, men close to the President, but in the end there was no athletics Watergate, just a very bad taste in the mouth.

As morning dawned on the final day of the championships Britain still had not won a gold medal. Stuttgart seemed an age away. There were three hopes on this day – Cram in the 1500 metres, Jack Buckner in the 5000 metres and Fatima Whitbread in the javelin. Coming into the championships Steve had shown excellent form, winning the *Weltklasse* in Zurich in 3:31.43. The field was a strong one – it included Gonzalez, Herold and the new African star, Abdi Bile of Somalia, the first great distance runner to emerge from that country.

The first lap was slower in pace than in the women's race earlier. The lead jigged around from runner to runner over the second lap, completed in a slow 2:03.90. The pace livened over the next lap and with 350 metres to go Cram took the lead and made his bid for home. The next 200 metres took him 25.41 but the Somalian was with him. To the great despair of every Briton in the stadium Steve withered on the vine as Bile stormed past on the final bend and runner after runner passed him. He finished eighth. Gonzalez was second and Jim Spivey third. It was the end of another era. British athletes had won every championship 1500 metres since 1978 and now the run was ended.

Jack Buckner ran bravely in the 5000 metres but could not match Said Aouita and the Portuguese Castro and had to be content with the bronze. Steve Ovett, who had overheated in the heats, finished tenth. Seb Coe had been injured and was a spectator. The three men who had thrilled the world in the first half of the eighties seemed to be coming apart.

Good tactics by Frank Dick in the 4 x 400 metres relay ensured a silver medal for the British team. Roger Black had been injured all season and had only recovered when he came to Rome, thanks mainly to the efforts of the team doctor, Malcolm Reid, who nursed him quietly along. Roger missed the first two rounds, came into the final and helped the quartet home in second place, behind the Americans.

Fatima had been nursing a damaged shoulder and there was some doubt, as the team arrived in Rome, as to whether she would compete. Petra Felke, the new world record holder, was the main danger and led for four of the rounds. In round five Fatima unleashed the third-biggest throw of all time, 76.64 metres, to take the lead. There was an anxious wait in the sixth round as Felke threw after Fatima but there was no repeat of Helsinki and the gold medal was hers.

At the end of the home straight is the green area where the TV crews are, ready to interview the triumphant or the fallen, if they are willing. Here are BBC, NBC, ITV, ARD and CBS. Jim Rosenthal for ITV, Kevin Cosgrove for the Beeb and, hyping it up with fixed smiles for NBC, the very smooth Dwight Stones, ex-world high jump record holder. The athletes come there under the hot Mediterranean sun to tell of gallant deeds or not, as the case may be. Crammy looks mournful and says there was nothing there. John Walker tells me that it is the worst tactical race he has ever seen Steve run. "You cannot front-run a man like Abdi Bile like that after a slow-run race," John says.

After her win and the round of TV interviews, dope-testing and the medal ceremony Fatima climbs the stairs to the interview room. She sharply rebukes a journalist from the States who asks about drug-taking in track and field. All week Carl Lewis has been running around hinting that Ben Johnson is on drugs but no one takes him seriously. "Not the appropriate moment to ask about that," snaps Fatima. "Your name?" asks an Arab reporter. "Do you possibly have connections with our part of the world?" "My mother," says Fatima, tongue firmly in cheek, "had an indiscretion with Omar Sharif."

The lovely Anna smiles immediately and rattles off a perfect translation in Italian and French but her coolness evaporates when Fatima gives her the flowers she had received at the medal ceremony; Anna bursts into tears.

And then it is over and we pack and leave the Stadio Olimpico *amidst the dances of the closing ceremony and the fireworks; footsore, red-eyed and sunburnt. We haven't been stung by the wasps but by the Italians (laundry for two, £38); we've drunk the vineyards of the Roman hills dry of Frascati and we've seen the greatest athletics meeting in the world. Back then to the Village to eat at the small restaurant half a mile away that has kept us going for a fortnight and whose owner can definitely afford to spend the winter in Bermuda. And then to bed and to sleep the sleep of the just.*

At 3:30 a.m. the phone shrills by the bed. It is Andy Norman.

"Tell Tony," he says, "that Fats can't make TV AM."

15

ZOLA: T'INGS ARE GALLOPING

In November 1986 Tossie Budd and her husband were divorced and Frank went off to indulge himself. At least when Zola returned to the homestead there would be no more embarrassing chance encounters with her father – and they could use the garage again. The ensuing year was as fraught as the previous three had been. More commuting between Guildford and Stellenbosch, break-ups, injury, new coaches; her life seemed in a turmoil. Late in the year Andy Norman flew to South Africa to talk through the problems and made some snap decisions. He decided that Harry Wilson, the man who had guided Ovett, should be Zola's new coach. Labuschagne had decided on the quiet life back in South Africa and was coaching some new athletes.

Zola came back to Guildford with one of her companions, Minke van de Walt and in the New Year came the announcement: Zola was to spend nearly all her time in England and her new coach was to be Harry Wilson. At a Press conference the three of us sat and faced a large group of photographers and journalists. I had a distinct sense of *déjà vu*.

The coaching relationship with Harry never got off the ground. Wilson had an approach different from the high-volume-mileage philosophy of his South African counterpart. Neither Wilson nor Zola had been consulted in advance about the arrangement. It was doomed to failure. At their first training session together in Woking, he asked her why she had chosen him and she didn't know what to reply.

Her hamstring injury did not improve and she began the desperate search for a cure that so many athletes will have empathy with. She went to Freiberg in Germany where she received a course of injections, but they seemed to do little good and she was beginning to face up to the fact that she might never run again. Her relationships with people were fluctuating wildly. She was worried about Momberg's association with Worrall in South Africa, thinking that the politics might rub off on her; there were increasing tensions in the

Zola Budd with coach Pieter Labuschagne, an important prop in her life who decided in 1986 to return to a quiet life in South Africa.

Another false start for Zola: announcing her new coach, Harry Wilson (right) with the author (left).

house in Guildford with her friend Minke. She flew home to South Africa to celebrate her twenty-first birthday.

Whilst at Bloemfontein she met with Fanie Van Zijl, one of South Africa's greatest-ever distance runners, who was now a successful businessman and the Mayor of Randfontein. Van Zijl had nearly been crippled for life by an injury at the end of his running career and he had turned to an applied kinesiologist, Dr Ronald Holder, who had cured him. Holder had practised in the States, mainly on ballet dancers, who face horrendous injury problems, but he found that runners there also needed his help. His work involved testing the body to find the muscular imbalances that can cause injury and then proceeding to right them through orthotics, using the pages of a telephone book; so precise was the treatment that one page could make a difference. Zola was introduced to him by Van Zijl and was almost instantly cured.

Van Zijl became more and more involved with her career and this sparked off antagonism with Momberg. In July, no doubt prompted by her new adviser, she decided to terminate her relationship with the "Uncles" and dissolve the Trust. Whilst she was staying with the Mayor and his family she attended cross-country races as a spectator. In June, at Brakpan, Van Zijl, now acting the part of her coach, told her to run two laps on the outskirts of the course. Zola reluctantly did so. She was rightly concerned about her status.

Holder worked wonders and in the autumn she felt fit enough to return to England. She ran some low-key cross-country and road-races, one incognito, which gained her unwanted publicity. Van Zijl came to England with his family and stayed at Guildford, engaging in the usual cloak-and-dagger operations that South Africans, with their siege mentality, cannot resist. The trouble was that they fooled nobody.

Zola flew to and from South Africa later that autumn, the second time in a panic because her injury had returned. Holder gave her further treatment, and she stayed over Christmas; then on New Year's Eve she went to watch the Van Zijl road-race, which she followed by bicycle. At the prizegiving she was summoned to the rostrum over the public address system, where she was handed some flowers. The crowd cheered and clapped and chanted her name. She drove back to Bloemfontein the next day, the first of Olympic year, unaware that she had performed the action that would end her international running career.

It was the first year that Great Britain, as an entity, was sending a team to the World Cross-Country Championships, to be held in Auckland, New Zealand. Previously all the home countries had sent teams, a legacy from the days when it was a very limited, closed-shop affair. Now the International Federation decreed otherwise and at Gateshead, on a damp, chilly last day of January, the trial races for places in the team were held. Zola had flown in earlier in the month, still recovering from her injury, accompanied by Holder, who agreed to be on hand. She arrived in Gateshead with him and John Bryant, who had returned to the scene. She had asked him to be her "British coach" earlier in 1987 and he had agreed, but had then been struck down by a car whilst running – he was a two hours twenty-one minutes marathon runner – and almost killed. Months of physiotherapy, grit and painful exercise were returning him to normality but he appeared in Gateshead, in the huge grass bowl that had staged the World Cross-Country race in 1983, on crutches that sank heavily into the mud.

"I am genuinely happy to phase any South African coach out," Zola told Bryant, "and let you take over."

The shadow of Van Zijl, a loud, brash character, was still evident at the trials, however. He had told Zola to wear needle spikes; viewing the wet, muddy conditions, Bryant recommended longer ones. A telephone call was made to Randfontein; Zola wore the needle spikes.

The clouds of controversy were gathering around her like the black cumulus of a tropical storm. The New Zealanders began a campaign to have her excluded from the World Cross-Country meeting. The issue of a Commonwealth Games boycott was much nearer to home this time. Auckland was the venue and there were problems in obtaining sponsorship. They could not afford to offend the sensitivities of the African nations. The New Zealand group HART (Halt All Racial Tours) demanded that Zola be banned from entering New Zealand. Twenty years before, Mandy Rice-Davies, the woman at the centre of the John Profumo scandal, had been refused entry, on the ground that she would cause offence to the people of New Zealand. Zola, said the organisers of HART, fell into the same category.

At Gateshead she ran a slippery, sliding race, ignoring the demonstrators, who this time were prevented from encroaching on to the course; she came fourth and qualified for the Great Britain team. The noise from New Zealand intensified. The training run around the cross-country course at Brakpan, the previous June, reared itself. The BAAB accepted Zola's explanation. In New Zealand the issue became more political with Peter Tapsell, the Federal Minister for Sport and Recreation, siding with HART, calling for a change in the IAAF rules of eligibility. Each day and night telephone calls came from the New Zealand Press and radio, all asking the same question. Why wouldn't we ban Zola Budd?

Our attitude was unequivocal. Zola Budd had a British passport, she was eligible for the team, she had won two previous World Cross-Country Championships. The IAAF concurred. "We have ruled that she is fully entitled to compete and as a passport-holder is entitled to travel abroad as she likes," said the General Secretary, John Holt. On the evening before an indoor meeting in Glasgow, Les Jones and I were engaged in a bizarre radio phone-in on an early-morning New Zealand sports programme. Les sat at the telephone in his room, I sat in mine and we were both speaking into a studio in Auckland.

The telephone rings. "Hallo?" says a strong antipodean voice, "is that Tony Ward? Radio Adelaide here." It is an expected call. I have agreed to take part in an interview for another radio phone-in programme, this time to the good citizens of South Australia.

"We're plugging you in now," says the voice; "the next person you speak to will be George Murphy, on the Georgie Murphy Breakfast Show." Loud pop music, seventies-style, emerges and then advertisements before a voice says:

"And now, folks, we're going live to Tony Ward of British Athletics all the way over there in London, England." (If I thought the first voice was unmistakably Australian, it sounded positively cloistered Cambridge compared with the undulcet tones of Georgie Murphy.) "Tony? Thanks for agreeing to talk to us all the way from London, England. Can you fill us in on the problems surrounding this little girl Zola Budd? I hear those queer folks over there in New Zealand are trying to stop her running."

I explain the problem as succinctly as I can. Georgie listens well, asks one or two pertinent questions. Then he says: "So you poms are insisting that she runs. Well done. Thanks for talking to us Tony Ward, all the way from London, England . . ."

I remain tuned in. Georgie now sounds very indignant as he addresses his audience, toiling over their morning toiletries. "Did you hear that folks? That poor little bitch is being prevented from running by those Maoris for innocently running around the edge of a field in some little one-eyed hole in South Africa. Phone in, tell me what you think . . . The number to ring, Adelaide . . ."

The British Board announced that if the New Zealanders refused access to Zola as a legitimate member of the Great Britain squad, it might withdraw the whole team. HART were threatening huge demonstrations to stop her running. She was receiving conflicting advice from both her coaches. Van Zijl in South Africa would tell her one thing, Bryant in England something else. When John asked to see her training diaries he found them all written in Afrikaans.

They went to Belgium to run in a cross-country race, won by Angela Tooby; Zola was third, over half a minute behind. Angela told her, in a friendly way, that she thought that she ought to withdraw from the championships for the sake of the rest of the team. On her return she went to Bryant's house and was in the process of giving his children some Belgian chocolates when the telephone rang. Bryant answered it. It was Les Jones. "A problem has blown up," he said. He had been at an international match at Cosford that day and had been shown a letter by Marea Hartman and the Chairman of the British Board, Ewan Murray. There was pressure being mounted by the IAAF; allegations had been made that Zola had competed in a race in South Africa, a New Year's Eve road-race at Randfontein. "There is," said Les, "a degree of difficulty."

When Zola heard the news she was distraught. "They're trying to ban me," she shouted, "they're trying to stop me."

The IAAF wrote to the British Board and said that as they could not guarantee Zola's eligibility they should drop her from the Auckland team. Board officials frequently called Zola in for questioning about the Brakpan and Randfontein affairs. In the end they asked her to sign an affidavit, which she did. Britain then wrote to the IAAF asking for sight of the evidence. We did not receive a reply. There is no doubt that the IAAF wanted the Board to carry out its dirty deeds, our Tyrrel to their Richard the Third.

A number of serious discussions went on in the ensuing days. It was obvious that if Zola went to New Zealand (the government had now given an assurance that she would be admitted and that they would do their best to contain the demonstrations) she would be subjected to extreme harassment, as would the whole British team. She was not in her best form and was unlikely to figure among the medallists. Surely the aim should be the Olympics in Seoul in September? Informal discussions were held with the IAAF. John Bryant believed, as a result of those discussions, that the IAAF had indicated that her withdrawal from the team would engender enormous goodwill and that there would be no problems regarding Seoul, provided that she stayed in Britain. Les Jones went further. He believed that if she withdrew from the race in Auckland there was a tacit understanding with the IAAF President, Nebiolo, his assistant, Barra, and the General Secretary, Holt, that there would be no problem relating to the Olympics. A week after her race in Belgium, she withdrew from the British team. Both Jones and Bryant were convinced that the New Zealanders had concluded a deal with SANROC, a piece of horsetrading: "You keep her out of Auckland; we'll ensure there is no boycott of the Commonwealth Games." Scandinavian and African countries wrote to the IAAF and asked them to investigate the activities of Zola Budd.

Van Zijl came to join Zola and Holder in Guildford. Bryant, meanwhile, had been talking to her about moving, buying a house near where he and his family lived in Kingston. In Guildford, frictions increased and Zola began making invidious comparisons between the cultured, practising Buddhist, Holder, and the oafish Van Zijl. Then on 24 March, the IAAF announced that Zola was to be suspended until their Council meeting, ironically in London, on 15 April, when they would decide whether she had broken Rule 53(i), a rule forever engraved on my heart. A competitor, it says, who "has taken part" in any meeting or event in which any of the competitors were, to his/her knowledge ineligible to compete under IAAF Rules, renders him/herself ineligible. All meetings in South Africa came under that category. Zola was in New York with Holder to run in a road-race in Central Park, but the ban prevented her from competing. She rang Van Zijl in South Africa, where he had returned. By now the whole affair was becoming too hot for the Mayor of Randfontein who was so non-committal and unhelpful that it was the last contact that Zola had with him. Her only prop now was John Bryant.

The story had now become world-wide news. Television crews arrived from France and Finland. Journalists from country after country kept telephoning. There seemed to be this constant battle between French justice and British justice. We believed that Zola was innocent until the IAAF could produce the evidence that would prove her guilty. They thought the opposite. From this moment on the attitude and actions of the IAAF and especially its President, Primo Nebiolo, were totally reprehensible. Nobody emerged with much credit from the Zola Budd affair but the international governing body of the sport emerged with most disrepute.

They constantly refused to let the Board see the new evidence which they said they had, which proved irrefutably that Zola had actually raced in South Africa. The officials and staff would only have done this under Nebiolo's instructions. In the weeks between 24 March and 15 April it somehow emerged that the IAAF's "evidence" was a curiously ambiguous story in an African newspaper and a photograph of her allegedly running in the race at Brakpan. Bryant, then an executive director of *The Times*, used his newspaper connections to ask a journalist to investigate the incident. He found the venue and date and Zola's apparent number. The journalist found the address of the athlete who actually wore that number, went to the house and found that the woman who answered the door had run in the race and had frequently been mistaken for Zola Budd.

The IAAF then changed tactics and said that "taking part" in a meeting did not necessarily mean competing. John Holt talked vaguely of taking part as being "part of the scene". It was obvious now that the IAAF were determined to ban Zola Budd from international athletics, no matter what it took. She was a pawn in a much bigger game.

The IAAF Council gathered at the Park Lane Hotel, in London's Piccadilly, as had half of the world's media, it seemed. Nebiolo was in a deep quandary. His power-base in world athletics were the Third World countries, nations upon whom, through his offices, the IAAF had heaped financial help and patronage. SANROC and Sam Ramsamy had been having a field day over Zola Budd, relishing the publicity; now Abraham Ordia, the long-serving president of the Supreme Council for Sport in Africa called for a boycott of the Olympic Games in Seoul by the African nations, if Budd was included in the British team. Also on the agenda of the Council meeting was the Evangelisti affair. It had been conclusively proved that Italian officials had cheated in Rome to gain the long-jumper the bronze medal. There were calls in Italy for Nebiolo, also the Italian federation president, to resign. His assistant in Rome, Luciano Barra, seemed also to be involved. In such difficulties, Primo could not afford to offend his power-base.

There was the additional problem of the Olympic Games. Every gathering since 1964 had suffered from political interference and boycotts of one kind or another. The Olympic movement was at a crisis point; another boycott would probably bring it to an end altogether. Zola could be the focal point of such a move by the African countries. Athletics would again be at the centre of disruption of the Olympics. Nebiolo and Samaranch were determined that such a problem must not arise. Budd must not be in Seoul.

John Bryant and Zola arrived at the Park Lane Hotel just before nine o'clock on the morning of the first day of the Council meeting. They were there for nine hours in a bedroom on an upper floor. They had an understanding with John Holt that Zola would appear before the Council for questioning. I had conveyed to Bryant that the Board felt that if she had legal representatives present it would be provocative and so they went with none. They had been assured that the IAAF would not have lawyers on hand. In the event they did, but it did not matter. Nebiolo determined that Zola would not be called and she was not. It was a matter, he stated, strictly between the IAAF and its member country, Great Britain. Ewan Murray and Mike Farrell, the Board's Acting Secretary, were called before the Council.

"What can you tell us of this matter, Mr Murray?" Nebiolo asked the British Chairman.

Murray was in a belligerent mood. "Why are we here?" he said.

The meeting dragged on through the day. Lamine Diack, from Senegal, Council member and President of the African Amateur Athletic Confederation, resplendent in the blue robes of his national costume, led the attack. He was backed by Hassan Agabani, from the Sudan. There was little or no support for Zola Budd; there was resentment at the British attitude. That attitude was that natural justice must prevail, that the evidence must prove conclusively that she had broken Rule 53(i) before she could be condemned. It seemed to us that for many of the IAAF Council, including the lawyer who was its President, this was a legal nicety that they could not afford to consider.

During the lunch-break Bryant and Zola Budd left the hotel and travelled across to the London Marathon Exhibition. It was the last day for runners to register and collect their numbers, and the marquee was heaving with people crowding round stands, watching videos, buying last-minute requirements and souvenirs. Zola immediately relaxed; she was in an environment that she understood and in which she felt at home.

"One day," Bryant said to her as they walked around, returning the smiles of hundreds of people who recognised her and knew of her plight, "you could be running this race. I've run 2:21, you can run faster than that." He was convinced that Zola was capable of running under two hours twenty minutes for the race, a time that no woman had ever achieved (and still hadn't by the end of 1990).

They went back to the hotel, returned to the room and drank many cups of tea, to which Zola was addicted. The British representatives went back into the Council meeting but no progress was made. At seven o'clock Zola left the hotel with the news that the IAAF Council did not wish to interview her. We held a Press conference under television arc lights and reiterated the British position. The Council adjourned until the next day, forming a five-man group to come up with a plan of action. It was becoming clear that the IAAF were having difficulty in deciding what to do, given that the British attitude was so intransigent. They had arbitrarily interpreted their own rule in a manner that had no precedent. They said that Zola had transgressed their eligibility rule by running around the cross-country course at Brakpan and by receiving flowers on the podium and acknowledging the plaudits of the crowd at Randfontein. In so doing they decreed she had "taken part" in the meetings.

On the Sunday morning a notable figure in the by now over-familiar lounge of the hotel was Abraham Ordia, who had flown in from Nigeria. He did not have to wait too long for a decision. Just before lunch, representatives of the IAAF Council (but not the President) appeared to make a statement to a packed Press conference. The first one they read out was an earlier draft and someone had to return hastily to the council room to collect the revised version. This error seemed to me to encapsulate the whole affair. The Council said that it was not satisfied with the manner in which the BAAB had regulated the conduct of their athlete, Zola Budd. Their statement went on:

"The Council requests the BAAB within one month from today's date to report to it on the matters that concern them and on what action it has taken. If, in the opinion of the Council, it is evident from the BAAB's report and/or representations that the BAAB has failed to take such action as is necessary, the Council will have to consider exercising its suspensive powers against the BAAB.

"During this one month period, the BAAB is requested not to permit the athlete to take part in international competition.

"Having regard to the interests of international athletics, the Council is of the view that the BAAB ought to consider a suspension of the athlete from international athletics for a period of at least twelve months beginning from today (13 April)."

Then it was the turn of the African AAC to face the world's media. Diack welcomed the IAAF Council's decision. "We understand," he said, "that some people see Miss Budd as a young girl with her life ahead of her, going through a confused and at times unhappy phase of her life. It is also plain that she has been manipulated by South African interests. This may explain her conduct but it does not excuse it." He added a couple of what could only be construed as sinister riders, calculated to keep the IAAF's and Britain's minds concentrated on the issue. Certain federations wanted the IAAF headquarters to move away from London, and if Britain failed to carry out the IAAF's request, then an Olympic boycott was still on.

We held the third conference. What did we think of the decision? What about the threat to suspend Great Britain? What were we going to do? We were going to call a BAAB Council meeting the following weekend.

Doubtless Primo Nebiolo had a glass or two of champagne on his flight back to Italy. Now there would be no boycott of the Olympic Games; Zola Budd was finished, no matter what the British did. And the Council had not had the time to deliberate on the World Championships long jump for too long. They had merely given Myricks his rightful medal.

Tossie arrived, accompanied by Quintus; Madame Defarge, knitting needles at the ready, arriving at the guillotine for the axing of her daughter's running career. Zola was feeling the strain; she was not well, and suffered from insomnia and lethargy by turns.

The Board Council meeting was at the Grosvenor Hotel by Victoria Station in London. Cameras awaited my arrival. I spoke but said nothing. They filmed the Council about to debate one of the most serious matters in its history and then left, adjourning to another hotel a few hundred yards along the road. The Board were angry and not inclined to be browbeaten by the IAAF or the African AAC. The Council wished Great Britain to act on Zola Budd's "conduct" without giving any real proof of her misdemeanour. We decided to set up an investigative committee to elucidate the facts. Headed by Edward Cazalet QC and assisted by Charles Woodhouse, the Board's legal adviser, the committee hired a firm of solicitors in Johannesburg to obtain affidavits from people who had been present at Brakpan and Randfontein. The committee would also meet with Zola and her legal advisers. We issued a statement. We were concerned that the IAAF resolution had been framed when they were not in a position to reach a conclusion fairly and properly. We had asked our enquiry team to report back on 21 May – a week later than the IAAF deadline. In other words we were saying to the IAAF that as they hadn't held a fair and proper enquiry, then we would. Zola was asked not to compete at all in the interim.

Ironically, the setting-up of this investigation proved the final blow to Zola's hopes. "Come 21 May," she said, "and they'll put it off again." Her health and mental state were deteriorating rapidly now. She could see no light at the end of the tunnel, no way in which she could ever compete internationally again. John Bryant was to write that Zola said to him: "Why do they do this to me? If I were black, they wouldn't let this happen. It doesn't happen to Sydney Maree, it doesn't happen to other people. Why should it happen to me?"

Tossie fussed around the house like a hen. All her misgivings about her youngest daughter embarking on this dangerous venture had come true. Her health and Zola's animals back on the homestead were a constant topic of conversation, part of the emotional blackmail that she had exerted ever since Zola had begun her travels away from South Africa. Daily she would bring out photographs of all the babies and children back home, saying how much she missed them and how much they missed Zola. And the animals, especially the dog Fraaier, who was moulting and pining away, and her blood disease and how she had a nightmare of dying with Zola so far away and thus not able to "say goodbye".

Bryant visited the house frequently. One evening, as they sat around the lounge, he asked Tossie how long she intended to stay. Tossie sipped her glass of Blue Nun wine, her favourite drink, and smiled.

"I'll stay here, man, until it's all over. Until all the trouble is over."

A few days later Tossie telephoned Bryant. "Her doctor says she's got to stop running altogether," she said. "She's given her pills to take. She mustn't train. It's all over, man. She won't run any more."

I am showering in the mausoleum that passes for a bathroom in Edinburgh's Caledonian Hotel. I am in Scotland to take part in a debate on politics and sport at Edinburgh University; among the other contributors is the West Indian cricketer, Clive Lloyd. The telephone in the room rings and I move quickly to it, water pouring down my face. It is Les Jones.

"Tony!" he says urgently. "Zola. Stand by your phone. T'ings are galloping."
He rings off before I can say a word.

I eye the mobile telephone that I have hired in anticipation of events, lying alongside the evening suit that seems the convention for this sort of debate. It was not my intention to take it with me but now it seems I must.

We stand around, sipping sherry with various dignitaries and University Union officers. I try to keep the mobile telephone as inconspicuous as possible but everyone has seen it and they keep eyeing me in a peculiar fashion. I resolve not to take the phone into the debate. A telephone call about Zola Budd in the middle of a debate on politics and sport, which has to include her, would be going too far over the top.

The debate is interesting and energetic. Clive Lloyd and I, opposing a motion that politics and sport do not mix, lose the vote. As I move into the reception, the mobile phone rings. It is Les again. "Tony!" he says, "the bird has flown!" He rings off again.

The calls start coming through at 1 a.m. I am in a taxi to a television studio by 6 a.m. and receive five calls on the way. I do three radio interviews at Glasgow airport. I reach the offices of the Board in London and all day long, it seems, everyone there is holding up a telephone, with a call holding. Zola has gone as she came, in a whirlwind of publicity.

John Bryant had met her again the day after Tossie's telephone call. They walked together in the woods near her home. She looked utterly beaten.

"I can't sleep, I can't eat," she said. "I don't think I'll ever run again."

"Not even in South Africa?" Bryant asked.

"Well," she sighed, "there I suppose I'd be a big fish in a small pond but at least I'd be able to swim."

The household – Zola, Tossie, Quintus and Dr Holder – were in a deep pit of despair and people were now extremely concerned at Zola's state of health. Dr Ken Kingsbury, a successful doctor well-known in sport, had arranged to see Zola on a Monday morning but her state was so bad on the Saturday that Bryant telephoned him and asked him if he could come earlier. Kingsbury arrived the next day. He spent four hours with Zola. He telephoned Bryant and said that he was very worried by her condition. She needed to leave Guildford immediately and spend a long period back in Bloemfontein with her relations, in a sympathetic environment. That was it. On Monday night, 9 May, four days before she was due to meet the enquiry team (which rumour had it was likely to find in her favour) she flew out of Heathrow, back to the homestead that she had first left just over four years previously. Tossie stayed behind to clear up the pieces. The *Daily Mail* had paid £100,000 for the scoop of her arrival; John Rodda, for the *Guardian,* received a tip-off and scooped her departure for nothing.

Few came out of the Zola Budd affair with much credit. John Bryant, perhaps, for being the only man to treat her as a person and not as a commodity. In the years that she competed on the world stage she was just that, someone to bring medals and glory to Britain, someone to "put bums on seats". She was a typical young Afrikaner, with all the paranoia members of that beleaguered tribe seem to possess. She was tight-lipped, secretive. She also had that ruthlessness, that deep aggression that Peter Coe had said Seb possessed. She was selfish to a degree that in ordinary society is found intolerable but which we suffer from those with genius. These are the downsides of greatness in any sphere, and especially in running. John Bryant thought that Paavo Nurmi, the great Finnish runner of the twenties, possessed many of these same qualities. A secretive man, ungracious, who took all of his training secrets with him to his grave. Few liked him as a man but as an athlete he was the hero of Finnish crowds.

Zola too was the darling of the athletics public, because they delighted in the greatness of her running. Her insensitivity to the situation of the black man in her country and to the problems that she was creating by her continuous visits there, and her unwavering determination not to condemn apartheid, were of no concern to those who, at stadia around Britain, rose to acclaim her enormous talent, her obvious love of running.

Bryant had almost been killed by a car whilst running. His legs had been crushed and he felt that the IAAF, by their iniquitous actions, had done the same to Zola. They had attempted to stop her from running, which had been and was her life. If both of them had sat in a room with Erich Segal and Dick Beardsley there would have been an immediate empathy.

"I don't like being alone," she said to Bryant at the end, and yet this is what, from 1984 on, her father and coach and British athletics inflicted upon her, this seventeen-year-old child of the veldt. She was expected to cut all ties with her country, with family and friends, all in the name of running. With hindsight one can see that it was asking too much. Les Jones admits that they weren't forceful enough with her, didn't spell out to her the consequence of all her actions. She exuded a fragile air and everyone felt a wave of protectiveness in her presence.

Double standards were applied by those who vehemently opposed her competing in Britain, who found it an affront and who believed that she provided succour to the racist South Africa régime. Tennis players, golfers and other men and women from sports that the rest of Africa did not generally compete at travelled to and from South Africa with impunity. Yet one memory remains. Her world cross-country win in 1986 was one of her greatest triumphs, beating the greatest distance runners barefoot in the muddy, slippery conditions of Neuchatel. At the post-race party a crowd of Kenyans and Ethiopians, winners in the men's races, crowd around her. They pose and take it in turns to have their picture taken with the women's champion. Everyone wanted to be with Zola Budd.

16

BRITISH TRIALS AND JAPANESE NIGHTMARES

After Zola's departure, relieved minds turned towards the Olympic Trials in Birmingham, but a new controversy arose over the British Board's selection policy. The administrators had veered from one opinion to the other. Many felt that the pre-selection policy, advocated by Frank Dick, had somehow failed in Rome and no athletes were selected for the Seoul Olympics before the trials in Birmingham, which were also the first-ever combined men's and women's championships. The policy decided upon was that the first two in each event, provided that they had achieved the necessary standard, would automatically be selected for Seoul, leaving the selectors one place to fill.

Sebastian Coe was a bitter opponent of this policy. Throughout his career he had always prepared for the main event, gauging his training towards an Olympic Games or other championship. He pointed to 1984 and the fact that, though beaten by Peter Elliott in the AAAs, he had reached peak form at the right time and in the right place. He believed that pre-selection of the best athletes was the right policy and other top stars, including Steve Cram, agreed with him. Seb had an additional problem. Injuries and illness had plagued him and he found himself approaching the trials without having achieved the necessary qualifying mark. In the end he had to find a local race in deepest Switzerland in order to achieve it. Also, in the weeks leading up to Birmingham, he had gone to altitude for training and some felt that the timing had not been right.

I thought that the best trial system was where the winner of each event was selected and the next two were picked up by the selectors, but you could not get away from the fact that the vast majority of athletes approved of the Board policy. Those travelling to the AAAs would know exactly what they had to do to go to the Olympic Games in Seoul. Seb and I both went on BBC2's sports magazine programme, *On The Line*, though the interviews were shot separately and intercut. The result was very fair. During my piece I said that I thought that Seb, who had not really run much since 1986, ought to prove himself against the younger men who were pressing for a place. "It's like the old lion," I said, "the leader of the pack. There comes a time when he has to defend that position against the younger cubs."

This mortified a lot of Seb's defendants in the media and I was attacked by David Miller and Chris Brasher for that remark. Brasher called me "two-headed and gravelly-voiced"; others suggested that I was the Bernard Ingham of athletics and still others that I was to the sport what Inspector Clouseau was to the French judiciary! Many believed that I was expressing personal opinions rather than those of the sport, but my job has always been to articulate policy in the most positive way possible.

The weather in Birmingham was brilliantly fine and hot and there was drama all weekend. Fatima Whitbread had been injured and elected not to contest the women's javelin, believing rightly that as World Champion she would be selected for the third place. Tessa Sanderson, the defending Olympic champion, was also severely injured but could not be so sure of selection. Only Sharon Gibson had achieved the necessary qualifying standard but Julie Abel was particularly close to it. Tessa arrived at Birmingham determined to throw. She went out to the warm-up track with Joan Watt, the team physiotherapist, and attempted to prepare. She kept breaking down and was in tears when the Assistant Team Manager, Joan Allison, went out and told her it would be a nonsense to attempt to throw and that she might do herself further damage. All this, of course, was grist to the mill of the television cameras and assembled media.

Never before has a women's javelin event been so avidly watched. If Julie Abel achieved the qualifying mark then the BAAB, adhering to its by now increasingly discredited selection policy, would have to omit from their team either the current world champion or the defending Olympic champion, both of whom were ranked in the top five in the world in 1988. In the end Julie did not qualify and acute embarrassment was avoided.

The other drama came in the 1500 metres where Seb, clearly out of sorts, failed to qualify for the final. He looked wretched and forlorn as he left the track. He knew that Steve Cram, who ran in the 800 metres, would almost certainly be awarded the third spot. Steve Ovett won his heat in his old manner, waving to the crowd. It was his last fling, for he did not run well the next day in the final.

The question now was, would the selectors pick Seb for the 800 metres? Both Cram and Peter Elliott wanted to double up, that is, run the 800 and 1500 metres in Seoul, so each ran one race in the trial, expecting to gain the third spot in the other. Cram won the 800 metres and Elliott the 1500. On the

Sunday night the selectors picked Coe for the 800 metres and on the Monday morning the Board Council reversed the decision by one vote. It was never going to be easy. Peter Elliott had run brilliantly to gain silver in Rome the year before, Coe was still the world record holder and European champion.

So Sebastian Coe would not be at the Seoul Olympic Games, the dream of an unprecedented third gold medal shattered by a nasty virus and, perhaps, odd preparation. The Press had a field day. The *Daily Mirror* ran a scurrilous "Coe Must Go" campaign, described by its sports editor as "a bit of a lark". Badges were issued, votes taken and a dreadful cartoon drawn, depicting Coe as a fine racehorse and Peter as a carthorse. Being the gentleman that he is Peter took it well but it must have hurt. Meanwhile Samaranch, a Coebophile, launched the idea of giving Seb a "wild card" entry to the Olympic Games and he was swiftly supported by the British Olympic Association. On holiday in Somerset I could not believe what was going on; but the idea was soon scotched when notable athletes, Steve Cram among them, denigrated the idea.

At the end of August the first contingent of athletes flew out of Heathrow, bound for Tokyo via Anchorage. The Holding Camp in San Diego had been so successful in 1984 that Frank Dick had organised another, this time at the Nihon Centre, sixty miles east of Tokyo, near the city of Chiba. Frank had been Director of Coaching since 1978. A Scotsman, he brings a very academic approach to his job. His pre-planning for major events is probably unequalled in the world and his team-talks before championships are marvellous feats of inspiration that were to reach their apogee the following year. Controversy, of course, follows him around. I say of course, because that has always been the lot of those professional coaches, from Geoff Dyson onwards, who actually want to achieve something.

Nihon was an extraordinary place. Its normal clientele were Japanese business executives who paid huge membership fees. It had every facility that our athletes could have asked for. There was a 400-metre synthetic running track, just outside the huge building that housed weight-training facilities, a swimming pool and courts for racket games and volleyball. There were saunas, jacuzzis, lecture and physiotherapy rooms and a large restaurant that provided food that any five-star hotel in Britain would have been proud to serve. Frank had chosen brilliantly again, though he had come in for some criticism for selecting somewhere outside South Korea. But he was right; the needs of the athletes, preparing for the most important competition of their lives, were paramount. There was only one snag; the media were to be staying with us for a good period of the time that we were there and no one had informed the athletes beforehand. It was to give me a nightmare of a fortnight. The sponsors of our camp were Minet, the finance company, and Frank was naturally

Director of coaching Frank Dick, an honorary Falklands Islander for the Auckland Commonwealth Games of 1990, where a bureaucratic muddle left him without British accreditation!

anxious to see that they obtained the maximum coverage possible. Both Penny Dain of APA, the company's press officer, and I warned Frank of the possible dangers of having the media housed with the athletes but he felt, I suppose, that it was worth the risk to obtain the coverage.

On the day our jumbo jet flew out of Heathrow, Tom McKean had suffered particularly at the hands of the *Sun* who ran a noxious story about a night out that he had had in Glasgow. Remembering his nightmare experiences in Rome it was hardly the start required to keep him cool and calm for Seoul. On the flight to Tokyo there were a number of journalists and as always one or two kept the stewards busy with round-the-clock drinking. One of these staggered up to a swimmer, believing him to be Tom, and began an interview. The swimmer strung him along and it was some time before he realised that he was being made a laughing-stock. He then staggered over to Linford Christie and unknowingly taking his life into his hands, put his face close, breathed alcohol fumes and slurred: "Are you on drugs?" With remarkable self-composure Linford told him where he could conduct himself and embarrassed colleagues came up and escorted him away. Later this upstanding member of the Fourth Estate wrote a piece about the IRA and the Japanese Red Brigade combining to wreck the Olympics.

With the "Seb Must Go" campaign, the Tom McKean piece in the *Sun*, the drunken journalist on the plane and a later incident at Nihon, we were suffering from the facile mentality of the tabloid editors and their journalists – not the athletics corps but news journalists and a vile breed known as "sports-news" journalists who are inflicted upon sport every Olympic Games, when anything seems permissible. In Seoul they revelled in their notoriety, wearing T-shirts emblazoned *Rotters*.

The team therefore arrived in Japan in a belligerent mood towards the Press and then found that they were about to encamp with us at the Centre. Daley Thompson had arrived ahead of the pack and was also angry to hear this news. Like Steve Ovett, some incident with a journalist in the past had rankled for years and his interviews, except for those he gave to the BBC (who, to my mind, over-eulogised him), were as rare as an Egyptian Vulture nesting in Woolwich. He was fully entitled to ignore the Press if he so wanted but he was not entitled to impose his antipathy upon the team.

Finally, infiltrating our vetting system came John Chapman, of the *News of the World*. He jumped into the showers when he saw Tom in there to ask for more details of the *Sun* story. Finally he filed a piece about Linford and Tessa Sanderson that was so ludicrous that no one took it seriously. It suggested that they were so infatuated with each other that they were "bonking in the bushes", an impossible feat given the number of armed guards all over the grounds. With, I suppose, an acquired unerring instinct for self-preservation, he left before the paper was published.

But no one could doubt the magnificence of the Nihon Centre and its efficacy for preparation for the Olympics. It was the nearest equivalent to the German Democratic Republic's élite sporting clubs. We were able to acclimatise gradually, and then the athletes moved into their final preparation for Seoul. Most of them had their personal coaches with them so they had every convenience. Some of the distance runners decided that training conditions were better some 300 miles away at Fukuoka, home of the world-famous marathon, and a number went there, including Peter Elliott. It was all part of the new-found flexibility on the part of the administrators: the prime consideration was the best possible training conditions for the athletes.

The weather was mostly overcast, often damp and always extremely humid. We had all the television networks present, and radio too; if it spoke or photographed, we had it. Then the Americans arrived, amidst police sirens and flashbulbs, and attention was partially diverted from our beleaguered (and in some cases slightly paranoid) athletes.

Throughout our stay there is an infestation of Japanese television crews and photographers, their camera shutters sounding like a plague of locusts. This reaches its zenith at the Press conferences held for Carl Lewis and Florence Griffith-Joyner.

In charge is the highly inscrutable public relations man for Nihon, Ichiro Kawato. I have never known a man so totally lacking in humour. Carl Lewis and his manager, the diminutive Joe Douglas, pose as millions (apparently) of pictures are taken. The British Press, by now shell-shocked at their week, sit bemused. Mr Kawato, in a dark suit, speaks.

"Ladies and gentlemen, we would like to begin. Stand up Mr Lewis please."

Carl stands up. "What is this?" he asks. "The Dating Game?"

"Stand up, Joe!" cry the British Press to Douglas, "stand up!" He is standing already.

The clicking becomes frenetic, then dies away, but never, during the whole conference, actually ceases. Carl gives the usual replies to the usual questions: he is pleased to be here, he thinks Nihon is wonderful, he is in good shape and believes that after racing him in Zurich he has the beating of Ben Johnson. Linford Christie is a fine sprinter. The conference ends with a final flurry from the photographers and then Carl is gone.

The Flo Jo conference is an entirely different affair. If possible the desperation of the photographers is even more intense, for Flo Jo, in track and field terms, is glamour personified. Her husband, Al Joyner, the Olympic triple-jump champion, is now relegated to a secondary role. Florence sits there posing, like a model on the front cover of Vogue, *not an eye blinking, not a muscle twitching. She is heavily made-up, her fingernails long and blood-red.*

"Tell us, Flo Lo, how you keep so pletty?"

Florence smiles and turns towards the questioner, still keeping her head in absolutely the best profile. She says she believes that personal appearance (I think for one moment she is going to say "personal hygiene") is very important, that it helps the image of women's track and field and so on. Then she resumes her pose, inscrutable as Mr Kawato, waiting for the next equally inane question.

On a day towards the end of our stay, Tessa Sanderson ripped open her heel whilst training on a top field and was rushed back to the Centre by two of the heavy throwers. They carried her at a run through the main lobby, blood flowing on to the floor, past startled journalists and other team members and up to the medical centre. It was of course a major story and there then followed a cat-and-mouse game, Daley to the fore, to keep the media at bay. Frank wanted to call the gash a "nick" and play down the incident. It all served to heighten the tension between the two groups at the Centre. In the end the Press got their story but the hassle beforehand had been entirely unnecessary. In all this the two women team managers, Pam Piercy and Joan Allison, were magnificent and it was through their calming influence that we finally got Linford and Tessa to face the Press, in a belligerent conference, to complete all the team interviews. We had got there but it had been an agonising road.

"Can we," asks Mark Austin of ITN, "do a general piece with you about the Nihon Centre?"

I tell him that it is okay and we set a time. During the day the hour of interview is constantly changed but finally we gather some distance away from the Centre itself, on the far side of the track. It seems a bit remote to me but there it is.

Again the interview is postponed and Mark keeps talking on a walkie-talkie to his editor, Peter Wallace. I look at him as he awaits a reply and there is a happy, confident smirk on his face. I suddenly realise that this interview is not to be about the Nihon Centre at all but something more earth-shattering. ITN think they have a scoop. What can it be? Suddenly and luckily my mind clicks. Seconds before the cameras start turning and the question comes, I know the subject.

A couple of days beforehand the officials back in Britain instructed our administrator in Seoul, John Brown, to add to our 4 x 400 metres relay squad the name of Sebastian Coe. The well-intentioned idea was that if Cram or Elliott dropped out of the 800 metres then his name could be transferred. It was based on a false premise and as soon as we in Japan had been alerted to it, the action was rescinded. But the media have access to the computer-list of competitors.

"Is it true," asks Mark Austin, "that Sebastian Coe is on . . ." It has been a close-run thing.

The time had come to leave Nihon and the magnificent attentions of Toshi, the owner, and Tadashi, the manager. Their farewells to the advance party travelling to Seoul were effusive and kind. They looked absolutely shattered. They had done us proud and despite all the setbacks with the media, the athletes had had magnificent preparation. But now the Games were almost upon us and I was glad to be leaving, to be where the action was. The threats against both the Great Britain and USA teams had been taken seriously by the authorities and security at Nihon was very tight indeed, inducing a feeling of claustrophobia in most of us. It was pouring with rain as we left Nihon and the enormous, frantically busy Tokyo airport. Two hours later the sun was shining as brilliantly as the welcome when we landed at Seoul's Kimpo airport and were driven along the south bank of the Han River to the Olympic Village, past the huge stadium proudly displaying the five rings. At every major international meeting there is always excitement, tension and crisis but none of us realised the drama that was to come, that was to shatter us all in the country that was called The Land of the Morning Calm.

17

OLYMPIC INFAMY

Drama came early to the athletics events of the Seoul Olympics, as the world awaited the expected clash between the two great protagonists of sprinting, Carl Lewis and Ben Johnson. Their rivalry had transcended sport; millions of people not normally interested in athletics had been drawn into the event by saturation television and Press coverage. A page of athletics' history had been turned and the fastest men on earth now held centre-stage. Johnson had been injured and when he had arrived at the *Weltklasse* in Zurich he was not ready to meet Carl Lewis. Both sprinters were allegedly sharing $250,000 appearance money, much to the anger of the other runners. Lewis won, with Calvin Smith second and Johnson third. It was a serious psychological setback for the world champion, who immediately flew back to Canada to try and recover his form.

Lewis had had a remarkably successful season and was undefeated in his run-up to the Games. He was arrogant and confident. He had rented a flat in Seoul and was staying there with his family and advisers. Johnson had been subdued on arrival, hiding himself away from the media and world attention in the Hilton Hotel. Christie, Calvin Smith and Dennis Mitchell were housed in the Village.

All the major contenders qualified easily from the first round, the fastest, as in Rome, being Carl Lewis. Linford Christie had been greatly worried about an abductor muscle but the niggle had disappeared completely, once he had run his heat. The second round, later in the day, produced a shock when Linford and Dennis Mitchell of the USA both beat Johnson and he was left in the galling position of having to qualify as a fastest loser. There was a mixed reaction to this. Most felt that Johnson was still suffering from injury and had not recovered his form; others recalled that he had been in a similar position in Rome.

The following morning the semi-finals were run. Lewis ran the fastest so far, 9.97 seconds. In the second semi-final, Johnson seemed to have recovered his pace and beat Christie and Mitchell and so the scene was set for the final, when only one would win the ultimate prize. There was not an inch of space left in the stadium for this race. The steps and walkways were crowded four or five deep and even those television technicians who could be spared had come into the arena. As the sprinters entered a huge buzz of excitement arose.

Around the world millions were transfixed to their screens, no matter what time of day it was. Former Olympic sprint champions watched intently as they saw the men come out on to the track and begin their preparations. They knew what was going through the minds of the athletes, knew the tensions that had built up, knew the trance that excluded all distractions that the finalists had created for themselves. They were there watching, as nervous for the athletes as they had been for themselves so many years before.

The starter called the sprinters to their marks. The nerves of the coaches and managers became tautened as they sat by impotently, like fathers at the moment of birth. Now their charges had to deliver. Joe Douglas, thinking dollars of triumph; Charlie Francis, hoping he had timed everything to perfection; Malcom Arnold, who had helped Linford with his final preparation and had accompanied him as far into the stadium as he could. Back in London, Ron Roddan, also in a television studio, bit his lips in apprehension.

They went to their marks, each man carefully following his routine. The gun went and Johnson, as if previously held back by elastic, shot away and was never headed, opening a yawning gap over the rest of the field. Lewis came in second, Linford third. Again the Canadian had triumphed and Lewis had succumbed when it mattered most. The times were sensational. Johnson had smashed his own world record with 9.79 seconds; Lewis had set a new American record of 9.92 and Linford Christie had become the first European to run below ten seconds with 9.97. It had been the greatest Olympic sprint race ever. For the first time in history four men had bettered ten seconds.

Later, under the great stands that ringed the Olympic stadium, I came across Carl Lewis and Joe Douglas, desperately trying to find an exit that would not be blocked by Pressmen. They seemed dazed, bewildered even. The scenes after the race had been traumatic, frantic television interviewers tugging at their arms to snatch a word and in the drug-testing room coaches, team managers and Korean officials, all shouting like Bedlamites, the Confucian spirit of gentility of the hosts shattered by events. I led them out by a quiet route to the sanctuary of the warm-up track. Neither spoke; Lewis just stared ahead, his dreams of Olympic immortality, of being the first sprinter to win two 100-metre titles, smashed by this red-vested man of his nightmares.

Seoul is an ancient city, as was magnificently portrayed in the opening ceremony of this XXIV Olympiad, and the home of an immensely cultured people. Most of that heritage and culture had developed on the north side of the free-flowing Han River. Seoul was founded in 1392 and over the years the Korean people had battled for their freedom. They had been conquered by the Japanese but with United Nations help had fought off the Communists of North Korea in a bloody conflict. It was paranoiac fear of North Korean terrorists, together with the still-fresh memory of the Munich Olympics of 1972, that engendered a security operation that would cost millions of dollars and many hours of frustration. I was living in Olympic Town, an annexe of the over-crowded Village, with British coaches and physiotherapists. Transport between the Town and Village was mostly by taxi, the drivers neat and tidy, wearing white gloves, their English limited but functional. The subsidised charges were immensely cheap.

All except a handful of the British team missed the opening ceremony and I believe that this was a mistake. Many, watching it on television in the lounge of the Nihon Centre, were missing their only chance to savour the unique atmosphere. There was some resentment amongst the British Olympic Association staff, for it seemed that athletics was again adopting an attitude contrary to the Olympic spirit. The original idea of sportsmen and women from all around the world coming together in a great spirit of love and harmony has long since become a myth. I saw very little mixing between the various sports in the Great Britain team, let alone between international teams. The competitors were there for one purpose only, to compete and do their best, and they wanted no distractions. The athletics team in Seoul was housed in one block, the rest of the British team in another. It was not conducive to fraternisation. I was informed very early on that my role would be subservient to the BOA press officers and I was unable to gain access to the media areas of the stadium, as I have usually managed to do. Thus the resentment that had built up on all sides in Nihon was continuing in Seoul.

The early days saw mixed fortunes for the British team. John Regis, distracted by a falling athlete, had been eliminated in the heats of the 100 metres. In the second round of the 800 metres, disaster had struck. Steve Cram inexplicably lost form and trailed in sixth in his race, failing to qualify, and Tom McKean had been disqualified for barging his way through when he had found himself boxed in. This had led to further argument and disquiet in the British team, with Frank Dick and Mike Turner disagreeing over whether to appeal. Frank felt that we should support the British athlete; Mike, having viewed a video recording of the race, felt that he could not in all honesty make a protest. News of this disagreement reached the media almost immediately.

Tom had failed again in a major championship and one had to view his continuing limited racing programme with concern. Tommy Boyle, his coach, had an almost mesmeric effect on his athletes – Yvonne Murray seemed to have undergone a personality change since moving to him – but Tom's talent

"Tell them that the carthorse has made it to the final." Peter Elliott, who won the 1500 metres silver, in action in Seoul.

was not coming to fruition and we began to wonder if it ever would.

Peter Elliott was the saving grace. He had come to Seoul determined, like Steve Cram, on a middle-distance double. In the 800 metres he qualified easily through the heats and semi-final and then, warming up for the final, he pulled a muscle in his groin, osteitis pubis; only a very painful local anaesthetic injection, given by one of the team doctors, got him to the start line. The pace was fast; the Brazilian Barbosa led through the bell in under fifty seconds and the final showdown was between the Kenyans, Kiprotich and Paul Ereng, the defending champion Cruz, Said Aouita, with a heavily-strapped thigh, and Peter. Ereng won, to continue the Kenyan renaissance, Cruz was second and Aouita just beat Peter for third. On the rest day, Peter received a cortisone jab and then further local anaesthetic jabs on each day of the 1500-metre races. It was a testimony to his courage that he was to qualify through to the final on the last day. "Tell the *Daily Mirror*," he quipped, "that the carthorse has made it to the final."

Liz McColgan gained a silver in the 10,000 metres and Yvonne Murray salvaged Tommy Boyle's (and Scottish) pride with a bronze in the 3000 metres. But there no doubt that medals were extremely hard to come by in the fiercest Olympic competition ever.

The persistent ringing of the telephone finally pierces deep sleep in Olympic Town. It is still dark. I patter across the floor to answer it.

"Hallo," I say, and loudly clear a husky throat.

"Tone?" says a familiar voice. "It's Jim Rosenthal. Sorry to ring you so early."

"Jesus, Jim," I say, "what time is it?"

"It's five-fifteen," he replies. "The reason I'm phoning is that Ben Johnson has been caught for taking drugs."

"For God's sake! What sort of gag is this at this time of the morning?"

"No gag, I'm afraid. It's horribly true." Jim sounds very serious. "They got me up an hour ago," he adds, by way of compensation, perhaps. "Look," he continues, "we'd really like to speak with Linford."

"Not yet, surely," I say.

"No, no. Perhaps about eight o'clock?"

"I'll try," I say. "I'll go over to the Village now. Jim, this is awful."

"You're dead right, mate," he says and rings off.

I dress swiftly and make my way out into the deserted streets of Olympic Town. Only the security guards are stirring and they eye me a little suspiciously as I hurry along. There is one taxi waiting at the rank and the driver stirs from a snooze as I approach.

"Olympic Villagee?" he asks. I nod.

We drive off and I try desperately to get my thoughts together. We pass the

"Cheer up, you've won the silver!" Coach John Anderson with Liz McColgan after the Olympic 10,000 metres.

Kajyale Market, the shadows of the fish and vegetable vendors moving under the pale lighting, the haggling already under way. I hardly notice the scene, my thoughts are confused. I remember the buzz of excitement before the 100 metres in the stadium; I remember the roar and excited voices afterwards. It was the race of the Games. Someone said that Ben had been congratulated, on television, by the Canadian Prime Minister and he had told him how proud everyone at home was. And now, disgrace, ignominy, infamy, notoriety . . . my mind is like a Thesaurus. Now, I think, we all know what the Games of the XXIV Olympiad would be remembered for.

I pay off the taxi and enter the deserted Village, passing the sleepy guard, who smiles, and hurry to the British team headquarters. The first person I awake is Les Jones, who sleeps on the left by the door, in what appears to be a glorified broom cupboard. He too comes out of sleep and is incredulous, thinking it is all some elaborate hoax. Then he awakens fully and other team managements come out of bedrooms, staring in disbelief at the news.

The first thing we do is try to confirm the story. It is difficult, people are reticent and evasive. Then we learn that the night before, Primo Nebiolo quietly called an emergency meeting of the IAAF Council for early this morning, to discuss a matter "of grave importance". We believe this is the clincher and at half-past seven Les and I climb the stairs to Linford's room, to try and get him on to ITV. We creep in and he and Colin Jackson, with whom he is sharing, are sleeping peacefully. It seems a shame to waken him, to shatter his dreams with the news that he is now the Olympic silver medallist and his friend Ben Johnson is in deep disgrace.

The sequence of events had begun when Ben had given a urine sample following the 100 metres. It had been taken, along with many others, to the testing laboratory in Seoul. Late the following evening, a Sunday, the International Olympic Committee were informed that the sample given by the winner of the 100 metres had shown a positive result. The Canadian team in the Village were informed by a hand-delivered letter, and their officials were totally stunned. An emissary hastened to the Hilton Hotel at five.o'clock, woke Charlie Francis, Johnson's coach, and told him the news. Francis must have known at that moment that this was when the cheating was going to stop. He told Ben the news and they talked through the rest of the night.

Just after dawn the next morning a Canadian contingent including Francis went to the laboratory, as they were entitled to do, to be present at the testing of the B sample (each tested athlete's urine sample is divided into A and B samples for this particular situation, or in case something goes amiss with the first test). It proved positive. That evening the IOC Medical Committee met and recommended that Johnson be stripped of his medal and disqualified. In

The red-vested man of Carl Lewis's nightmares smashes his own world record. But the fastest man on earth had cheated.

the middle of the night, once more, the Canadian team were informed of the decision and they knew that, for them, something akin to Armageddon would break the next day. The Johnson entourage were told of the result; he handed back his gold medal and hasty arrangements were made for him to leave Korea.

By 8:30 a.m. on the Tuesday morning, the IOC Executive Board had confirmed the decision to disqualify Johnson. They announced a Press conference for ten o'clock to tell the world what it already knew, through massive leaks from the Seoul testing laboratory – that Ben Johnson, the hero of the hour, the man whom billions had watched on television earlier, had taken drugs and had lost his title. The fastest man on earth had cheated. A statement told the world's media that a substance had been found in the sample given by the sprinter Ben Johnson, namely "stanozolol, an anabolic steroid". The statement continued: "The IOC Medical Commission discussed all arguments presented by the Canadian delegation, especially the statement that the substance in question might have been administered after the competition by a third party. The steroid profile, however, is not consistent with such a claim. The IOC Medical Commission recommends the following sanction: disqualification of this competitor from the Games. The decision is unanimous. No right of appeal is given."

It was over. As the Press conference ended Ben Johnson was leaving Kimpo airport on a Korean Airlines flight bound for New York. He looked, as he was carried along on a tide of screaming humanity, as if he were being taken to a lynching. He seemed stunned and bewildered; his whole world had fallen apart in thirty-six hours.

The Village was a quiet place that day. There were no noisy scenes. Officials and athletes of the Canadian team looked pole-axed, confused, hurt. They felt that the disgrace inflicted on them by Johnson, Charlie Francis and the strange figure in the background, the doctor Jamie Astaphan, had been enormous. Nobody knows why Ben Johnson, with one of the most carefully planned drug programmes in the world (certainly the equal of that of the East Germans) tested positive. Charlie Francis, as confident and cocky as ever on a visit to Britain in February 1991, was still espousing the "sabotage" theory that had been his immediate reaction in Seoul. Could someone have "spiked" Ben's drink? Given the chaos and lack of security in the drug-testing area after the race, such an action was certainly possible. There are many who believe that this theory is wildly far-fetched, but they are ignoring the fact that millions of dollars in endorsements were at stake and that cheating at the highest levels of track and field is not unknown, as was shown in Rome in 1987.

Francis, who is now banned for life from officially coaching, has nothing to hide. He insists that Ben came off his "drug protocol", as he is fond of calling it, the requisite 26 days before the 100 metre final and had never taken

A bewildered Ben Johnson returns to Canada in disgrace...

...to be greeted by a "welcome" party of enraged protesters.

stanozolol. This is, of course, an academic exercise, because Ben was and had been on drugs for years, but it remains a mystery, and, I suspect, the relevant authorities will wish to keep it that way. Other athletes trained by Francis came under suspicion. Mark McKoy left Seoul early after the hurdles final without permission.

Les Jones and I were concerned with a solely British problem. John Regis, the bronze medallist of the World Championships of the year before, had a bad draw for the semi-final of the 200 metres, in the inside lane. We made every attempt to get it changed on the grounds that John had run fast enough times in the second round, under the new IAAF rules, to be given one of the four central lanes. Our efforts were all in vain and we returned to the Village. John was sitting alone at the table in his room, staring forward, clearly obsessed with the draw. He had had an unfortunate experience on the first morning of the athletics events; a man overbalancing in the lane next to him had distracted him and he had expected a recall gun. It hadn't happened and he had failed to reach the next round of the 100 metres; he brooded. It is at such times that a tiny, fatal percentage of doubt creeps into the mind, insidiously planting itself there, and this is what happened to John. He did not qualify for the final the next day, but he had learned an important lesson.

Self-doubt must have tormented Steve Cram as he waited in his hotel for the opening rounds of the 1500 metres. His two runs in the 800 metres had been lacklustre and he had not qualified for the semi-finals. He had developed an Achilles tendon injury in a race in Rieti, a few weeks before the Games, and had missed valuable speed training. Nevertheless for a man who was the fifth-fastest of all time and had been so impressive winning the Olympic Trial, progressing to the final should have been a foregone conclusion. He had some blood tests after his 800-metre runs and they revealed a vitamin and iron deficiency. He went on a course of treatment but it was a desperate state for the world mile record holder to be in. Karen was with him, feeling a sense of *déjà vu*. So was that wise campaigner of many championships, Brendan Foster.

Steve ran well in both heat and semi-final and lined up in the final with a field that he would have beaten with ease in his heyday, no matter how the race was run. This was his great chance, maybe his final chance, of crowning his illustrious career with Olympic gold, to emulate, indeed surpass the achievements of Coe and Ovett. Elliott was there, the final painful jab inserted in his groin to counteract the pain. He did not know, would not know until he had had an operation on his return to Britain what the long-term effects would be, but he knew the risks and was determined to race, remembering 1984 when he had had to withdraw through injury from the semi-final of the 800 metres. Peter Rono was there, the most diminutive of the Kenyans, who had seen his country's distance-running reputation rise race by race during the week. Steve

Scott was there, still looking for his supreme moment, and so was the East German record holder, Jens-Peter Herold, a staff sergeant in the army, who had followed Gonzalez and Cram home in the European Cup a year earlier.

In the end it was a disappointing affair. Rono it was who finally took the race by the scruff of the neck on the second lap, threw down the gauntlet and led and was never headed. Cram, Elliott and Herold mounted their attack around the final bend but there was no catching Peter Rono. Cram ran out of steam, Elliott took the silver and Herold the bronze. Steve was fourth in a race that, really, was tailor-made for him. In contrast it was Peter Elliott's finest hour.

A crucial moment is reached in the qualifying rounds of the women's javelin. All week Britain's gold-medal chances have floated away. Now, our biggest hope, Fatima Whitbread, who has been injured for most of the season, is in crisis. She has had two no-throws and has only one left to reach the qualifying line. Margaret Whitbread and I sit in the competitors' section of the Olympic stadium and wait for Fatima to take her third throw. It is early evening and the sun is setting fast. There isn't much to be said. Stuttgart seems light-years away. As Fatima lines herself up on the end of the runway and stares ahead, concentrating now, knowing this is one of the most important throws of her life, Margaret looks away from her and shades her eyes with her hand. She is looking directly at me.

"I'll tell," I say. Margaret is supposed to watch every throw and analyse it. Fatima runs hard down the runway, lets the javelin soar high over the infield with a cry and it lands safely, beyond the qualifying line.

"Don't you dare," Margaret says, and she makes her analysis from the action replay on the giant scoreboard.

The next day Fatima wins the silver medal. Petra Felke is the Olympic champion.

Linford Christie had exhausted his supply of ginseng between the final of the 100 metres and the opening rounds of the 200 metres. He took this and other vitamin supplements to replace the energy he would expend in the ten races he was expecting to run during the week. He ran well in the 200-metre final, just missing a medal but lowering Regis's UK record. Now he was preparing himself for the sprint relay. Throughout our stay at Nihon and even during the early days of the Olympics, the running order of the sprint relay team was a subject that had not been raised. The problems in Rome were well-remembered.

On the night before the heats he went with a group of athletes to the main Village restaurant. It was an enjoyable night, with lots of fun and good-natured discussion. They left by the main entrance, glanced idly at the group at the meeting-place opposite, where the market in lapel-pins was in full swing, and headed towards the British compound. Linford saw Mike Turner, the team manager, and smiled. Mike, looking worried, stopped him.

"Can I have a word, Linford?" Mike asked.

The rest of the group – John Herbert, Sally Gunnell, Colin Jackson among them, moved on, giggling like schoolchildren, one of whose number has been stopped by the headmaster.

"Serious news," Mike said. "We've had a letter from the IOC indicating that there is an illegal substance in your test sample."

Linford was aghast and at first refused to believe it. In the end he was convinced; a messenger had again come through the night, bearing a letter to the BOA stating that two of its team members had illegal substances in their samples. He was immediately grilled by the athletics team management and by that of the BOA itself. The problem was that there had been no indication as to what the substance was; after the Ben Johnson affair, most people thought of steroids. Linford was sometimes hysterical, sometimes angry, sometimes even suicidal. In the end Malcolm Read gave him sleeping pills but he still slept fitfully. There were two positive samples from the British Olympic team; the other was from Kerrith Brown, the 1984 bronze medallist from the Judo events.

The next morning a delegation from the BOA headed for the testing laboratory. Encamped outside were television crews and photographers. Since the sensations earlier in the week the media knew where the action would be if another positive test showed up. The moment the BOA group arrived for the testing of the B samples, the television crews and reporters were galvanised into action, the cameras began filming. Clearly British Olympians had tested positive and one of them was an athlete.

I am ignorant of Linford's situation as the taxi takes me towards the Village. On my way there my mobile telephone rings and I pick up the news. For the second time in a few days I am totally dumbfounded. What is happening to these Olympic Games? Surely not Linford? Surely a terrible mistake has been made?

The BOA management issue a strict order that no one shall speak on the subject to the Press. It is a naive instruction, creating nothing but a news vacuum. I take a bus to the stadium and on arrival find total chaos outside the warm-up track, the British team under close scrutiny. Unbeknown to most of us, Linford has been confiding his predicament to a number of close friends and team management. About a hundred journalists, television reporters and camera crews crowd behind the rope that blocks the entrance to the warm-up area. Their eyes are concentrated on the two tents that house the physiotherapists and where the team members competing that day gather. High above, looking down on the area, ITV have a camera pointing directly at the British. Speculation as to the identity of the athlete is rife around the stadium. The British team management are finding it impossible to operate.

It seems to me that the BOA instruction has to be ignored in the light of the circumstances prevailing at the track. Rumours are quickly spreading as to the possible identity of the British athlete; too many people already know who he is, and the previous night Daley had returned from another brave but unsuccessful attempt in a major decathlon, to say to Linford: "You're in trouble, aren't you?" I walk over to the large crowd of reporters.

"Okay," I say, "I'll talk, but I won't say anything."

And I do so for five minutes, stalling and evading direct questions, promising more information as soon as possible, confirming that a British athlete has been found positive, that we don't know what the substance is. I promise to let them know as soon as possible when we have any news. The cameras, microphones and notebooks are put away, the crowd disperses. The news vacuum is filled and the team management can resume their work. An hour later ITV tells the world that the athlete is Linford Christie. One of Linford's confidants, himself or herself the subject of speculation, has spilt the beans.

Everyone was very supportive of Linford, especially Frank Dick. It was as if their very public disagreement of the previous year had never occurred. It was an armistice, rather than a peace, but it has held for nearly three years. Though Linford warmed up with the sprint relay squad it was never intended that he should run in the opening round. In the first place, he was under tremendous stress and therefore could suffer injury and in the second, though everyone was careful not to mention it, if the very worst came to the worst the whole relay team would be disqualified if he ran.

By lunch-time we knew that the offending substance in Linford's sample was pseudoephedrine, a stimulant, and that the amount was just over the allowable limit. We also knew that Linford's case was not nearly so serious as that of Kerrith Brown. As the sun beat down on the warm-up track, Malcolm Read and I circled the inner perimeter whilst he talked on the mobile phone to his colleague Malcolm Bottomley in the Village. We learned from that conversation that the stimulant was almost certainly in the ginseng that Linford had been taking. Events moved fast and in the evening the BOA party again left the Village for the Shilla Hotel, across the Han River, to meet with the IOC Medical Commission.

What happened at the Shilla that evening was a total disgrace and an indictment of the Olympic movement. Hordes of television crews, journalists and photographers thronged around the British party as they arrived, milled around them in the hotel, tried to accompany them into the lift and followed them down the corridor of the floor where the enquiry was being held. Hot television lights beamed down on the party and reporters yelled constant, mostly incoherent questions. Linford felt as if he were walking to the electric chair. No attempt appeared to have been made to keep the hearing confidential. It seemed that the publicity of the Johnson case had gone to the IOC's collective head.

Kerrith Brown was duly stripped of his bronze medal. He had been injured and had taken a drug to help him recover. Linford met the committee next; his case was presented by Robert Watson, not only the treasurer of the BOA but also a QC. Linford then answered some questions and they left. The media stayed on.

The IOC Medical Committee reached their decision. The Prince de Merode, one of the many and varied titled people who grace, or not, as the case may be, the International Olympic Committee, appeared in his shirt-sleeves to tell the assembled hacks that nothing would be said until the official statement was released. After a barrage of questions he said that Linford had been cleared to run in the relay the next day and that he "had been given the benefit of the doubt". It was an extraordinary and totally misleading phrase to use. Linford's twenty-four-hour nightmare was over.

The way that the drug-testing was carried out in Seoul was a scandal. From the first day there were leakages from the laboratory to the media. People in Britain and other parts of the world knew, via television, what was happening in these cases before we did in Seoul. Why notification had to be by letter at night, necessitating an all-night investigation, was never made clear. Why indeed the tests had to be carried out so swiftly and the results announced within hours was never clarified. The case of Linford was examined in a noisy glare of publicity that no athlete should have to suffer. Even the Ben Johnson affair was appallingly handled, the attendant uncontrolled media scrum worse than at an American murder trial.

Ben Johnson cheated on his peers at the Seoul Olympics and deserved the punishment that he received. But it was the International Olympic Committee, through its gross mishandling of the affair and by seeking maximum publicity for Johnson's fall from grace, that ensured that the XXIV Olympiad will always be remembered as the Games of the drug cheat.

The anxiety to leave Seoul, once the Games were over, was intense; some of us had been away from home for almost a month. Kimpo airport could hardly cope with the exodus and going through the immigration and customs procedures was a painfully slow process. Finally though, the first batch to leave the South Korean capital were safely aboard the Boeing, bound for Tokyo, Anchorage and then home.

It was time for reflection as we headed first east and then north. The Games had been an enormous success; all the world had been there and for the first time in twenty-four years, they had been free of politics. Many felt that the Olympics had been saved. For a country that had no real tradition of sport the Koreans had done a magnificent job. There was little to fault in their organisation, though their security had been over-intense. As we sat in the stadium and watched the panorama of the closing ceremony, the young men in neat blazers who had accompanied us everywhere, in the buildings, on the buses, around the stadium, suddenly opened their jackets and revealed the automatic weapons that they had been carrying, presumably since the first day. None of us would miss the interminable queueing that you had to endure each time that you wished to enter the stadium. But in their eagerness to ensure the total success of the Olympics, they had worked themselves to a frazzle, and on that last day each official that you met, each security guard, each interpreter looked ready to lie down and sleep for a hundred years.

Britain had done well but had won no gold medals, such was the intensity of the competition. The memories that would remain were manifold: Jurgen Hingsen, seemingly cracking in the 100 metres of the decathlon competition, breaking three times in his heat and being disqualified, then running around the stadium, appealing frantically to every official in sight, including Nebiolo; a man demented, at terrible odds with himself. Track and field would see him no more. And Daley, again succumbing to injury, battling through the decathlon, strapped and injured and in pain, finally losing the bronze medal in the final event. And on that last day, Paula Ivan, who ran a solo 1500 metres of determination and courage and won by a street. We watched her down the home straight and then switched back to the race for the silver and bronze medals and leapt to our feet, for battling there was Chrissy Cahill. We yelled and shouted but she could not quite grab a medal and finished fourth. In the evening she came into the office area of the British athletics' block, dressed to the nines, and stamped her foot and waved her arms like a flamenco dancer, still on a high from her achievement.

And Flo Jo. This amazing woman had revolutionised women's sprinting, setting a world record in the 200 metres. In both the sprints over fifty men had run slower and she showed power in her sprinting that no woman had ever displayed before.

Between them, the two close friends Linford Christie and Colin Jackson had won three silver medals. Colin had chased home the burly American Roger Kingdom in the high hurdles and Linford, in the final of the relay, had released all his pent-up energy, his fears, his frustrations and anger with an anchor leg of 8.95 seconds, the fourth-fastest of all time. He just failed to pip the Soviet runner for the gold medal.

Colin Jackson (right) chases home the USA's Roger Kingdom (in hood) to take the silver in the high hurdles.

Then there was the great street market of It'aewan where you could buy imitation Rolex watches or Reebok shoes at a fraction of the cost of the real thing, where they hassled and you haggled and where you could have a suit or a pair of shoes handmade in two days. We reckoned that if you had stood in It'aewan for the whole period of the Olympics every visitor to Seoul would have passed you by.

The Boeing took off from Anchorage and headed for London. Linford sat and wondered what reception awaited him there, not knowing of the great outpouring of sympathy that his problems had generated. Peter Elliott gazed out at the black night, sore from his injections, uncertain if he had inflicted any lasting damage upon himself but certain that he had done the right thing. Mike McFarlane, the Haringey sprinter, slept contentedly. He had served his country well for a decade, had served it for the last time with a relay run that had given Linford the chance to snatch, for the team, the silver medal. Now the running would be over and the living would have to start. For Mike Turner and Pam Piercy too this was the end. They would now retire from being Olympic team managers into athletic oblivion. They would take with them their memories of their days and nights in Seoul, which would never fade, for still the Olympic Games is something very special indeed.

It was that "specialness" that had made Ben Johnson's Olympic infamy felt so keenly by sport itself. We felt somehow unclean, rather like those whose houses or churches have been burgled and defiled. The publicity surrounding his success and downfall reverberated around the world. Sport, in millions of people's minds, was in disgrace and Ben was going to have to pay for it.

18

SPORTING SALEM

In the summer of 1990 I went to see the National Theatre's excellent production of Arthur Miller's *The Crucible*, the story of the witchcraft trials of Salem in 1692. It is, like all Miller's work, a compelling drama, in which communal hysteria leads to witch-hunting and persecution. It was written in 1953 and its relevance to the McCarthyism that gripped America at the time makes it a classic parable. It also stirs within me a distinct unease about drug abuse in sport, about the innuendo and sometimes hysteria arising from undue zealotry, and the lives and reputations that can easily be besmirched, sometimes permanently. In the interval I discussed this with Gwenda. I reminded her of the drama that had been enacted two and a half years previously, when two journalists, Pat Butcher and Peter Nichols, had written a series of articles in *The Times*, alleging connivance by prominent officials in the avoidance of drug tests.

It had been almost Christmas when the articles appeared and I remembered calling a Press briefing in a Bloomsbury hotel to give the sport's reaction. The room was not well lit and throughout the meeting a photographer moved around to take flash pictures; affected as I was by the paranoia that had gripped us since the articles appeared, I suspected he was looking for my worst side. It was a difficult sixty minutes and when it was over we rather bizarrely all moved off to drink at a Yuletide get-together.

The substance of the articles centred around the Grand Prix meeting at Crystal Palace in 1985. It was alleged that Russian athletes had been assured by Robert Stinson, the IAAF treasurer, that they would not be tested and that Andy Norman, with Les Jones in attendance, had assisted the hammer-thrower Martin Girvan to avoid a test by providing him with a container of "clean" urine. It was Girvan who had named names to the journalists. The AAA set up an independent enquiry under Peter Coni QC, and Robert Stinson sued *The Times*, a case which was settled out of court with substantial damages and costs to the plaintiff. Martin Girvan appeared before the Coni enquiry team and not only confirmed his story but told another of similar skulduggery at a meeting in Gateshead. Investigations of that allegation, however, showed it to be a complete fabrication, with some of those supposedly involved hundreds of miles away on the day.

Coni reported: "We cannot possibly find that the accusation made by Girvan is substantiated." All those who were accused in *The Times* articles were exonerated and Butcher and Nichols were shown to be no Woodward and Bernstein.

In the programme notes to *The Crucible* there was an extract from Miller's autobiography, *Timebends,* where he wrote that the main point of the McCarthy hearings, as in seventeenth-century Salem, "was that the accused make public confession, damn his confederates as well as his Devil master and guarantee his sterling new allegiance by breaking disgusting old vows – whereupon he was let loose to rejoin the society of extremely decent people ... an act of contrition done not in solemn privacy but out in the public air." Surely, I said over the malt whisky, this is what the Dubin Enquiry, the Canadian multi-million-dollar purging of its sporting soul, had been all about? That Johnson make public confession and be contrite, condemn Francis, and Astaphan, ask Canada for forgiveness for the disgrace he had brought upon it. And hadn't Francis with his unsubstantiated mass allegations of world-wide drug abuse delivered in his slick, streetwise manner, projected his (as Miller had written) "own vileness on to others in order to wipe it out with their blood"?

The bell rang, a three-minute warning for the second half of the play. As we left the foyer I remembered another man, who in the very early eighties had always smiled slyly when drugs were mentioned and given half a wink; he had recently been on television wrathfully condemning to hell and damnation an imaginary army of drug abusers.

In the second half of the play, Abigail Williams and the other young women who make accusations of witchcraft against the townsfolk of Salem suffer from mass hysteria. It is gripping stuff, and as the main character, John Proctor, went to the gallows for refusing to name "what persons conspired with you in the Devil's company" and the curtain came down, we moved to the theatre restaurant to continue our discussion. I wanted, like Miller, to discover a visceral connection with all this.

Though *The Times* articles had not provoked hysteria they did provide hysterical outbursts. They had quoted a high-jumper, David Abrahams, as saying that eighty per cent of British athletes were on drugs. This he based on conversations overheard on the flight back from the 1982 Brisbane Commonwealth Games. Even if he had managed to overhear everyone on the plane, it transpired that a goodly proportion of the England team had gone on to other venues in Australasia. Daley Thompson bandied about percentage figures that fluctuated wildly. Zealotry abounded, and self-styled crusaders appeared on television and in the Press to demand, with Calvinistic sternness, the suspension of the accused officials until the enquiry had reported. According to the Press and magazines British athletics was rife with drug cheats.

What was interesting, Gwenda felt, is that these same commentators, two years later, had conveniently forgotten their statistics and accusations. At the European Cup in Gateshead where the standards, especially in the women's events, had fallen away sharply, they were now saying that random testing in eastern Europe was working and this was why Britain had become so successful. The significance of the fact that our standards, with a rigorous random testing programme, had not fallen away, had been studiously ignored. But what, my wife wondered, had stirred up this hornets' nest of gossip and tittle-tattle and why did the subject invoke such evangelical fervour?

I replied that the answer to her second question is that drug cheating strikes at the very core of a lifetime's belief for so many people; belief in the ethos of fair play, in the purity of equal competition. If Britain was the mother of modern sport and its Olympian ideals it was felt right that we should impose the most Draconian penalties upon those who abuse the concepts that we invented. The danger in our approach would come – and there were some so passionate about the issue that they could take us there – when, as Miller had written, "the repressions of order were heavier than seemed warranted by the dangers against which the order was organised."

The answer to the first question, I went on, is historical. Coni had indicated that drug abuse, in the late seventies and early eighties, was probably as rife in Britain as anywhere else, which was why when David Jenkins was arrested in California in 1987 for black-market trafficking in anabolic steroids, there was some acute nervousness in British athletics. He had confessed to taking steroids himself from 1975 onwards; the worry for some was whether, like the simple folk of Salem, he would absolve himself of moral guilt by intoning the names of fellow-sinners and recant former beliefs.

Jenks. We had both known him. A supercharged, frenetic individual, always shooting for the stars. Like Zola Budd, like Mary Slaney, a hapless child, looking for father-figures. He had a father, of course: Arthur Jenkins, a successful Scottish businessman; but a man, by all accounts, who was more the hard taskmaster than the loving parent, who insisted that his family worship at the icon of success. He was to rubbish Jenks all his running career and afterwards, and to many this would explain the path that the son took. The first prop was the tough, often irascible coach, John Anderson, from working-class Glasgow, about as far removed as you can get from the effete Edinburgh neighbourhood where the Jenkinses lived. Under Anderson he won his only major title, in 1971 at Helsinki, where at just nineteen years of age he became European 400-metre champion, setting a British record. That, though, was it; for the next ten years he would remain, like Brando's punch-drunk boxer in *On The Waterfront*, not quite a contender. After his failure at the Munich Olympics he dropped Anderson to be advised by David Hemery. I told Gwenda what David had said, that Jenks vibrated on a much higher frequency than most of us, that he himself had felt shattered and drained after coaching sessions, trying to absorb some of his stress and anxiety. It was the classic anxiety of a son seeking of a father the love and approval which he would never receive. When Hemery left to work in America Jenks turned to a chemical prop, anabolic steroids. It was the dark side of the drive for sporting success.

In those days the taking of drugs was not viewed with the same antipathy as it is now. It was another likely short-cut to success, like altitude training or some technical innovation. Testing procedures were slack and easily avoidable. Promoters were as relaxed about drug-taking as about money. If part of the deal for an athlete to appear was that he or she would not be tested, no problem. The voices that spoke out then, like Sir Arthur Gold, were in the wilderness. Drug abuse, in the seventies and even early eighties, was not viewed as a serious problem.

There was a few moments' silence as the waiter cleared some plates away and prepared for the main course. Then we resumed our conversation, and Gwenda played Devil's advocate. In the play programme there was a sentence: "There are Communists, but there never were any witches." In her view the same applied with my theory – there were and are drug abusers.

Yes – but I pointed out that Miller gives an answer to that as well. When several hundred thousand people had been executed in Europe for witchcraft, it was hardly wisdom to say that the cause was merely imaginary. People, Gwenda said, would believe that we were going soft on drugs and would say so. I replied that if that were the case, then we were in a more paranoid state than I thought we were. There is no subject that cannot be debated, there is no stance that should not from time to time be reviewed. What I was worried about was not the actual fight against drug abuse but the innuendo and slander that accompanied it. Athletes and others pointed fingers of damnation at fellow competitors just as effectively as Abigail Williams and Susanna Walcott had at Goody Proctor. Carl Lewis had done so against Flo Jo and because she had not sued him, the assumption was that she was guilty by omission. The same thing had been said about Andy and Les after Coni had cleared them. Their refusal to sue *The Times* was seen as some sort of admission of guilt. There was an element of paranoia in a society where gossip by influential people was accepted as gospel.

Though I believed that there was a connection with the theme of *The Crucible*, it was with Salem in the seventeenth century and not Washington in the 1950s. McCarthy's witch-hunts against real or imaginary Communists had no moral basis; the fight against drug abuse in sport had. In addition sport had an equally strong duty to protect its participants from their often overwhelming passion for success, a passion that would tempt fate, even risk death, in its quest. If it needed just one incentive to take a tough stance against performance-enhancing drugs, the case of Birgit Dressel would be enough.

On Friday 10 April 1987, the West German heptathlon champion, twenty-six-year-old Dressel, died in the Intensive Care Ward of the Urological Hospital of Mainz University. For two days she had lived in considerable pain as almost twenty doctors and surgeons desperately tried to diagnose the cause of her illness and in so doing pumped into her a whole series of drugs that may have compounded her death; because, for years, Birgit had been swallowing, drinking and injecting drugs by the thousand. Many of these had, for the previous six years, been prescribed and administered by the so-called guru of West German sports medicine, Armin Klumper. In addition Dressel pumped and injected drugs into herself, including the anabolic agent, Megagrisevit, which, supposedly, arrived anonymously through the post. The truth was that Dressel, like most athletes, was not only addicted to success, she was also hooked on any drugs that she thought would get her to the top in her event.

In the February of the year she died Klumper noted that she was "an athlete who was capable of good performances, strong and of the greatest fitness". The subsequent investigation of her death revealed quite the contrary. The German magazine, *Der Spiegel*, reported that the joint medical-legal document on her death said: "... in truth a chronically sick young woman pumped full with hundreds of drugs. Sport had made a cripple of her long ago, and destroyed her joints, ruined her internal organs prematurely. In her search for such contradictory things as help and pain alleviation, increased performance and world records, the athlete became more and more dependent on doctors and drugs of all types, including 'doping drugs'." Birgit Dressel had died of a cocktail of drugs taken over many years, finally compounded to breaking-point by those applied by the doctors at the Mainz hospital. She had died, bewildered and in pain, from chasing a sporting excellence that her normal body could not attain.

The only person to suffer, Gwenda said, was Birgit Dressel. Her coach and boyfriend, Thomas Kohlbacher, and her doctor must have known what she was up to.

I agreed, but I reminded Gwenda that in the end the state attorney's office decided that there was insufficient evidence for prosecution. Birgit had been a free agent who had known of the dangers. This was where drug abuse in sport differed from drug abuse generally. In society the pushers and illegal importers of drugs are punished much more severely than the addicts; in sport, only the users incur penalties. In the world at large Jenks's was a rare case. He had thought that he could at last impress his father by becoming a millionaire, but there was little likelihood of doing that in the small vitamin business he had set up near San Diego, so he began illegally importing steroids from Tijuana in Mexico. He hadn't been very successful at that either; within months the authorities had begun to investigate him. Ironically he had been arrested just ten days after Dressel had died. I wondered if he had heard of her death and felt any qualm of conscience. There were those in Britain who, on hearing of Jenks's arrest, were demanding that an independent assessor take evidence from athletes on the extent of drug abuse here, because of Jenks's close connections with British athletes staying in California – David always threw open house to such people. Arthur Miller had known about that sort of thing; he called it "guilty of familiarity with the Unclean One", an offence in old Salem.

We talked about Ben Johnson, Charlie Francis and Jamie Astaphan and their appearances at the Dubin Enquiry. Ben had purged himself publicly and been duly rewarded – Judge Dubin criticised the Canadian government for their stance – they would not allow him back into international competition. The government relented and very promptly both Athletics Canada and the Canadian Olympic Association announced that they would select him, once his two years' suspension was up. Francis, smooth-talking and cocky, used the Dubin Enquiry to salve his conscience. He, the villain of the piece, a proven cheat and liar, became the star of the show. It was the Oliver North trial all over again, when the prosecuted becomes, in the public's mind, the prosecutor. He convinced many Canadians – eighty-two per cent if a television poll is to be believed – as he had convinced naive, shy Ben Johnson, a Jamaican emigrant to Toronto, that drugs had to be taken to achieve the sporting success that the public craved, because everybody else was taking them. Public confession in Salem was made before a handful of people; Francis adroitly appealed via television to millions.

Early in 1991 Ben Johnson returned to track and field and Charlie Francis bounced into Britain with a well-worn line in plausibility to be wooed, mostly with reverence, by the media.

It was a leaner Ben that faced the world and five other sprinters in an indoor 55 metres race in Hamilton, Canada in January. Gone was the intimidating, drug-induced upper body muscularity. The hype surrounding his return was immense, culminating in an hour-and-a-half programme on Canadian television for an event of less than six seconds' duration. The public welcomed him back with open arms, the redeemed sinner, the prodigal son. Only one man spoilt the occasion and that was the tall American, Darren Council, who won,

Back on the track. Ben Johnson (second left) in the second race after his comeback in 1991, in which he made a slow start and was beaten by Andre Cason of the US.

beating Ben into second place, a particularly inauspicious defeat because Council was not even a specialist indoor runner. Yet already, around the world, promoters were rushing with lucrative offers – he was, like Jesse James, the most wanted man in the west. Many were repelled by the unsavoury nature of it all, the unacceptable face of athletics' capitalism. I was repelled, not by Ben Johnson, who had served his time, but by those eager to cash in on his notoriety. Of his first three comeback races he won only one.

In February, Charlie Francis breezed into London to promote his book. The man was articulate and plausible and conducted over forty interviews in a week. Very rarely was the moral issue of drug-cheating discussed, always he managed to turn the conversation to the wider issues – national and international hypocrisy, drug-abuse in the GDR and the USA – on which he was on stronger ground. In the end, though, Francis, a self-confessed drug user as an athlete and as a coach, had debased his calling by inciting his athletes to embark on drug-taking. For this he has rightly been ostracised for life by Athletics Canada.

The fact that he was able to justify his acts to the world is an indictment of the international federation and some national federations whose fight against drug-abuse has been less than forthright and whose wholesale commitment has been lacking. "What is not realised", an IAAF official said to me, "is that the battle to convince my colleagues of the evil of drug abuse has been a long hard one." That said more about the problem than he could possibly have realised.

"So," said Gwenda, as we drank our coffee, still playing Devil's advocate, "you feel the penalties are tough enough."

They palpably are not, I said. Two years is not a deterrent, it is a penalty worth the risk. People look at Ben Johnson, about to finish his sentence and think, "Why, it doesn't seem any time at all since he was caught." And he doesn't miss the next World Championships or the Olympic Games. Only the Commonwealth has passed him by and for an athlete of his calibre that is hardly a penalty. There doesn't seem to be a collective will at international level to impose any stronger measures; the international administrators are so intent on giving the sinners a second chance that they have forgotten that they have a responsibility as well to the great majority who do not cheat. (Since our conversation, at the end of the year came further proof that the two-year ban is an insufficient deterrent with the positive tests and two-year banning of American world record holders Randy Barnes and Harry "Butch" Reynolds, who is currently involved in litigation with the TAC.)

Then was I in favour of our life ban for using steroids, Gwenda asked.

I said that it seemed to work, but that I worried that there was no room for redemption. Forgiveness of sins is a key element of most religions and yet we cannot take it upon ourselves to do so under any circumstances. In the Bible it says somewhere that joy shall be in heaven over one sinner that repenteth, more than over ninety and nine just persons, who have no need of repentance. Ben repented of his sins and for his pains had his world title and records taken away. In Britain we are stuck with what we have; we cannot go back now. But internationally the authorities must be realistic and a four-year ban, an Olympiad, would seem a fair penalty. It would take a dedicated athlete indeed to train for that sort of period without competing; it would be a proper purging of his or her soul and yet it could offer, for such a person, a chance of redemption.

We went down the steps to the car park and drove out. It was another clear, warm night of a brilliant summer, and the Embankment lights shimmered across the Thames. The night before I had been in Gateshead, where Britain had faced East Germany and Canada. The Canadian team had been very weak – they were still recovering from their traumas of 1988. Whilst we were there a small incident had occurred in the drug-testing room in which some wild and unfounded accusations were semi-publicly uttered. As we drove home a late-night radio sports bulletin spoke of further rumours of a million-dollar race between Ben Johnson and Carl Lewis, once the Canadian had served his time. The Bible had it wrong; the wages of sin were lucrative indeed. I sighed. We still had a long way to go.

19

THE GAME ISN'T OVER TILL THE FAT LADY SINGS

The continent's top athletic teams flew into Newcastle airport the day before the 1989 European Cup final. Out on the Sunderland Road in Gateshead, the finishing touches were being put to the International Stadium, about to enjoy its finest hours. The track had been inspired by Brendan Foster's running in the seventies and improvements encouraged by Steve Cram's brilliant achievements in the eighties. The winning of the bid the year before to stage the European Cup, ahead of Frankfurt, had encouraged the Council to make the stadium an all-seater, a show-piece for the area. Linford had said that this was his favourite stadium and many of us felt the same.

The Great Britain team were gathered at the Swallow Hotel, the closest to the track, and the athletes arrived from the Wednesday onwards. Expectations were high; we stood an outside chance of gaining a place in the first two in the competition, thereby earning a trip to Barcelona for the World Cup a few weeks later. The Soviet Union, we believed, would win the competition, but we could perhaps beat the East German men, if everything fell into place. Much depended on the performances of our field-event athletes, who had done so badly two years earlier in Prague. Crucial to the team's success would be the support of the crowd and so in the days leading up to the competition we urged, via the media, those who were coming to the meeting – it was sold out on both days – to bring Union Jacks and their voices and cheer us home. In the women's competition there were those who were deeply pessimistic, who forecast that we could finish last and be relegated; but they had not reckoned on the great changes that had taken place in overall standards because of the random drug-testing procedures now operating in Europe.

On the Saturday morning we held the team meeting and Frank Dick and Les Jones gave pep talks. Frank, especially, was at his very best, instilling in the team a belief that they could, as many of them put it, "go out and do the business". He recalled Stuttgart, and proved that in Seoul we had again emerged as Europe's top nation. As the athletes left the meeting there was none of the usual jocularity, but instead a steely determination in their eyes; already they were preparing mentally for the battle ahead.

The Princess Royal opened the meeting and as the teams entered the stadium each was greeted with enthusiastic applause. Then, marching on to the red synthetic track, last in line as befits the host nation, came Great Britain, the Union Jack to the fore, and a mighty crescendo of noise lifted from 12,000 throats. Gateshead had heard our pleas, they were going to yell the British athletes home.

In any major championship a good opening event is an essential requisite for subsequent success. It lifts morale, it throws down a challenge to the rest of the team to equal the performance. At Gateshead the first track event was the 400 metres hurdles. Kriss Akabusi had been injured for a good part of the year and his fight back to fitness had been protracted. On paper he was expected to finish third but no one, least of all Kriss, knew how much his injury had affected his competitive edge. The favourite was one of the greatest one-lap hurdlers of all time, the West German Harald Schmid, who for ten years had dominated the event in Europe, three times European champion and five times winner in the Cup.

Each competitor was introduced to the crowd and each received his due acknowledgement, Harald perhaps a little more than the rest. But when Kriss's name was announced, another mighty roar erupted, enough to bring a lump to the throats of the most cynical. Schmid led for the early part of the race but as it unfolded around the second bend it was apparent that Akabusi was pulling the German back, stride by stride. The crowd roared again, and rose to their feet to urge him on; he took the lead, crossed the final hurdle and won. It was a perfect start.

The next race was the 10,000 metres. This had occasioned some controversy before the meeting, when the British record holder Eamonn Martin, along with steeplechaser Mark Rowland, had declined selection, preferring to concentrate on the following weekend's AAA Championships, which were also the Commonwealth Games Trials. Tim Hutchings, a leading cross-country runner, had also performed well at Olympic and European level and he didn't let anybody down, finishing second to the outstanding Italian, Francesco Panetta. After two events Britain led Spain by five points, but most importantly, the GDR had had a disastrous start and were in last position with only six points.

In the field events Steve Backley, whose family roots were in the area – he had brought his grandfather to a pre-meeting Press conference – led in the javelin, Stewart Faulkner in the long jump and Dalton Grant in the high jump. This is what had been missing in previous European Cup bids, the field eventers matching the track men, point for point. Steve led from start to finish, a pattern he was to follow in competitions over the next year, and Dalton was ... well, Dalton. He had an initial failure at 2.20 metres but then went on to match Europe's best and win with a British record of 2.32. No British high-jumper had finished higher than sixth in previous Cup competitions. Stewart slipped to third in the long jump but still gained valuable points.

Linford stepped forward to his marks, confident that he would be the first man to win a European Cup 100 metres for a second time, and he did, ahead of the Frenchman, Sangouma. Now Britain had scored four wins in seven events and were seven points ahead of the Soviet Union and an extraordinary fourteen in front of the GDR. The whole stadium was buzzing with excitement and so were the team who were round the events urging and cheering each other on. British athletics had never seen anything like it. But now a curious fear gripped everybody: surely this couldn't hold? Surely something would go wrong? The momentum slackened a little as Brian Whittle in the 400 metres and Tony Morrell in the 1500 metres both ran fifth, but even in those events the Russians and the East Germans did not gain many points and we came to the final event of the first day, the sprint relay, still well ahead. We remembered the same race in Prague, two years previously, when a bad change-over had led to Britain's disqualification; but this was a different quartet and an inspired run by Linford on the last leg overhauled the Frenchman, Marie-Rose. No team had ever run faster in Britain and it was another initial Cup win for us. At the end of the first day Britain led the Soviets by eleven points and the GDR by thirteen!

The European Cup is like a decathlon, where there are strengths and weak-nesses, and when we gathered again for a meeting on the Sunday morning it was with the knowledge that the first day had been our strongest and that on the second the Russians and East Germans would come through. Gwenda and I went out early and bought every newspaper in sight. Sometimes you curse the tabloids when they go over the top but on this occasion nobody minded. Huge banner headlines like "YOU BEAUTS!" and "GREAT BRITS!" shifted all other sports out of sight. We pinned them up on a notice-board just to let every-one know how the country felt.

Les and Frank began the meeting by congratulating the women's team who had confounded all their critics by finishing third on the opening day, behind the Soviet Union and the GDR. Though no British athlete had won, four of them – Paula Dunn, Sally Gunnell, Linda Keough and Yvonne Murray – had finished second. Fears of relegation had fast receded. Now they had to hold on to equal their best-ever showing. Frank analysed the men's match. It was going to be a strong day for the Soviet Union and to a lesser extent the GDR. We were eleven points ahead, but a couple of disasters could soon erode that lead. Every point, in every event, must be fought for. If a pole-vaulter or hammer-thrower or triple-jumper could gain an unexpected place, that would be a bonus.

"So if you're lying seventh and can get to sixth, fight hard for it," Frank said. "That point is just as vital as those gained by the track guys. Everyone must perform to their best. The World Cup in Barcelona is the prize." He took off his spectacles and gazed at the group. "Remember," he said, "the game isn't over till the fat lady sings."

Frank was referring to an American adage arising from baseball. At the end of every game a superbly built mezzo-soprano comes into the arena and sings *God Bless America*. The implication was clear.

Afterwards we chatted about what would happen if everything was down to the final event, the 4 × 400 metres relay. There was jocular speculation that we might have a shit-or-bust selection and throw in John Regis and Linford Christie. John, who had run a few one-lap races in his time, looked philosophical but Linford, to whom the distance seemed like a marathon, looked appalled and his leg was pulled for quite a time, until the team dispersed to their own pre-event thoughts.

The stadium was again alive with excitement and anticipation when we arrived. The day was overcast but, for Gateshead, not at all cold. The first event was the hammer and the point Frank had made that morning was emphasised. Astapkovich of the Soviet Union unexpectedly lost the event to the West German Weis and the British thrower, Shane Peacock, went close to his best and came sixth, one position higher than we had forecast. Then came three wins in a row for Britain, which set the crowd roaring once more. Colin Jackson ran a steady, taking-no-chances hurdles and Tom McKean ran faultlessly to win his third European Cup 800 metres. He came off the track, his arms spread wide.

"Where were they?" he said excitedly to me as he came in from the finish. "It was so easy."

The pressure was mounting on our track athletes, not from other countries but from their team-mates. As each win went by, an intense feeling rose within the remainder that they weren't going to be the one to let the team down. So it was with John Regis, who hit the straight first; the roars of his fellow athletes and the crowd, hundreds of whom rose to their feet waving their programmes, seemed to almost physically carry him to the finish line.

"There was no way," John said later, "that anyone was going to pass me."

Normally athletes are unaware of crowd noises. They put it out of their minds as a distraction, but the tumultuous cheering of these days broke through to give an emotional touch to their determination. Now we were seventeen points ahead of the Soviets and twenty-one ahead of the East Germans, but still fearing a disaster that would bring our edifice crumbling down. In the steeplechase Tom Hanlon ran fourth, behind the GDR man and ahead of the Soviet. Nineteen points ahead. Now the Russians came with a rush, winning the pole vault and the triple jump and finishing second in the discus. In the 5000 metres one clear decision was made. A GDR gamble with Kunze, who had won ten years previously, failed and he trailed in seventh. Jack Buckner came in second to the brilliant Italian Antibo, with the Russian, Dasko, third. The GDR could not catch us – we would be going to Barcelona! But the Soviet Union, through their brilliant field-event athletes, had narrowed the gap to just one point, with the relay to go.

"Hey," Les Jones says suddenly, "we could win this thing."

"It's looking possible," I say cautiously.

"We need a captain," Les says. We look at each other; there is only one man.

We move to the walkway above the competitors' enclosure, where all the team have gathered. Linford is sitting in the front row. I shout his name, he turns round and both Les and I wave him up. He looks mightily suspicious, remembering what had been said about the relay in the morning. One point in it; it is shit-or-bust. He comes slowly up the steps and looks warily at us.

"Linford," says Les, "if we win this cup we'd like you to go up and collect it." His face loses its suspicious look and is wreathed in smiles.

"Thank you," he says, and goes back down for one more shout. A lot of the team are quite hoarse. But this really is the moment of truth.

In the warm-up area the relay squads gathered together. Frank talked quietly to our quartet; Igor Ter-Ovanesyan, the former world record holder for the long jump and now chief Soviet coach, was in a huddle with his men. Britain had a fine international record in the 4 × 400 metres. We had won Olympic and world silver medals and were the current European champions from Stuttgart, but in Seoul our star had waned. The squads marched into the arena, past the competitors' enclosure. All the team rose to their feet, shouting encouragement. "Go boys!" "Let's go, Kriss!" "Peter!" "Todd!" The four runners stirred not an eyelid, their concentration complete. If they ran well, Great Britain would make history; *they* could make history.

Peter Crampton, the European Junior champion of the year before, ran the opening leg. At the end he was down on the leaders but that didn't really matter, for he was three metres clear of the Soviet runner. Then Kriss Akabusi called upon his vast experience and speed to put us into contention. We moved to fourth. The Soviets were still trailing, the crowd noise, once more, rising.

A glorious moment for British athletics: Linford Christie collects the Bruno Zauli Cup after the Great Britain team overcame twenty-five years of GDR and Soviet domination with a superb victory.

Todd Bennett ran a magnificent leg, took us up level with the Spaniards and West Germans and handed the baton over to Brian Whittle; the Soviets were trailing badly – they were out of the race. We had won the European Cup! Les Jones and I were dancing a jig of joy when a voice yelled: "Look at this!" We turned. The battle was really on at the head of the race; Ralf Lubke the German and Whittle the Scotsman, the spikeless hero of Stuttgart, locked together. The crowd noise was worthy of a measurement on the Richter scale; people in Sunderland, it was later said, looked fearful. Whittle struck at the beginning of the finishing straight and, like John Regis, would not be passed. People were literally screaming. Whittle won, threw the baton in the air, and his team-mates embraced him. The applause went on for minutes, while we all hugged and danced together. It was the most glorious moment in British athletics history – if *Boy's Own Paper* had written it, no one would have believed it.

It took a very long time to clear the stadium. The closing ceremony, the hundredth mighty roar of the weekend as Linford went up to collect the Bruno Zauli Cup, the laps of honour where the whole team, men and women, management, coaches, physiotherapists, doctors joined in and returned the applause to the crowd, all passed. Then people just milled about, wanting to savour the moments, to wave to any British athlete that they saw.

At the hotel the champagne flowed. The women's team had finished third, equalling their best-ever achievement in the competition. Short speeches were made and finally Linford spoke. He singled out for praise those who had also served – the pole-vaulter, Michael Edwards; the hammer-thrower, Shane Peacock; the triple-jumper, Vernon Samuels, all of whom had earned valuable points to keep us ahead. In such an individual sport as track and field athletics the team spirit generated that weekend in Gateshead was extraordinary. On the Friday morning they had assembled as twenty or thirty individuals, often highly competitive amongst themselves; by the Sunday evening, they had fought for and cheered and urged each other until they had gelled together as a unit, the Great Britain team. They had achieved something that had begun to appear impossible; they had broken the twenty-five-year hegemony of the GDR and Soviet Union in the European Cup.

One week later we gathered in Birmingham for the national championships, which were also the England trials for the Commonwealth Games to be held in Auckland, New Zealand, the following January. Neither Cram nor Elliott was fit enough to take part, but Sebastian Coe, now free from injury, had decided to run his last championship and try for selection. Also entered was Steve Ovett and some of the media became a little excited at the prospect of Coe and Ovett finally meeting on British soil. As far as I was concerned such a clash was at least nine years too late. They had skilfully avoided each other around the big meetings in Europe, presumably for marketing purposes, and whilst they might have gained individually from such a situation the sport itself had suffered. More frequent races between the two in the early eighties would, I was sure, have reduced the world mile record considerably and I do not believe that one of them would have been the sole victor in such a series.

The fact was that anno Domini had caught up with Steve and he was now in no shape to match Coe, nor quite a few others entered in the 1500 metres. To many it was a tragedy to see him running so much below his best, a shadow of the superb runner of the late seventies and early eighties. But he loved running, it was his life, and to keep on competing was his prerogative. There had been talk of the two meeting in the final event of the season, at Crystal Palace, definitely Seb's last run in Britain before he entered the political arena, but again to have them both battling it out around the final bend would have meant a considerable diminution of the standard of the rest of the field. Still, newspapers never let facts like these get in the way of a good story and in the days leading up to the Championships the tabloids made a fuss, ignoring the fact that one or both might not reach the final. The heats were on the Friday night and both did make it through.

The three-day meeting went smoothly. During the early Sunday afternoon, whilst I was having a quick lunch in the Kodak hospitality tent, Stuart McConochie and Richard Worth of ITV hurried past, clearly very agitated.

"What the hell is going on?" I heard Stuart say.

What was going on was that at that moment Steve Ovett was holed up in a room at the Post House hotel, some two miles north of the stadium, refusing to run in the 1500 metres final. McConochie's concern and interest was that Ovett was part of the ITV commentary team, when he wasn't running. Officers of the sport were hurrying to the hotel to try and sort the problem out. A major scandal was brewing yet again for British athletics, just one week after its greatest moment in Gateshead. With hindsight it was easy to see that there had been a problem from early that morning. In the lobby of the Holiday Inn I had wished Steve good luck for the afternoon and he had given me a rather gaunt look and said nothing. He had already made his mind up not to compete and hinted as much to two journalists, Colin Hart of the *Sun* and Neil Wilson of the *Independent*. The problem, in his mind, was money.

It had been the policy of the Joint Standing Committee, a group that handled the televised promotional events for the sport, that no subvention payments should be made for the AAA Championships. If athletes wanted to go to Auckland, they had to compete, so a financial incentive was not required. Steve was now saying that Andy Norman had offered him a considerable sum to run in the Championships and that he had discovered, just a couple of days beforehand, that Seb Coe had not been offered any payment. Steve said that he

A distressed Steve Ovett tells his story to a strained Jim Rosenthal.

was shocked and distressed by this and during the time they were in Birmingham had approached Seb on a number of occasions to discuss the matter. Seb, embarrassed, told him that it really didn't matter and suggested that Steve really ought to be thinking more about the race. Steve was clearly in no mental condition to do so.

Negotiations at the hotel persuaded Steve Ovett that he ought to run. He returned to the stadium but was clearly in a distraught state. Some who saw him thought that he might have been close to a breakdown. Rachel too was distracted. Andy Norman maintained that no negotiations had taken place and that no money had been offered. The media were now wise to what was going on and the Championships were building to a sensational climax. The race itself was also dramatic, though Ovett played no real part in it. Coming down the home straight for the penultimate time, with the field clustered together, Steve Crabb was tripped and crashed to the ground, immediately in front of Seb Coe. Coe leapt into the air and somehow managed to hurdle the fallen Crabb and maintain his balance. By the time he had landed the rest of the field were away, led by Tony Morrell. Seb set off in pursuit and with immaculate pace-judgement overhauled the leaders and sprinted home to win. It was, in the circumstances, one of his greatest-ever runs. Ovett trailed in at the back of the field.

I stood in the Press room at the Alexander Stadium, waiting to make a statement concerning the Ovett allegations, which were now widely known. A large television attached to a wall bracket displayed the ITV coverage. On screen came Steve Ovett, being interviewed by Jim Rosenthal. He was clearly in a distressed state, telling Jim that he had been misused, and then he began to cry. Between sobs the story came out. It was a long, painful business and, in my estimation, ITV should have cut short the transmission, not because it might have damaged the sport but because it was damaging the reputation of one of our greatest-ever athletes and one of their commentators. Everyone in the Press room was stunned. One might have expected a babble of noise and questions but there was silence. Nobody could believe what they were seeing and hearing. Andy came on and denied that any money had been offered to anybody, and that closed down the television coverage of the 1989 AAA Championships.

A week of intense media activity began. It was August, the silly season for news, and Ovett crying his heart out on television became a big story. The *Insight* team from the *Sunday Times* began a lengthy investigation, to be published the following weekend. Until the Monday morning the remarks that I had made on behalf of the sport had been circumspect and no direct attack was made upon Steve. However, on his return to Scotland he widened his criticism to include the whole sport and so a vigorous reply was needed. I went to the Howard Hotel at 11 a.m. for a Junior Commission Press Conference and was unable to leave until 4 p.m., such was the intensity of the calls. I went to ITN to make a direct riposte to Steve's remarks. Many people found it amazing that Steve was angry and distressed, not about the fact that he had been offered money, but that Seb Coe hadn't. To those who had known Steve over the years this seemed totally out of character. Seb himself was completely mystified. And yet Steve's breakdown appeared absolutely genuine.

Then the details came out and made the whole affair bewildering to those of us closely involved. Steve alleged that Andy had telephoned him making him an offer that he couldn't refuse – £20,000 to run at the Championships against Seb. He said that he had phoned him at the time of the Tuesday Press conference before the meeting. I was at that conference and I was convinced – still am convinced – that Andy could not have telephoned Steve Ovett at that time or at any time surrounding that particular gathering at the Mountbatten Hotel in Bloomsbury. And such an offer presupposed that both athletes would reach the final – in Steve's case quite a presupposition.

The AAA set up a two-man Committee of Enquiry – David Pickup, the Director General of the Sports Council, and Robert Reid QC. It reported early in 1990. Though the evidence read like an Agatha Christie novel there was no denouement. It was, in the end, one man's word against another's. The circumstantial evidence was almost equal. There was animosity between the two men, who had at one time been so close. Steve had dropped Andy, but there was nothing new in that; famous athletes were always dropping close friends and acquaintances for the most whimsical of reasons. It was supposed to be part of their genius. Many too thought it amazing that Ovett, so long reclusive with regard to the media, should go rushing to them with this particular story. On the other hand Andy Norman was a wheeler-dealer, and the language that Ovett said his caller had used was vintage Norman. Yet again, where would Andy have got £20,000? Prior to the Crystal Palace Grand Prix meeting he had had a considerable sum stolen from his hotel room, and this added to the speculation.

So the arguments went on. I liked best of all the comments of the former Olympic bronze medallist, Ian Stewart, who became involved with the world of professional cycling upon his retirement from athletics. He couldn't understand what all the fuss was about, he said. Ovett and athletics were making themselves look silly. It was now a professional sport, no matter what contortions it got itself into to prove otherwise. In a professional sport if you are offered £20,000, well, good luck to you. If someone else is willing to run for nothing, then that's his affair. After becoming a wealthy man on the back of athletics it was a bit late to start taking the high moral stance. During the week following the Championships all the anti-Norman brigade came out of the woodwork. Disgruntled athletes and agents, rival promoters, all pontificated. The whole affair was a sordid business in which the only loser was athletics. And the truth? Well, unless there is a death-bed confession, we shall never know.

To most of the athletics circus that arrived there, Barcelona was the same as any other venue – an airport, a hotel and a stadium. But to one member of our party it was also a seedy night-club. The team was strengthened by the inclusion of Sebastian Coe, who seemed genuinely delighted to be part of the international squad again. All the Gateshead heroes had been invited to the World Cup, though not all would compete. Vernon Samuels was replaced in the triple jump by Jonathan Edwards, who had not competed in the European competition on religious grounds because his event was on a Sunday. But, as in Gateshead, the reserves were a vital part of the team in such a competition. They warmed up with the main competitor and then as he left for his event, warmed down again. The reserves for the middle distances did it two or three times, but it was necessary in case of a late injury.

We had flown in with a problem. The pole-vaulter, Michael Edwards, who had done his duty at Gateshead solely by clearing the opening height and earning one point, had arrived injured. He had failed to inform the team management, as every international is instructed to do. For some years now, pole-vaulting has been at a low ebb in Britain. Foreign competitors despair when they come here – waiting for hours whilst our competitors struggle through lowly heights. Sometimes it takes two hours before they can enter the competition. It has not always been so – ten years ago Brian Hooper and Keith Stock were taking British vaulting to international respectability. Edwards did not give much hope for the future. His mental attitude, more that of soccer hooligan than an international athlete, was not conducive to giving Sergey Bubka sleepless nights. When we arrived at our hotel in Barcelona he was examined by the medical team; in their opinion he was unfit to vault and if he attempted to do so, his hamstring could sustain further serious damage. Edwards refused to accept this verdict, and became abusive to Les Jones, making threatening gestures of a head-butting nature. The team management withdrew him from the competition and sent urgent messages back to Britain to contact Andy Ashurst, the Commonwealth champion, asking him to fly out immediately. At the start of the competition the next day Edwards, accompanied by his veteran pole-vaulting father, a man of equally temperamental tendencies, rushed to the warm-up area to indicate to the media, to whom he had aired his grievances, that he was fit. He ran down the runway to vault and his hamstring went. He was carried into the physiotherapists, who began treating him, a very magnanimous gesture in the circumstances.

Later it transpired that Edwards had visited one of Barcelona's less reputable night-time establishments and performed acts on stage which, according to the British Press present, might have caused more permanent muscular damage in another area. For this and his conduct towards the team management he was dropped from the Commonwealth Games team. The Press, on that night, displayed a very commendable restraint, agreeing among themselves not to use the story, which could have been very damaging to the team's morale. In 1990 Edwards returned, less aggressive but still twitchy, and vaulted again for Britain.

The opening day of the World Cup was dominated by the "Freedom of Catalonia" movement and violent thunderstorms. As our coach took us up the long, winding road to the peak of a hill, on which the Montjuic Olympic Stadium stands, our heartfelt sympathies were already going out to the men and women marathon runners who would be making this ascent at the Olympics in 1992. It had been decreed that the races would end in the stadium – solely, I suspect, for reasons of protocol. It was such protocol that delayed the start of the 1989 World Cup. As the black thunderclouds gathered over the peaks of the Pyrenees just to the north, the arrival of King Carlos, who would perform the opening ceremony, had already been delayed. There was fervent Catalonian nationalism evident in the stadium and one wondered if the delay was in direct proportion to the intensity of feeling in the crowd. The least-considered people, as so often, were the athletes, who had to huddle together and warm up in the synthetic area beneath the stands. In the end, the programme on the first day finished two hours behind schedule.

Kriss Akabusi again opened well for Britain, finishing third in the 400 metres hurdles, behind Patrick of the USA and Amike of Africa. Of the nine competing nations four were from individual countries – Spain, the hosts, the USA, the German Democratic Republic (replacing the Soviet Union, who had lost their second place gained at Gateshead through their shot-putter failing a drug test) and ourselves. The rest were from continents. Two more track wins followed, both in lashing rain. The first was by Tom McKean, who again ran an impeccable race to beat Herold and Kiprotich. The change in demeanour in Tom since his marriage had been extraordinary; gone was the slightly oafish behaviour of Rome and Seoul, replaced by charm and wit. He was now some-one it was a delight to be with. The second win came from Linford, who though injured earlier in the year, was now coming into top form. He effectively beat the new United States hope, Leroy Burrell, and the Frenchman Sangouma, running for Europe. The first of many injuries to afflict the team over the weekend came in the 10,000 metres when Tim Hutchings had to withdraw and Gary Staines, the reserve, was drafted in. But Staines, an asthmatic, had an attack during the race and slowly drifted back to eighth place. It was a very brave run by Gary and he had finished ahead of the GDR runner, Wessel. At the end of the first day, Britain lay fourth behind the USA, Europe and Africa but ahead of the GDR. Our ambition was to be the second-best nation at the competition, behind the USA.

Brian Whittle came down to breakfast on the second morning looking as if he had battled ten rounds with Mike Tyson the night before. The Scottish 400-metre runner's nose was heavily bandaged. Ten days before, his young daughter had accidentally clouted him with a baseball bat while they were playing together. During the night it had started bleeding profusely and here he was, *hors de combat*. We drafted in Derek Redmond, who had been injured for two years, in a massive gamble that did not come off. He finished last.

Seb Coe was due to meet Abdi Bile, the world champion, who had been showing excellent form around Europe. Seb had been obliging, friendly and co-operative throughout the trip, holding Press conferences, patiently giving interviews to the media. The controversy of the previous year had, seemingly, been forgotten. At his Press conference I said that "the old lion had roared effectively again". I felt it was the least that I could say. We had chatted a little about the AAAs and I had said how angry I was that his truly great run there had been overshadowed by his old rival's behaviour. Seb shrugged his shoulders; his career had had too many ups and downs for him to worry too much about that. We talked about his retirement and how important it was to know when to go. He agreed. Of Ovett he said: "I wish that I had been closer to him, known him better, so that I could have told him, in 1986, that that was the time to go." Brendan Foster had said something similar. It was important, he felt, that the book close naturally.

Now Seb faced Bile. The race was controversial. As the field came off the final bend and Seb was starting to wind it up, Bile nudged him. Seb was thrown off stride and lost momentum. Bile went on to win. The arguments then raged – Peter Coe wanted us to protest, Seb did not. I had to scour the stadium for Ewan Murray, then BAAB Chairman. There was a mêlée of Pressmen behind the wire fence that separated their area from the official one. They seemed divided in their opinions but wanted to know what was going on.

I ask the BBC if I can see a replay of the race so that I can report back to Les, Frank and Ewan. I climb up and into one of the great transmission vans parked just outside the stadium. About twenty screens on one side of the interior show all the action. David Coleman's commentary can be heard. In Britain it is about three minutes before the nine o'clock news.

"Well," I hear David say, "we still haven't heard about the protest. Tony Ward is watching the replay on one of our videos now." Then he goes on to describe what is occurring in the stadium. I watch the replay. Seb, it seems to me, is definitely impeded by Bile. I mutter my opinion to someone on my right but clearly a microphone linked to the commentary point is near at hand.

Tom McKean, who achieved his win in Barcelona by running an impeccable race in lashing rain.

"We've just heard," I hear David say, "that Tony Ward says that Seb was definitely impeded and that there will be a protest." Oh, my God, I think and put out a hand in protest. Too late. "So that's the news as we say goodnight from Barcelona!"

In the end we did protest, but to no avail, though we understood that the decision of the three-man jury of appeal was not unanimous. The problem of cynical pushing and shoving, especially in slow-run races, was increasing and firm action by the IAAF was needed to combat it. It was not forthcoming this time.

On the third day the rain lashed Barcelona again; the thunder rolled and the lightning flashed around Montjuic. The events were postponed and the stadium, newly refurbished, leaked everywhere. At one time it looked as if the meeting would have to be abandoned, a tragic end to a fine competition. We stood and watched as the track flooded and the rain looked like silver stair-rods under the floodlights. A joker suddenly appeared and started running down the track over the hurdles; finally he crashed in a great shower of water, and was taken away. For a moment it alleviated the gloom. A rumour began that the event would continue, but with a limited programme, but Frank was adamant that this could not be so, since it would not ensure a fair result. Two of the events likely to be cancelled would be the hurdles and javelin, where we could score highly. A meeting of team managers and coaches decided that the full programme must be staged and as if in answer, the weather eased, a full moon shone and we could get down to the business that had brought us to Barcelona.

Colin Jackson ran a sub-thirteen seconds 110 metres hurdles, just behind his great rival, the double Olympic champion Roger Kingdom. The times were wind-assisted but on the very wet track it was a tremendous effort by the likeable Welshman and earned us seven points. We had another injury blow in the 200 metres when John Regis had to pull out. He was substituted by Marcus Adam who ran fifth. Our task now was to overhaul the East Germans, who had had a magnificent second day. We had succeeded in the preceding events and Jack Buckner kept ahead of Pflunger in the 5000 metres. Much now depended on the javelin and high jump.

Steve Backley threw 85.90 metres on his first attempt, effectively killing the competition. Much interest from the British contingent now centred on how well the GDR thrower, Hadwich, would do. In fact he did very well, coming third, so Steve's win only gained us a couple of points. The high jump was now a nail-biting competition; Dalton Grant versus Sjoberg, the Swede, the Cuban Sotomeyer and Wessig of the GDR, men who had all jumped higher than he. On the night he was magnificent, considering that the competition had been delayed three hours and the apron was soaking wet. I could hardly look as he attempted each height but at the close only Patrik Sjoberg finished ahead of him. Wessig finished fourth equal. We had overtaken the East

Seb Coe's last great run, in the World Cup 1500 metres in 1989, was marred by a clash with the eventual winner, Abdi Bile.

Phil Brown awaits the baton for the amazing run he will remember for the rest of his life.

Germans, but which team would seize the third spot, behind the USA and Europe, would depend on the last event of the night, the 4 × 400 metres relay. To overtake us the GDR had to finish two places ahead in the race. Our team was not at its strongest. Redmond had finished last in the individual 400 metres, Akabusi and Bennett would form a solid middle duet and on the anchor leg was Phil Brown, a man who had run some heroic races for Britain, gaining gold and silver medals all over the world in the eighties; but this year he was far from his best.

Derek struggled over the first leg and Kriss and Todd kept us in contention with the GDR. We had done well; Carlowitz, the runner-up in the individual event was in the GDR team and now on the final leg for them was Thomas Schonlebe, the world champion. Our hearts sank as he shot past Phil and then another athlete, putting the requisite two places between them. Coming round the final bend that is how it was, Schonlebe looking good, Phil seemingly making no impression. In the area near the finish the GDR managers and coaches began to celebrate. Les and I looked at each other and grimaced in disappointment, but all of us were being premature. An excited shout came from the BBC's Paul Dickenson. "Look at Phil!" he cried.

We looked at the television monitor. Schonlebe was dying and on the inside came Phil, easing his way through, running on memory, a touch of the old magic, past Europe, past the GDR and into the safe sanctuary of fourth place at the line. We had done it! Third team overall behind the USA and Europe but ahead of the GDR, the Americas, Africa, Oceania, Asia and Spain. Officially the second-strongest nation in the world. I don't think that Phil knows where that run came from. He had always been a different runner with a baton in his hand, but this was truly special. Such form has not been seen from him for years since and yet from deep down he had produced a run that he will remember for the rest of his life. And so will a lot of other people.

20

HAPPY EVER AFTER

Zola Budd met Mike Pieterse, a Bloemfontein liquor-store owner, on her return to South Africa and following a whirlwind courtship they were engaged within six months. The wedding was in April 1989. Pieterse's father gave her away. She had wanted her brother Quintus to do it but Frank Budd threatened to disinherit him if he did. The animosity that had totally split the family was, dispiritingly, continuing as Frank publicly attacked his daughter. "I no longer have a daughter called Zola," he said. "To me she's dead and I curse her." So Tossie, her son Quintus and her elder daughters Estelle and Cara gathered in Bloemfontein's Universitas Ned Geref Church to watch the youngest marry. The service, the speeches and conversation at the reception were all in Afrikaans.

In September Quintus received a telephone call from Mary Anderson, a farmhouse owner who was hoping to marry Frank Budd. She said that Frank, who lived in a tin-roofed stone outhouse on her estate, had gone missing. His *bakkie* (truck) was not there and his dogs locked inside the house were howling. Quintus rushed to the farm and kicked down the door. Inside he found Frank's blood-spattered body covered by a blanket. He had been shot and battered about the head. A few days later, an Afrikaans-speaking man, Christiaan Johannes Botha Barnard, who had been staying with Frank, was arrested for his murder.

At his trial in February 1990, Barnard told the court that Budd, for whom he was carrying out building work, had made sexual advances towards him whilst he was in the bath. Later Budd had said to him: "I want sex with you now," and made highly insulting remarks about his girlfriend. Barnard, enraged, grabbed hold of a shotgun and shot him twice at close quarters, hitting him about the head with the butt for good measure. Then he had driven off in the *bakkie*. The police had traced him through the truck.

Now the story of Frank Budd's homosexuality emerged. Hans van der Knokke, who had worked for Budd for seven years, said that he had known that he was homosexual from the first day he had met him in 1970 and others came forward to the court to testify that Frank had made sexual advances towards them. Zola confirmed, in a Press interview, that she knew of her father's homosexual proclivities. Christiaan Barnard was sent to prison for twelve years. It was a macabre ending to a bizarre story. The man who had dreamt of taking tea with the Queen had ended up a crumpled, bloodied corpse only a few miles from where the story had begun.

Zola began training and racing again in South Africa. She ran second in the 1990 South African 1500 metres championship in Port Elizabeth. Her best time was a modest 4:12.91. But in February 1991 she ran 8:42.27 for 3000 metres, a time that would have ranked third in the world the previous year. During the year there were signs that South African sport might be slowly returning to the international fold and there was speculation that the country might return to compete in the 1996 Olympic Games, or even, given the pace of change, well before.

It is possible, then, that Zola Budd-Pieterse might still fulfil the prophecy of John Bryant and run an Olympic marathon. If she competes in Atlanta in 1996 there are many who will feel, given Georgia's racist history, that that would be the greatest irony of all.

21

SPLIT: THE FINAL FRONTIER

As Steve Backley stood in the rain on the far side of the track, facing the javelin runway, its surface glistening under the floodlights, a number of people sitting around the stadium thought back over the years, almost to the very beginning of this great era in British athletics. Joan Allison, the women's team manager, sat in the stand; her mind returned to 1980, when she had taken the junior distance runners for training at her club, Cambridge Harriers. Amongst them was this very keen eleven-year-old with the slightly over-enthusiastic policeman father, himself a distance runner. The young Steve had shown a lot of talent despite being run over two years earlier, whilst out running in the rain in Bexley, where he lived. He had gone to Sidcup General and in his training diary, which he kept religiously, he had written: "Went for a run along Hurst Road and was knocked over by a car. Taken to hospital and spent 3½ hours in the theatre." Beside it some wag had written, "And didn't see a thing." He trained most days then, in all weathers. 1980 was the year he went back to hospital to have his pins removed.

Also in the stand, amongst the great crowd of British supporters, sat Steve's mother and father. They seemed a century rather than a decade away, those days when Steve pounded out the miles around the roads and parks near their home. He had run everything, from sprints to cross-country, in all weathers. John smiled when he recalled Steve arriving at the finish of a cross-country race at Parliament Hill, on a freezing day, wet and cold from the snow on the ground, crying his eyes out. He had lost his way, the thirteen-year-old, and it may have been then that his son's enthusiasm for distance running began to wane and John's ambitions of producing another Coe, Ovett or Foster had to fade as well. Steve had taken up karate and become a green belt and his father had wondered if he was going to be lost to athletics completely. Had he been over-enthusiastic with the boy? Well, it didn't matter now.

In the VIP section, Fatima Whitbread sat with Andy Norman. They

The young Steve Backley showed a talent for distance running, but the track's loss was the field's gain.

remembered 1983, when John Backley had telephoned Andy and asked his advice. Steve, he said, had substituted in the javelin in a Young Athletes League match, and had thrown it thirty-two metres. Clearly there was some talent there – could Andy help? Andy suggested that they drive through the Dartford Tunnel to Thurrock, where Fatima, along with Margaret, would be delighted to give them some tips. Four months later, when the family were on their annual trip north to visit his Nan and Grandad, he had thrown forty-six metres. A world record holder had been born.

It had almost ended before it had begun. David Cobb and his wife Madeline sat glued to the live BBC transmission in their home in Middlesex. She had been an Olympic sprinter, he a javelin coach who had helped and advised the Backleys in those early days. Steve had broken his elbow in a competition at Woking, which had put him out of action for months, not only from athletics but from karate as well. When he returned he could hardly throw twenty metres and there was a certain amount of despair. Steve had thought that he would be no good now that he had broken his elbow. But he had persevered and just beaten, by a metre or so, his best of the previous year.

Gary Jensen was trying to shelter from the rain in the open stand. He had been eliminated in the qualifying round but now he was here to support Steve and Mick Hill. He was twenty-three, two years older than Steve, and had preceded him through the junior ranks, a promising talent, silver medallist at the World Junior Championships in 1985. But Steve had overtaken him two years later and had never looked back.

In 1987 he had won the European Junior Championship and made his breakthrough. It was an important year; he had grown a lot, and from a technical viewpoint his good technique could be grafted on to longer levers. It was the year he had first met his coach, John Trower. John sat and watched anxiously. The expectations were high from everyone and that created greater pressure. It had been at Gateshead on a Junior Commission weekend that he had first worked with Steve and found that he was an easy learner who knew how to recognise the basics of the event, what was fundamentally important. They worked hard together that winter but the following year had been disappointing. Steve had set a world record but had been too confident at the World Junior Championships at Sudbury in Canada, and had let the bad organisation and confusion in the event get to him. He had led from the first round to the fifth and then a Russian thrower, Ovchinnikov, had gone two metres ahead and he could not respond. It had been a useful lesson. On his return Mick Hill was chosen ahead of him for the Olympic Games.

Mick sat alongside the runway as the rain poured down, just about protected by the small canvas tents. He was glad to be there; it had been a long road back from injury. He wondered if Steve would follow the usual pattern of the last two seasons with a long, challenging throw in the first round. Mick had been British number one right up until 1988 and the record holder. Then in 1989 Steve had come into his own, annexing Hill's British record, winning the World Student Games, the European Cup and World Cup. In all three he had reacted well to pressure, amazing for such a young man. Then Steve had won the Commonwealth title and earlier this summer had exchanged world records with the Czech, Zelezny.

Neil Horsfield watched and was glad he wasn't running at that moment. At the Crystal Palace, at the Grand Prix meeting in July, he had won his first major 1500 metres, beating a world-class field, and hardly anybody noticed. At a crucial point in the race, Steve had unleashed a mighty throw, the first over 90 metres, for a new world record. Who cared who won the track race? Some said that that moment marked the real end of the middle-distance domination of British athletics.

Steve raised the javelin above his shoulder, collecting his thoughts and energies to concentrate them on the great effort that would come at the end of the runway. His father suddenly remembered the trees in the park near their home, which had been their targets during the dark nights of winter when their efforts had been lit by the adjacent street lamps; he remembered the times he had climbed the trees to retrieve the javelins or pulled them from the trunks. He recalled the telephone calls to Cantabrian, the sports manufacturers, for shop-soiled javelins and the time he had been told that a Sandvik javelin would cost £220 and the family had pooled their resources and driven to Cambridge to find it was actually £250. The company had been generous that day. It had been a long haul, with plenty of toil, plenty of laughs and most of all, plenty of love.

Steve ran down the runway and unleashed the javelin. It sailed out over the green inner field, a shining silver dart in the floodlights. It landed well beyond 80 metres. Nobody was to better the throw, except Steve himself in the final round. He was the European champion.

We had flown into Split the previous Thursday on a Yugoslavian airlines Boeing, swinging in off the blue Adriatic for a smooth landing on the sunlit runway. The atmosphere was relaxed and easy but with underlying anxieties, for there were great expectations for the British team. This was the essential difference from Stuttgart; there the success had been quite unexpected; here, in Split, it was almost pre-ordained by the media. I felt that we were similar to the NASA technicians in Houston. Until the space capsule started to rise there was always the chance that there would be an embarrassing and very public flop. We were there as European champions. Three of the 1986 winners would be defending their titles. Seven of the European Cup winners were ready to

Yes, it's all there in black and white!

consolidate their position. The biggest danger lay in over-confidence, that we would believe what we read in the papers, that it was hardly worth the opposition turning up. It was never as simple as that.

Despite initial fears the accommodation at the Hotel Zagreb was fine and the food extremely adequate. The hotel faced the bay and the islands offshore and each morning you could gaze out on a quite stunning view. Even the local beer sufficiently quenched the almost continuous thirst. Each day we held a Press conference, determined not to cause a news vacuum. The tabloids were delighted when we informed them that, one morning, on returning to our rooms, we had found packets of condoms in the bathrooms, including that of seventy-year-old Marea Hartman, the Head of Delegation. When informed of the exact purpose of them, Marea said: "Well, you know, I think I'm getting a little too old for that sort of thing." When the story broke in Britain some male members of team management had to take the condoms back with them to prove fidelity.

The first day of the Championships was very hot indeed. An efficient bus service, running every ten minutes, took us from the hotel to the stadium. Whereas in previous days, in the trips to the training tracks, there had been noise and chatter and hilarity, now there was silence. The competitors looked out of the windows at the unprepossessing scenery on the outskirts of town, their minds already honed to the task in hand.

Our trepidation increased as we watched Linford in the heats of the 100 metres, when he ran in third to the Frenchman Moriniere and Krylov of the Soviet Union and qualified for the next round only as one of the fastest losers. In the end his was the fourth-fastest time of the day, but it was the manner of his running rather than his time that caused furrowed brows. In the warm-up area he had laughed and joked with the managers and physiotherapists. When he was going to his marks he heard, overhead, the helicopter that continually circled the stadium; his mind was distracted. In the badly-organised European Indoor Championships in Glasgow earlier in the year, he had had difficulty in motivating himself, in feeling the necessary adrenalin pumping through his veins. It had taken the posturing of the Italian sprinter, Pavoni, to jerk him into the right frame of mind. Motivating himself is an increasing problem for this thirty-year-old, and it was a measure of his greatness that the next day he came into the stadium for the semi-final and final a different man. His face was a mask of stern determination. He was angered by what he considered to be a "bad Press" and perhaps this was the catalyst for his motivation. He won the semi-final, and in the final, again stamped his authority on European sprinting. It was his forty-eighth race of the year, stretching back to the Commonwealth Games, which he had won with ease. His time of 10.00 seconds, marginally wind-assisted, was his fastest of the summer. Britain, like France, had three sprinters in the final. John Regis won the bronze medal and twenty-one-year-old Darren Braithwaite, possibly the champion's heir-apparent, ran in sixth.

"Yesterday," Linford said after the race, "I didn't have any adrenalin or respect for the opposition and they didn't have any for me. It was the kick up the backside I needed."

Two gold medals on the second day. Maybe everything was going to be all right after all.

In Stuttgart Kriss Akabusi had glanced up at the scoreboard at the end of the closing ceremony. "Good-bye from Stuttgart. See you in Split" flashed across the screen. "You won't see me," he thought. He had been there for the relay and had only run in that because Todd Bennett had been injured. He was twenty-seven, nearly twenty-eight. At these championships new, younger men had come to the fore. Roger Black had won and Derek Redmond, injured for most of the season, had come fourth. Both were just twenty years of age. There was no future for him at 400 metres. He was not to know, of course, that Black and Redmond were to suffer horrendous injury problems necessitating surgery, and were not to figure in the next three years. He looked carefully at the other events. He saw Britain take all the medals in the 800 metres; there was no hope there. But then he noticed that in the 400 metres hurdles, no British athlete had reached the final. Maybe this was an avenue to explore.

Kriss was an orphan-boy made good. His parents were Nigerian; Ibos, from the east of the country. They had christened him Kriss Kezie Uche Chukwu Duru-Akabusi. Sponsored by their respective villages they had come to Britain to study, then returned, leaving him and his brother here with foster-parents to get a good education. The Biafran war had intervened, the money from Imo State had dried up and contact was lost. After five years with foster-parents the brothers had to be transferred to an orphanage. Kriss was eight years old. He remembered going from foster-home to foster-home until finally his uncle went down to Portsmouth to take him to the orphanage. All that experience had hardened him; he realised, as he grew older, that the most important thing was not to become attached, either to people or objects, that if you did you would be hurt. There must be no love-bonds, no intimacy.

I looked at Kriss as he punctuated his story with a sip of Coke. I had empathy with what he was saying. The important thing is to recognise what has happened. Behind us the huge lounge of the Zagreb teemed with activity like an anthill; the day's track and field events were still hours away.

"I haven't cried since I was about twelve," Kriss said. "I've never allowed myself to cry. I am determined not to get hurt. If I felt that those closest to me, whom I love dearly, were going to hurt me, I would cut them off." He made a scissoring gesture with his fingers.

"Do you have contact with your parents?" I said. "I mean, what do you feel about them?"

"Well, I feel no emotional ties at all. They're just people. Monika resents them though."

Monika is his wife. They met and married in Germany when he was there in the army. He had made a successful career that was now coming to an end – had been a PTI sergeant at twenty-one. Being at the orphanage had made him very competitive in all things in life.

"Everyone thinks," Kriss said, "that because you were an orphan you somehow are not equal to them. There's a tendency to patronise."

In 1986 Kriss thought that he was at the crossroads. Athletically he saw no future in 400-metre running. He had been to most of the top championships and had earned medals as a relay runner. Now he had to make a decision – retire, or try the hurdles. Spiritually too, he was dissatisfied. He had all the material things of life, a family, his own home, cars, but he felt a dissatisfaction.

"I had everything," he said, "but I had nothing. Nothing that brought me happiness."

At the Commonwealth Games in Edinburgh he picked up a Good News Bible by his bedside and began to read. Its straightforward language appealed to him and he became fascinated by the character of Jesus. He researched his life, and visited a whole gamut of different churches.

"Once I had convinced my intellect that Jesus had risen from the dead," he said, "then I was ready to make the commitment." He became a born-again Christian.

"I prayed to God, I prayed that he come and show me. That night I had a vision or a vivid dream. Jesus came to me in a special way. When I woke up I knew, without a shadow of a doubt, that I was a Christian."

He is evangelical and quite a number of the team are now Christians, meeting regularly at matches and championships. Monika is not religious and this has led to obvious problems.

"Monika thought," he said with a grin, "that it was something I would get over. One of Kriss's little whims! Suddenly she realised that the man that she had married was not the man she was seeing before her."

In Split, he cruised both heat and semi-final. The pressure of being the favourite had got to him a little. His religion helped.

"I realised that it wasn't in my hands. If the Lord wanted me to win, I was going to win anyway."

His main opposition in the final would come from two Swedes who had both come to their top form at the right time in the semi-finals. His main opponent was Sven Nylander but he had head-hunted him earlier in the season at

Malmo and given him a decisive beating. The next day a journalist asked him if he prayed before his races.

"Today I used Philippians chapter four, verse thirteen," he said.

The assembled hacks looked sideways at each other. Did they have Good News Bibles in their hotel rooms? The text was: "I can do all things through Christ who strengthens me."

It was his prayer as he went to his marks. He ran a classic race, pulling back the stagger on Nylander by the half-way mark and then, as agreed with his coach, Mike Whittingham, running hard over the next three or four hurdles. By the time he reached the straight, the race was over and he crossed the line metres ahead. By the finish there was a huge party of British supporters, taking up the whole of one section of the stand. They stood and roared their applause, waving their Union Jacks. Kriss moved to them, waving and clapping in return. He had remembered that when he had walked into an almost empty stadium to run in the very first race of the Championships on the Monday morning all these hundreds of supporters had been there ready to give him encouragement, so he went to thank them. As he waved they shouted at him: "Look at the time, Kriss! Look at the time!" He couldn't decipher their shouts above the din so he just smiled and continued waving. Nylander, who had won silver, came up to congratulate him. They put their arms around each other and over the Swede's shoulder he spied the digital clock. It read 47.93. The time was later confirmed as 47.92 seconds – Kriss had made history as the first British athlete below forty-eight seconds. He went berserk, dancing madly with elation, waving a clenched fist in the air. Then he sank to his knees and prayed and thanked the Lord before leaping up again and running around in a great circle of complete joy.

"If I had to finish the chapter there and then," he said to me later, "then I would have been happy."

The pressures on Tom McKean were enormous, despite all his European and World Cup wins, for he knew that it is by your championship record that you are measured, and his was dismal. Following Rome and Seoul, he, like Sebastian Coe, had mysteriously flopped in the Commonwealth Games. Only in Stuttgart had he run true to his form. If he did not win here then the media would write him off completely as a championship contender.

He was drawn in the outside lane and as the break came, at the end of the first bend, he went into the lead. Tom McKean was going to run it from the front, as he had done to win the European Indoor title in Glasgow in March. But there the crowd were totally behind him, here there were a thousand British voices against twenty thousand shouting for the Yugoslav, Slobodan Popovic. Tom led at the bell and we joined Kriss Akabusi in prayer as he still

An overjoyed Akabusi gives thanks for his epoch-making 47.92 seconds in Split.

led down the back straight. The challenges came and went. David Sharpe ran second and then slipped back to fifth. Then came Popovic, then the Italian Vialli, but Tom wound up the pace and as he did so the opposition faltered and suddenly we knew that he had won it. Behind him there was a fierce battle for the silver and bronze medals and in a run that was so reminiscent of Phil Brown's relay leg in Barcelona, David Sharpe came on the inside and with a huge grin snatched the silver medal. Later they stood together on the winner's plinth, while the anthem was played and the flags raised. They looked at each other and smiled, and you knew somehow that it was the greatest moment in their lives.

Yvonne Murray was conscious of all this as she waited for her race, but she tried to erase it from her mind. She had talked over the tactics for her 3000 metres with her coach, Tommy Boyle. She knew when she was going to make her bid, knew how she was going to achieve it. The race was run at no exceptional pace, all the runners bunched together and then suddenly, with 550 metres to go, Yvonne sprinted to the front and in thirty metres had opened up a gap which grew and grew. She caught the field by surprise, including her main opponent, the redoubtable Soviet, Yelena Romanova. Swearing undoubtedly in her native tongue, Romanova gave chase, but the gap was too wide and although she felt that she was treading water as she came towards the finish, Yvonne kept glancing up at the stadium scoreboard and knew that though the Soviet runner was closing fast she would not catch her. She crossed the line, European champion, and punched the air, then cried and cried and cried. She went to Tom McKean and hugged him and cried. She put on a T-shirt that had stitched carefully on to the back the words "We Did It Mum" and back in Edinburgh, Mum started crying too. Finally, as the Union Jack rose into the black night sky and the anthem was played for the third time, she wept again. "I'm so sorry," she kept saying, but we knew these were tears of joy. Five gold medals now for Britain. We were well and truly on our way.

It was on this third day that the exploits of the British athletes in Split began to catch the public imagination back home. People were asking each other if they had seen what had happened on television the night before; the Championships became a conversation-piece in pubs. Once again British athletics was doing the nation proud.

In the Hotel Zagreb the atmosphere was marvellous, and as in Gateshead the year before, the pressure to do well was now coming from those who had been successful. The days were long, hot and tiring for the whole of the team management, but success added bounce to tired limbs and drooping eyelids. So we threw back our curtains early on the fourth morning of the Championships, thrilled again at the calm blue waters of the Adriatic, not realising that a day of high drama was in store.

A moment of euphoria for Yvonne Murray as she crosses the line to win the
3000 metres final in the 1990 European Championships.

More medals flowed into the team's coffers as the Thursday night wore on. First, John Regis and Linford Christie lined up in the 200 metres. As the gun went Linford, running inside John, seemed to cut down the stagger as he ran a brilliant bend but the power and almost brutal strength of the younger sprinter came into play from there on. Regis reminds one of the great Bob Hayes, a man of similar physical attributes. He crossed the line and celebrated as all the others had done. He had set a new Championship record of 20.11. Linford just lost the silver to the Frenchman, Trouabal. Britain had won four of the six medals available in the sprints.

The story of Roger Black is a remarkable one. It seems amazing that he is only twenty-four years of age, for he has suffered a whole lifetime of anguish and pain. In 1986 the world of 400-metre running seemed at his feet; he had won both the Commonwealth and European titles, and had set British records. Then came a hamstring injury, which meant that he could run only the relay in Rome and had to watch as the man whom he defeated in Stuttgart, Schonlebe, took the World Championship title. Then came a stress fracture that threatened his whole athletics future and he began to rue his decision to quit medical school to become a full-time athlete. In 1988 he had an operation in which the surgeons inserted screws into his right foot. He spent six months on crutches and then right at the end of the 1989 season, in Jersey, he ran 46.2 seconds to rank fourth in Britain. He went to Auckland to run in an ill-fated relay team that was disqualified, and now here he was in Split to defend his title.

His problem all season, as he acknowledged, had been to re-learn the event. In 400 metres, pace-judgement is a key element in success and at Grand Prix races throughout the summer he worked at it. In Malmo, he went off too quickly, in Zurich likewise; but in Brussels he got it right and was rewarded with his first run below forty-five seconds for three years. In Split the atmosphere got to him and he ran the first 300 metres too fast and so, inevitably, his muscles protested violently down the home straight. The pack closed and closed but could not quite make it. Roger Black was again European 400-metre champion, the first man to win the title twice. Amazingly it was Schonlebe, who had shown no form at all that summer, who came nearest to snatching the title from him.

"I ran like a plonker," Roger said afterwards, "but I'm a plonker with a gold medal."

As he stood on the victory rostrum and the flags were raised and the anthem played, a happy smile flickered on his face. He is a quiet and unassuming man, not over-emotional, but watching him you knew that this was a very personal victory that he would savour all his life. He, and he alone, had defeated pain, anguish and frustration and had had to live with the thought that he might never run again. As he stood there he knew that the torment of Erich Segal was not for him.

I crouched on the steps of the media area in the main stand. Around me the television commentators were relating, in various languages, the story of the heat of the 1500 metres that was, slowly it must be said, unwinding before us. The field was bunched, it was cat-and-mouse, and then with 200 metres to go to the bell, the runners seem to concertina abruptly and one sprawled on to the track. It was Peter Elliott. I picked up the walkie-talkie, one of six loaned to us by ITV, and shouted: "Tony to all mobiles! Elliott is down and out!"

Les Jones had already witnessed the incident. He was in the Jury of Appeal room considering whether to make a protest on behalf of Nigel Walker, the Welsh sprint hurdler, who had claimed he was baulked in his semi-final, where he failed to qualify. He was just concluding that it would not be valid when, on the other television screen, he saw Peter crash down.

"Tony, get Marea," Les said. "Frank, can you hear us? Let's meet in the mixed area."

The invaluableness of the walkie-talkies was proved at that moment. We were the only team in Split to have them and they indicated the excellent relationship we had with both television channels in Yugoslavia. I rushed towards the VIP stand where Marea Hartman had been faithfully sitting every hour of the Championships, in case of a moment such as this. Les, Frank, Marea and I gathered in the mixed area. Already Peter had walked off the track and in to collect his gear. Steve Cram had qualified from the same race. They had both been interviewed by television and were now, their sweat glistening in the lights, surrounded by the Press and radio, analysing the race. Marea agreed that if we felt it necessary we should protest. Next we went to the BBC and viewed the incident in slow motion. There was no doubt in our minds that Peter had been deliberately pushed by the East German runner, Hauke Fuhlbrugge. It was decided that we should make a protest, first of all to the track referee and then, if necessary, to the Jury of Appeal.

The initial protest was dismissed and Les wrote formally to the jury. By this time, Neil Horsfield, the third British entrant, had qualified in the second heat. I rushed around the stand informing the Press (who were on tight deadlines), radio and television, that we were making a protest, asking that either the race be re-run (an unlikely proposition) or that Peter should be reinstated into the final. The reaction of the Press was unanimously favourable; that of two ex-distance runners commentating for television was not. Brendan Foster, for the BBC, said that the protest was invalid and that there was no way that it would succeed. Steve Ovett, for ITV, said much the same thing. They were invoking the curious camaraderie of distance runners; in their view such incidents were part of the game, part of the rough-and-tumble of the event. If you went down, that was bad luck and you accepted your fate. Peter, in television interviews, had said much the same thing. Yet there was a rule – Rule 141.1 – which allowed for such a happening and permitted the reinstatement of the athlete.

Meanwhile, on the track, we were witnessing a brave run by the steeplechaser, Mark Rowland. In the closing stages of the race it was down to a battle between him and the Italian, Panetta. With 250 metres to go he had taken the lead and we rose to cheer our eighth gold medal. But the Italian, full of unexpected bounce, sprinted past Mark on the run-in, waving his arms about in excitement, whilst the mentally and physically shocked Englishman could only jog in, dazed and bewildered by the Italian's speed, for the silver medal.

Les stayed outside the jury room and kept up a string of comments in his attractive Irish lilt. "There is very heavy discussion ... they've called in the referee and the marksmen ... the officials have left ... there's more heavy talking ... I've just had a thumbs-up ..."

"I'm not going on a thumbs-up," I said.

Then suddenly: "Les to all mobiles. Elliott reinstated, repeat, Elliott reinstated. Fuhlbrugge disqualified."

It was amazing and unprecedented but it came with the full authority of Rule 141.1. I rushed around the media area again with the news, stopping off for a BBC interview with David Coleman (Brendan sat by looking stunned) and with radio. Peter, battered and bruised from the incident, was in the Press area, phoning the bad news to Rotherham. When he received the good news, a great smile lit his face. He still had a chance of a Commonwealth and European double. He was pleased to be back in, he said; now the priority was to get ready for the final, two days hence. However, doubts over the fairness of the decision were to creep into his mind in the ensuing forty-eight hours.

Just as we were getting our breath back news came through from the Zagreb that there had been an accident involving Kerry Shacklock, Steve Backley's girlfriend. According to the message from the hotel, she had fallen off the bed and landed awkwardly and seemed in very bad shape. One of the team doctors was urgently needed. Steve Calvert was instantly available, but how to get him out to the hotel? To the rescue came David Bedford, looking like a middle-aged Easy Rider, on his high-powered motor bike.

We arrived back at the Zagreb exhausted, to hear that Kerry had been taken to hospital. It was now well past midnight and we persuaded the equally exhausted hotel staff to serve us a meal. Suddenly, we remembered that we had arranged for some athletes to visit the British supporters at their hotel. We checked and found that the transport arrangements had broken down. It was too late, there was nothing we could do. It had been another one of those days.

Down and out. Peter Elliott falls in the 1500 metres semi-final, but was controversially reinstated for the final after a protest was made.

Colin Jackson had not been showing his usual impeccable form in recent weeks, and in the heats of the hurdles he had not seemed the dominant force that he should have been as one of the world's top hurdlers. In Split he had been receiving massage from a hard-working private masseur, who had a number of clients amongst the athletes and had been absorbed into the medical team after a great deal of heart-searching and compromise. In the previous forty-eight hours, though, Linford had given his friend some strong advice: let the official physiotherapists have a look at his knee, which seemed to be causing a good deal of pain and trouble. This presented a major headache for the medical staff and for team management, for Colin's only real opposition in Europe was his fellow-hurdler, Tony Jarrett from Haringey. If Tony received any intimation that his great rival had an injury it would give him a psychological advantage.

In the hours leading up to the final of the hurdles the physiotherapists and doctors worked flat out to get Colin in reasonable shape for the race (though it was obvious that he would require a cartilage operation post-Split). The cloak of secrecy surrounding this treatment was extremely successful and Tony was unaware of the problems facing Colin right up until they went to their marks. Colin, though, was wearing a knee support and there was the additional problem of when to tell the media. If we did not tell them at all then we would be accused, rightly, of witholding information of vital importance. If we told them too early then there was the danger of Tony Jarrett getting the information on the grapevine. In the end we decided to tell the story after the athletes had been marched away to the report room, underneath the main stand. It worked well. When the athletes divested themselves of their tracksuits the most surprised man was Tony Jarrett.

It was a great battle between the two and there was little to separate them at the line. Both dipped so low at the finish that they failed to break the photo-timing cell and the digital clock in the stadium registered the time of the third athlete, Koszewski. Colin just won, Tony came second with a new English record. We now had eight gold medals, the equal of Stuttgart, and we had three big chances on the final day to set a new record.

Peter Elliott received successful treatment for his physical ailments during the forty-eight hours between the heat and final of the 1500 metres, but there was no one to help him with his mental torment. In the cold light of another brilliant Adriatic dawn, on the final day of the Championships, he began to brood on the fairness of the decision by the Jury of Appeal and perhaps to pay heed to the remarks of his running peers. He sat in the garden of the Zagreb and contemplated his options. He did not want to be known as the man who had won a European championship by default, a stigma (in his eyes) that he might have to carry for the rest of his career. On the other hand he did want to prove, at least to himself, that he was the best in Europe. He finally came to an extraordinary conclusion. In Auckland he had won the Commonwealth title by a good margin, winding up the pace over the final lap, in much the same way that Tom McKean had in Split. If he found himself in a similar situation, he told himself, he would run off the track ten metres from the line. He would thus have proved himself the best in Europe but he would not have taken the title. Honour would be satisfied all round.

On the warm-up track before the final, Peter was subjected to some abuse by Spanish athletes, which he ignored as he carried on his preparation. In the end the final was an anti-climax, tailor-made for the fast finishers. A funereal pace for the first three laps was then enlivened by Steve Cram, who moved to the front in a brave long run for home. Peter fell in behind and, momentarily, so did Neil Horsfield, so that for one fleeting moment a British clean-sweep seemed a possibility. Cram still led with half a lap to go, digging in now, the frustration of his lack of speed – caused by a severe curtailment of his training by injury – showing on his face. Peter shadowed him, his wrist bandaged after Thursday's fracas, and seemed poised to challenge, when the younger guys came roaring through. First, Gennaro Di Napoli edged ahead, hoping to give conclusive proof of Italy's dominance in distance events; but then Jens-Peter Herold swept through and scored a triumphant victory for the GDR, at their last major championships before reunification.

That both Cram and Elliott were short of race fitness was proved in mid-September by their superb running at the end-of-season meeting at Don Valley Stadium in Sheffield, venue for the 1991 World Student Games. Cram, in particular, had run with a decisiveness and courage that we had not seen for four years. Injury, that curse of so many major British international athletes, had deprived them of their true destiny.

The row over the reinstatement of Peter continued (nine countries made official protests) and many fallacious arguments were put forward against the practice, in particular that Peter had not finished the race and therefore should not have been in the final. Others felt that in future runners might deliberately dive in order to gain reinstatement. But these were conservative arguments intended to maintain a practice that had been accepted over the years. Nobody in international competition had ever actually implemented Rule 141.1. That rule was clear-cut and Luciano Barra, the technical manager of the meeting, summed up the European AA's conclusions when he said: "If people want a limitation of the scope to reinstate an athlete to those who finish the race, then it should be inserted in writing in the rules."

Would Peter really have run off the track if he had been leading ten metres out? Afterwards he assured me that he would have, even when I said to him that no matter how many Olympic medals and world records he would set in future, it would be the one thing he would have been remembered for. But there were some provisos in his thinking. I asked him what he would have done if, ten metres out, it had been just he and Steve Cram battling it out and he smiled and gave no answer. It is all hypothetical now, and we shall never know.

The final day gathered momentum. Gary Staines ran a valiant race in the 5000 metres but could not hold off the Italian, Antibo, who scored a magnificent distance-running double. Gary's silver medal, though, brought him out of Eamonn Martin's shadow. In three of the relays Britain did well without striking gold. The women took a bronze medal in both their races. In the 4 × 400 metres it was gained through a fine run by Linda Keough. In the men's sprint relay the French team won with a new world record, 37.79 seconds, and it took that run for them to stay ahead of the British quartet, who set a new national record of 37.98. If Marcus Adam on the third leg had possessed the fitness that had gained him a Commonwealth 200-metre win in January, the title and a world record would undoubtedly have been ours.

So we came to the final event of the Championships, the 4 × 400 metres relay. A quick count told us that we were one gold medal short of a record and likewise one medal short of an overall best. We were the clear favourites but we had taken a gamble. John Regis had been quickly secreted away from the medal celebrations for the sprint relay and quietly prepared for the 4 × 400 metres, in which he was to run the third leg. Many thought that we were taking an unnecessary risk, but we were confident that we were not. John was in the form of his life and had gained three medals so far. Now he too could go for a record.

Paul Sanders led off with a fine leg, his fastest ever, and then Kriss Akabusi, using all his experience, took the team into the lead, handing over to John Regis. John stormed the first half of his leg and there was a gasp in the stadium as the gap between him and his pursuers grew and grew. We became a little tense – had he, through inexperience, gone off too quickly? Would he now fade and let the chasing pack overhaul him? If anything he seemed to accelerate over the next 100 metres and he entered the home straight in splendid isolation. He was timed at 43.9 seconds. Roger Black was the anchor man and he maintained a steady, cool, relaxed pace, yet ran 43.96. The thousand or so British supporters rose as one, many hoarse now from a week of cheering, the Union Jacks waving, the excitement intense. The time of 2:58.22 was a new European record and the squad and supporters celebrated. It was a marvellously fitting end to a totally extraordinary week, a memorial to a decade of mounting triumph.

EPILOGUE

Hans-Joachim Waldbrol had taken pages of notes, which, he said later, he found it difficult to encapsulate into his piece for the *Frankfurter Allgemeine*. Now I had to compose my thoughts succinctly. What had been the reason for our success this week in Yugoslavia? It has to be a subjective viewpoint, I said, because there is no British system and many theories abound. My ideas had been clarified by work I had been doing to narrate a Channel 4 *Equinox* series programme on the science and system behind the success of the East German athletes, particularly their women. In the GDR athletes had had an unrivalled opportunity to prepare properly for the major competitions. Millions of Deutschmarks had been spent to ensure that they had the best coaches, the best sports scientists, the best sports medicine available. Their facilities and their sports monitoring equipment were highly practical. In other words, the athletes of the GDR were, in reality, full-time athletes. For the women, it was a unique example of equal opportunity.

Against such competition our athletes, part-time at best, were struggling. To use a cliché, they were fighting with one arm tied behind their back. So the first factor in British athletics' success was the move by the international federation, in 1982, to allow payments to athletes. Already our best middle-distance runners had had that possibility, with clandestine appearance money being paid by European promoters. From 1983 onwards this opportunity was available to a wider selection of talent. A year later we had signed a highly lucrative television contract and sponsorships began to roll in which enabled us to stage more meetings in Britain where the athletes could be paid. All this brought about the second factor in our success – increased competitive opportunity both at home and abroad for our men. This programme meant that our athletes came to Split having taken on, throughout the season, the very best in the world. Christie had met Leroy Burrell, currently the world's fastest man, more than once; Akabusi had raced all the top American one-lap hurdlers; McKean had run against the very best Kenyans. The Europeans held no fears for them.

The third factor was that the great influx of black sprinters and hurdlers with West Indian and West African roots (they represented one-third of our team) that had come through in the decade were also able to benefit from the wealth of the sport. They too could become professional. Only the United States, in the developed world, had a greater proportion of blacks in their team.

Since 1948 we had had a coaching scheme that had produced thousands of coaches and from this enormous base it was inevitable that men who had gained great technical knowledge and who possessed the flair to use it had risen to the top and were available to the best athletes. Not always, but often. This was the fourth factor.

Finally, I said, the team management today bore no resemblance to that of yesteryear when the positions were mostly sinecures, rewards for years of faithful service. Today's management – and I used the word in its widest sense to include coaches, physiotherapists and doctors as well as managers – were highly professionalised, hard-working and dedicated to success. Frank Dick's pre-planning for a major meeting was meticulous.

It was, I stressed, only a personal theory but I felt that it was borne out by the flip-side of all this, the comparative lack of success of our women. Up until the Athens Congress, which changed the face of athletics, the East German men had been almost as successful as their women, dominating with the Soviet Union the European Cup competitions. Their star had begun to wane after 1983 as the sport in the West became more professionalised, a process which culminated in the British win in the European Cup in 1989. The East German women, operating in an area which is still not fully developed, had continued to dominate because hardly any women in the West were full-time athletes. In Britain in the mid-eighties, for reasons best known to themselves, the autonomous women administrators had chosen to stay outside the bonanza that had struck athletics. Now that the GDR system was about to vanish there was no doubt that world standards would fall because of that and the more vigilant drug-testing systems that were operating.

Hans snapped his notebook shut. "I hope that was okay," I said. He nodded and seemed pleased. "It's interesting," he said. The restaurant was filling up with other journalists anxious to fortify themselves before the frenetic chase after deadlines began that evening. The stadium was stirring with activity; the crowds arriving, some athletes already warming-up on the adjacent grass area, announcements in three languages floating through the balmy evening air. We stood and shook hands. "You must be proud," Hans said.

"I am," I replied, "proud to be a part of it."

INDEX